D0801451

HANDBOOK OF
Biblical
Social
Values

John J. Pilch & Bruce J. Malina, Editors

HENDRICKSON PUBLISHERS

HANDBOOK OF
Biblical
Social
Values

Copyright © 1993, 1998 by Hendrickson Publishers, Inc.
P. O. Box 3473
Peabody, Massachusetts 01961–3473
All rights reserved
Printed in the United States of America

Handbook of Biblical Social Values is an updated edition of *Biblical Social Values and Their Meaning: A Handbook,* published in 1993 by Hendrickson Publishers.

First Printing, Updated Edition — June 1998

Library of Congress Cataloging-in-Publication Data

Handbook of biblical social values / John J. Pilch and
  Bruce J. Malina, editors.
    Rev. ed. of: Biblical social values and their meaning.
    c1993. Includes bibliographical references and index.
    ISBN 1-56563-355-5 (casebound)
      1. Social values—Biblical teaching—Dictionaries.
  2. Ethics in the Bible—Dictionaries. I. Pilch, John J.
  II. Malina, Bruce J. III. Biblical social values and their
  meaning.
  BS680.E84H36   1998
  220.9´5´03—dc21   98-11537
                                                          CIP

The cover art is "Triumph of Mordecai," an engraving by Gustave Doré. It first appeared in *The Holy Bible*, with illustrations by Gustave Doré (London: Cassell, 1866–1870).

Unless otherwise indicated, scripture citations are from the Revised Standard Version of the Bible, Old Testament Section, Copyright 1952; New Testament Section, First Edition, Copyright 1946; Second Edition © 1971 by Division of Christian Education of the National Council of the Churches of Christ in the United States of America.

Table of Contents

PREFACE TO THE UPDATED EDITION ix

ABOUT THE EDITORS xi

CONTRIBUTORS xiii

INTRODUCTION xv

ACTIVENESS/PASSIVENESS (MCVANN) 3
AGONISTIC SOCIETY—SEE POWER 5
AGRARIAN SOCIETY (ROHRBAUGH) 5
ALMSGIVING—SEE ALTRUISM 8
ALLEGIANCE (PERSONAL AND GROUP)—SEE TRUST . . . 8
ALTRUISM (ALMSGIVING) (PILCH) 8
ASSERTIVENESS (REESE) 10
ATTACHMENT (PERSONAL AND GROUP)—SEE LOVE . . . 12
AUTHORITARIANISM (MALINA)—SEE ALSO DOMINATION
    ORIENTATION; POWER 12

BELIEF—SEE FAITH/FAITHFULNESS 19

CHANGE/NOVELTY ORIENTATION (MCVANN) 19
CHARITY—SEE LOVE 21
CLOTHING (NEYREY) 21
COMMUNICATIVENESS (MOUTH-EARS) (MCVANN)—SEE ALSO
    EQUIVOCATION. 27
COMPASSION (PILCH) 30
COMPLIANCE (MCVANN) 33
CONVERSION—SEE CHANGE/NOVELTY ORIENTATION . . 35

COOPERATIVENESS (PILCH) 35
CURIOSITY (MCVANN) 38

DECEPTION (NEYREY)—SEE ALSO EYES-HEART . . . 40
DEFEAT (FORD) 45
DOMINATION ORIENTATION (PILCH)—SEE ALSO POWER . . 48
DRAMATIC ORIENTATION (EXAGGERATION,
     OVER-ASSERTION) (PILCH) 50
DYADISM (NEYREY) 53

EMOTION/DEMONSTRATION OF FEELINGS (PILCH) . . . 56
END ORIENTATION—SEE PURPOSIVENESS/END ORIENTATION 59
ENVY (MALINA-SEEMAN)—SEE ALSO FATE 59
EQUALITY—SEE PATRONAGE; AUTHORITARIANISM . . . 63
EQUIVOCATION (SAYING ONE THING, DOING ANOTHER)
     (NEYREY)—SEE ALSO DECEPTION; COMMUNICATIVENESS . 63
EVIL EYE—SEE ENVY 68
EXAGGERATION—SEE DRAMATIC ORIENTATION . . . 68
EXORCISM—SEE POWER 68
EYES-HEART (MALINA)—SEE ALSO DECEPTION . . . 68

FAITH/FAITHFULNESS (MALINA) 72
FAMILY-CENTEREDNESS (MCVANN) 75
FATE (MALINA) 79
FAVOR—SEE GRACE/FAVOR 81
FEAST (MALINA) 81
FIDELITY—SEE FAITH/FAITHFULNESS 84
FIRST-LAST—SEE PROMINENCE 84
FREEDOM (MALINA) 85

GRACE/FAVOR (MALINA) 89
GRATITUDE (DEBT OF) (MALINA) 92
GROUP ORIENTATION (NEYREY) 94

HANDS-FEET (MALINA) 98
HEALING (PILCH) 102
HEART-EYES—SEE EYES-HEART 106
HOLY/HOLINESS—SEE WHOLENESS 106

HONOR/SHAME (PLEVNIK)   106

HOPE—SEE TRUST   115

HOSPITALITY (MALINA)   115

HUMILITY (MALINA)   118

HYPOCRISY—SEE EQUIVOCATION   120

IDEALISM (THE PRACTICE OF SAYING "YES" BUT NEGLECTING
    TO ACT ACCORDINGLY)—SEE EQUIVOCATION   .   .   .   120

INDIVIDUALISM—SEE DYADISM; GROUP ORIENTATION   .   .   120

INTROSPECTION/LACK OF INTROSPECTION—SEE
    AUTHORITARIANISM   120

JEALOUSY—SEE ZEAL/JEALOUSY   120

JUSTICE—SEE PATRONAGE   120

LAW-MINDEDNESS—SEE TORAH ORIENTATION   .   .   .   120

LIKABILITY (REESE)   121

LIMITED GOOD (NEYREY)   122

LOVE (MALINA)   127

LOYALTY—SEE FAITH/FAITHFULNESS   130

MANLINESS—SEE DRAMATIC ORIENTATION; PARENTING;
    AUTHORITARIANISM   130

MEDIATOR—SEE POWER   130

MEEKNESS (MALINA)   130

MERCY—SEE GRACE/FAVOR; GRATITUDE; STEADFAST LOVE   132

MIRTH (FORD)   132

MOUTH-EARS—SEE COMMUNICATIVENESS; DECEPTION;
    EQUIVOCATION.   136

NUDITY (NEYREY)   136

OBEDIENCE (SUBMISSION) (REESE)   142

ORDERING (OSIEK)   143

OVER-ASSERTION—SEE DRAMATIC ORIENTATION   .   .   145

PAIN—SEE AUTHORITARIANISM; PARENTING .   .   .   145

PARENTING (PILCH)   145

PATIENCE (MCVANN)   148

PATRONAGE (MALINA)—SEE ALSO GRACE/FAVOR .   .   151

PEASANT (ROHRBAUGH) 155
PITY (MALINA) 157
POWER (PILCH) 158
PROGRESS ORIENTATION (HANSON) 161
PROMINENCE (SEEMAN) 166
PURITY (PILCH)—SEE ALSO NUDITY; WHOLENESS . . . 170
PURPOSIVENESS/END ORIENTATION (OAKMAN) . . . 173

RELATEDNESS (OSIEK) 176
RELIABILITY—SEE FAITH/FAITHFULNESS 178
RESIGNATION—SEE PATIENCE 178

SECRECY—SEE DECEPTION 179
SELF-SACRIFICE (OSIEK) 179
SELF-SUFFICIENCY (OAKMAN) 181
SERVICE (MALINA) 183
SHAME—SEE HONOR/SHAME 184
SIN—SEE FREEDOM; PURPOSIVENESS/END ORIENTATION . 184
SOUL—SEE EYES-HEART; SELF-SACRIFICE. 184
STEADFAST LOVE (PILCH)—SEE ALSO GRACE/FAVOR;
    AUTHORITARIANISM 184
SUBMISSION—SEE OBEDIENCE 186

THRIFT (GREEK OIKONOMIA, MANAGEMENT, STEWARDSHIP)
    (FORD) 186
TIME ORIENTATION (MALINA) 189
TORAH ORIENTATION (LAW-MINDEDNESS) (DULING) . . 194
TRADITION—SEE GROUP ORIENTATION;
    FAMILY-CENTEREDNESS 201
TRUST (PERSONAL AND GROUP) (PILCH) 201

WHOLENESS (NEYREY) 204
WORSHIPFULNESS (REESE) 208

ZEAL/JEALOUSY (SEEMAN) 209

INDEX OF ANCIENT SOURCES 213

Preface to the Updated Edition

The editors and contributors are pleased with the critical acclaim and warm reception this book has received. Many reviewers noted the lack of a bibliography or list of resources for further reading. Bruce Malina conceived this project in 1988 precisely because no resources like it existed. Contributors to this volume researched basic social science resources in order to develop a cultural perspective necessary for writing their respective articles on biblical social values. There were precious few, if any, articles on biblical topics that adopted this perspective at that time. That has all changed, and in this updated edition we are able to supply bibliographic information.

Since 1988, a significant bibliography has accumulated. Contributors to this volume developed their respective topics and others in books, book chapters, articles, and book reviews. Other scholars employing social scientific criticism of the Bible have produced similar excellent studies as well. Each entry in this updated edition now lists key source material from the social sciences and articles on the Bible written from the social scientific perspective. This edition also includes new articles on "healing" and "limited good." Readers interested in additional research will profit from the extensive bibliography to 1993 compiled by John H. Elliott in *What is Social Scientific Criticism?* (Minneapolis: Fortress, 1993).

On the fiftieth anniversary of the publication of an encyclical promoting the use of modern, scientific methods in interpreting the Bible, the Pontifical Biblical Commission published a splendid document (*The Interpretation of the Bible in the Church* [Rome: Pontifical Biblical Institute Press, 1995]) summarizing the major approaches to interpreting the Bible in modern times and the beneficial contributions each makes to understanding the word of God. Perceptive readers of this document will recognize that the section on cultural anthroplogy reflects presentations made at a meeting of scholars in Spain by the contributors to *Biblical Social Values* and later published as articles in *Biblical Theology Bulletin*, a key resource for articles on biblical topics utilizing social scientific approaches to interpreting the Bible. It is significant that the Roman Catholic Church, one of the few Christian denominations that seeks to guide and direct the interpretation of the Bible among its adherents, finds the use of cultural anthropology to be very helpful in defining the message of the Bible.

John J. Pilch, Georgetown University
Bruce J. Malina, Creighton University

About the Editors

John J. Pilch, Ph.D., is a biblical scholar, author, and international speaker. Since 1993 he has been teaching Scripture in the Department of Theology at Georgetown University, Washington, D.C. He is widely in demand across the U.S. and Canada as a facilitator of seminars, workshops, retreats, and parish renewals on the Bible as well as on wellness spirituality. He serves as book-review editor for the *Biblical Theology Bulletin* and writes for Old Testament Abstracts and New Testament Abstracts.

His publications include *Introducing the Cultural Context of the Old Testament; Introducing the Cultural Context of the New Testament; The Cultural World of Jesus: Sunday by Sunday;* "The Transfiguration of Jesus: An Experience of Alternate Reality, in *Modelling Early Christianity: Social-Scientific Studies of the New Testament in its Context* (ed. Esler); "Family Violence in Cross-Cultural Perspective: An Approach for Feminist Interpreters of the Bible," in *A Feminist Companion to Reading the Bible: Approaches, Methods, Strategies* (ed. Brenner and Fontaine); and "Sickness and Healing in Luke–Acts," in *The Social World of Luke–Acts: Models for Interpretation* (ed. Neyrey).

Bruce J. Malina, Ph.D., is professor of biblical studies at Creighton University. He has degrees in philosophy, theology, and biblical studies. He received an honorary doctorate from the University of St. Andrew in Scotland (1995). He was a Fulbright Scholar at the University of Oslo (1986), visiting professor at the University of Naples (1990), researcher at the Consejo Superior de

Investigacciones Científicas, Madrid (1991), and visiting professor at the University of Stellenbosch (1994). He is associate editor of *Biblical Theology Bulletin*, Catholic Biblical Quarterly Monograph Series, and *Semeia*. Past president of the Catholic Biblical Association, he has been director of a task group on the social sciences and New Testament interpretation in the Catholic Biblical Association and a founding member and director of a similar group in the Society of Biblical Literature. He is likewise a founding member of the Context Group: Project on the Bible in Its Cultural Environment.

His books include *The New Testament World: Insights from Cultural Anthropology; Christian Origins and Cultural Anthropology: Practical Models for Biblical Interpretation; Calling Jesus Names: The Social Value of Labels in Matthew*, with Jerome H. Neyrey; *Social Science Commentary on the Synoptics*, with Richard L. Rohrbaugh; *Windows on the World of Jesus: Time Travel to Ancient Judea; On the Genre and Message of Revelation: Star Visions and Sky Journeys; The Social World of Jesus and the Gospels*. His recently completed work with Richard L. Rohrbaugh is *Social Science Commentary on the Gospel of John*, forthcoming. His works have been translated into Spanish, German, Japanese, and Afrikaans.

Contributors

Dennis Duling
Canisius College
Buffalo, New York
   Torah Orientation

Josephine Massyngbaerde Ford
University of Notre Dame
South Bend, Indiana
   Defeat
   Mirth
   Thrift

K. C. Hanson
St. Olaf College
Northfield, Minnesota
   Progress Orientation

Mark McVann, FSC
Lewis University
Romeoville, Illinois
   Activeness/Passiveness
   Change/Novelty Orientation
   Communicativeness
   Compliance
   Curiosity
   Family-Centeredness
   Patience

Bruce J. Malina
Creighton University
Omaha, Nebraska
   Authoritarianism
   Envy
   Eyes-Heart
   Faith/Faithfulness
   Fate
   Feast
   Freedom

   Grace/Favor
   Gratitude
   Hands-Feet
   Hospitality
   Humility
   Love
   Meekness
   Patronage
   Pity
   Service
   Time Orientation

Jerome H. Neyrey, SJ
University of Notre Dame
South Bend, Indiana
   Clothing
   Deception
   Dyadism
   Equivocation
   Group Orientation
   Limited Good
   Nudity, Nudity and Shame, Nudity
      and Purity/Pollution
   Wholeness

Douglas E. Oakman
Pacific Lutheran University
Tacoma, Washington
   Purposiveness/End Orientation
   Self-Sufficiency

Carolyn Osiek, RSCJ
Catholic Theological Union
Chicago, Illinois
   Ordering
   Relatedness
   Self-Sacrifice

John J. Pilch
Georgetown University
Washington, D.C.
  Altruism
  Compassion
  Cooperativeness
  Domination Orientation
  Dramatic Orientation
  Emotion/Demonstration of Feelings
  Healing
  Parenting
  Power
  Purity
  Steadfast Love
  Trust

Joseph Plevnik, SJ
Toronto School of Theology
Toronto, Ontario
  Honor/Shame

†James M. Reese, OSFS
St. John's University
Jamaica, New York
  Assertiveness
  Likability
  Obedience
  Worshipfulness

Richard Rohrbaugh
Lewis and Clark College
Portland, Oregon
  Agrarian Society
  Peasant

Chris Seeman
Box 1213
Novato, California
  Envy
  Prominence
  Zeal/Jealousy

Introduction

Every culture colors the way its members perceive and interpret reality. Though reality is always the same, cultural interpretations of it differ. What is considered important in Middle Eastern or Mediterranean culture may be considered quite unimportant in the prevailing culture of the United States. Even when both cultures use the same word to describe something important, like hospitality, the understanding of that item is very different. That is why a handbook of New Testament values is significant. The purpose of this handbook is to describe some of the values prominent in the New Testament and frequently referred to in the Bible in general. Each New Testament value will be contrasted with the understanding commonly held by United States citizens.

WHAT IS A VALUE?

The word "value" describes some general quality and direction of life that human beings are expected to embody in their behavior. A value is a general, normative orientation of action in a social system. It is an emotionally anchored commitment to pursue and support certain directions or types of actions.

For example, most Americans pride themselves on being efficient. (N.B.: In this handbook, the word "American" refers only to citizens of the United States and does not include Canada or Mexico.) But what exactly is "efficient" behavior in a concrete situation? What does it mean to clean out a garage efficiently? What sort of garage, with what procedures for the disposal of waste oil, for example? At an abstract level, values such as efficiency bear no reference to specific goals or specific situations. Giving a general value a specific content or meaning results from institutionalization.

In the example of efficiency, there are fixed ways of disposing of the usual waste found in a garage. Empty oil cans could be deposited at a filling station, while used air filters could be taken by weekly trash haulers. These fixed ways of realizing values are institutions. An institution is a somewhat fixed structure of procedures and behaviors that people follow while exercising a value. In sum, an institution is a general, abstract, social structure that gives shape to general and common values.

APPROACHES TO UNDERSTANDING VALUES

There are a number of ways to understand or view values. Consider efficiency again. While Americans do not expect one another to perform all tasks identically, they do expect one another to carry out those tasks with a maximum of practical sense and a minimum of wasted effort. It is considered stupid and foolish, at times even humorous, to do anything in an impractical or inefficient way, such as washing a car with a toothbrush or digging up a garden with a spoon. Americans constantly evaluate what they perceive in terms of its efficiency quality, even though they may not be aware of making such a judgment. The reason Americans are always making this judgment is that human efficiency is a central feature of the core American value called "instrumental mastery."

Instrumental mastery, which lies at the heart of the dominant U.S. culture, refers to the ability to control persons and things so as to maximize one's individual well-being. Being efficient is simply one variation on the value of instrumental mastery. Thus, the word "value" refers to the quality ("of what sort?") and the goal or purpose (directionality) of human behavior in general or of some aspect of human behavior.

Values are also qualities that inhere in "value objects." Value objects include: self, others, nature, time, space, the All. In the Bible, God is "the All." Values are consequently revealed in the way human beings behave as well as in the way they assess value objects.

SOCIAL INSTITUTIONS

In order to realize values, human beings create and utilize social institutions. A social institution is like a set of railroad tracks of a specific width laid out in a given direction toward a specific end or goal. To illustrate, kinship or family is a social institution that serves as the means for bringing new human beings into existence and then nurturing them for a lifetime.

Institutions mark the general boundaries within which certain qualities and directions of living must take place. Generating and nurturing human beings must occur within the boundaries of kinship, whether in the form of the U.S. style of a nuclear family, the single-parent family, or communal living of one sort or another.

Institutional boundaries delineate and define value objects, i.e., the objects that embody values. For example, the individual person is a value object. Institutionally, individual persons are usually delineated by social arrangements called roles and statuses. Take a moment to reflect upon the roles and statuses that most persons in the U.S. possess within the social institution known as kinship: husband, wife, mother, father, brother, sister, parent, grandparent, cousin, and in-law. How is each one delineated from the other?

Roles and statuses are replicated throughout a social system because their dimensions distinguish one individual person not only from another person but also from nature, space, time, and the All or God. For example, we commonly refer to "mother" nature, but in actuality motherhood is a role and status of a human being. On the one hand, plants do not enjoy a mother status or role, and animals are given this reference by analogy with human beings. On the other hand, plants play a role in the food chain or serve humans as decorative objects. These two roles delineate plants, one element of nature, from human beings, who do not ordinarily play a role in the food chain or serve as decorative objects.

As fixed forms of various aspects in social life, institutions focus on goals required for the maintenance of a social group. Institutions do not change, but the values which people follow in the pursuit of social goals (e.g., begetting offspring and nurturing related human beings) can and do change.

In any society, then, social institutions take on dynamic expression by endowing persons, things, and events with meaning and feeling. "Value" is another term for the meaning and feeling that inhere in persons, things, and events. To use our original example, efficiency is a value that can inhere in or be attributed to persons, things, and events. Precisely how a specific behavior or action will be assessed at any given time as efficient is not predefined. For example, an American who budgets time to accomplish goals within a predetermined period is normally viewed as efficient. By contrast, the Mediterranean native who values interpersonal relationships and cares little about how much time is spent on this aspect of life is also viewed in that culture as efficient. The fact that Americans would view this extravagance as a "waste" of time indicates that the meaning of "efficient" is rather fluid.

SYMBOLS

Further, the valued person, thing, or event, that is, the object endowed with meaning and feeling, is often called a "symbol." Thus, a person, thing, or event filled with some socially appreciable value bears the meaningfulness characteristic of a symbol. From this point of view, social institutions are systems of symbols which establish powerful, pervasive, and long-lasting moods and motivations in human beings. Social institutions accomplish this by projecting concepts of an adequately meaningful, social, human existence, and then clothing these concepts with such an aura of factuality that the moods and motivations seem uniquely realistic. A country's flag is basically a distinctively colored cloth. When this cloth is called a flag and accepted as a symbol, it stimulates meaning and feeling that the cloth alone does not.

The way in which values are affixed to value objects is the process of "symbolizing," or having some person, thing, or event serve as a symbol. Symbolizing takes place by means of drawing lines over, under, around, through, into and out of persons (self, others), nature (the non-human), time, space, superhumanness (transcendence), the All, and then investing the lines thus drawn with feeling, and finally perceiving meaning in the emerging configuration.

KINDS OF VALUES

There are many ways to categorize values; for example: core and peripheral, primary and secondary, means and ends, and so on. Values that are expected in all human interactions are core values, such as efficiency in the United States. In contrast to the U.S. core value of efficiency, honor and shame are core values in the Mediterranean world. Because this is a handbook of New Testament or Bible values, "efficiency" is not listed, but honor and shame are.

Values that are specific to given interactions are peripheral values. In the Mediterranean world, compassion is an example of a peripheral value because it is expected only in situations guided and governed by kinship considerations. Values that facilitate the realization of core and secondary values may be called "means values." Power, generosity, and eloquence are means values because they facilitate the realization of honor, which is the Mediterranean goal or end cultural value.

Of the major social institutions—economics, politics, religion, and kinship—the prevailing institution in
the biblical world was kinship. The rules of kinship controlled the main ways in which core and peripheral values of the society were realized. Because of the centrality
of the social institution of kinship, the value objects self,
others, nature, time, space, and the All (God) were assessed, in the first place, by gender.

In the Mediterranean world, where kinship is basic,
a human being is primarily male or female (husband//
wife, son//daughter, brother//sister: kinship terms) rather
than rich or poor (economic terms), powerful or powerless (political terms), pious or impious (religious terms).
The human universe of discourse is then patterned in
rhythms and stanzas which are primarily male and female in quality. The world of human affairs is gender-
based, with a moral division of labor which is equally
gender-based. Such an understanding, which is quite
normal in the Mediterranean world, can prove trouble-
some in the Western world, and particularly in the United
States, where some social movements would consider the
Mediterranean perspective to be sexist or oppressive.

Handbook of Biblical Social Values, therefore, takes up
words that linguistically embody meanings derived from
the Mediterranean social system. Thus, the entries describe the value-meanings in the linguistic register of cultural anthropology rather than in the linguistic register of
piety (as in a dictionary of spirituality), or the linguistic
register of religion (as in traditional Bible dictionaries).
The linguistic register of cultural anthropology requires a
description of the value-meaning: (1) in itself, (2) with reference to the broader social system, and (3) in contrast to
contemporary United States experience. Each entry strives
to present this kind of information.

The reader who consults the Bible passages listed in
each entry will notice that the values may be *explicitly*
referred to in a given passages or only *implicitly* present
as a feature of circum-Mediterranean societies. For in-

stance, the word "hospitality" is not mentioned explicitly in Matthew 25 (the last judgment scene), but the behaviors listed there and the context of these behaviors leave no doubt that hospitality is definitely implied.

As we shall point out directly, every human group has a set of major value-preference orientations. And, as a rule, the preferred values remain implied in native social interaction; they are implicit values. In this handbook, implicit values will be described at explicit entries. For instance, the implicit value "present orientation" will be described at the explicit entry "time orientation."

VALUE OBJECTS AS A REFLECTION OF HUMAN BEHAVIOR

Values deal with the general direction of behavior. What direction should behavior take? What should guide this behavior? What attitude should be present as a person behaves? Reflection upon the value objects (individual person, others, nature, time, space, and the All or God) helps illustrate this dimension of values. Take careful note that in what follows, the category to which the value objects are assigned is social and cultural rather than psychological. For example, while an "individual" may be any biological entity from a single cell to a complex human being, the "self" is most often a psychological concept, while the "person" is the social and cultural designation. The entries will focus primarily on the social and cultural category.

The Person: Consider the value object called "the individual person." When a person, "the individual self," acts, does society expect this person to be ever mindful of "self"? If the person performing some action can say, "I as an individual am responsible for what I choose. I am doing this present action as I react to this or that stimulus," such a manner of behaving is called "individualistic." The individual person conceives, implements, fulfills, or fails to achieve a very individual goal.

Now suppose an individual person were expected to focus on the group's priorities rather than the individual's preferences, goals, etc. "The group wants, the group needs, the group demands, it would please the group if . . ." The group may be a family or an association like "The Twelve."

Further, suppose society expects individuals to focus on people above and below themselves socially, that is, to focus on hierarchy. "The authorities command, the authorities want, my father wants, the bishop wants, the pope wants, the king wants, or anyone above me wants me to behave thus and so." Obviously, in this hierarchical viewpoint, those below the individual must listen to and obey that person. "They ought to do what I want, what my status demands. They should respect my status, my choices, whatever I do."

These are three general orientations of human behavior. According to the orientation selected, the individual person will be perceived and interpreted as individualistically oriented, group oriented, or hierarchy oriented.

God: Using this same perspective to focus on the All or God, three interpretations are possible. In an individualistic social system, God is viewed as a "junior partner," just another individual like any other individualistic self, albeit more powerful. In a group focused social system, God is perceived to be ever present. God is a member of the group and is present wherever the group is gathered. In a hierarchical social system, God is above everybody else in a role such as king or patron.

Others: In like fashion, when dealing with others, consider whether others in a given society exist to facilitate one's personal ("my") success. "Do I have to learn how to control other persons and things in my environment so that I might succeed? Must I learn how to use other groups in my environment so that I might make it?" This outlook characterizes American *individualism.*

Another way to look at others is to divide them into groups: those who belong ("us") and those who do not belong ("them"). The chief focus is "us." Usually in this perspective "others" may join and leave "us" in some way, hence the abiding concern among "us" will be whether those within our group are trustworthy and can be duly trusted. This is a description of group behavior, or group orientation. Such considerations and relationships are called *collateral*.

Finally, others may be perceived as belonging to statuses held not because of individual achievement but because of birth. High class people are "high class" because they were born into propertied families, born into "blue blood." In this viewpoint, the class above me is there because the families that constitute it have always been above me and my family. The class below me is there because the families that constitute it have always been below me and my family. This is a pyramid in which people attain their position by birth or fictive birth. Such relationships are obviously *lineal* or *hierarchical*. Slaves are such because they were born of slave parents. Others may be looked upon as markers in a hierarchy to which a person is expected to look in order to determine personal status. In such an instance, I mind my own family, or I attend to the members of my group, my faction, my coalition, my family over against other families.

Nature: Consider nature as a value object. When the main goal in society is to live in *harmony* with nature, there is very little concern to possess or own anything. Ownership is generally communal; things belong to everyone, and everyone seeks to fit into the scheme of nature.

On the other hand, when the main value or attitude to nature is *subjection* or *submission*, the chief concern is how to keep nature from doing harm. Nature divinities of various sorts are often involved in antagonistic relationships with one another and with human beings. Hence, human beings with this view of nature seek to develop propitiatory relationships to such divinities. If the divinities can be appeased, human beings can live in peace with nature.

Finally, when human beings believe that they have control over nature, possession or ownership becomes a major value. Ownership, whether by individual or by group, is both prized and sought, and *control* also becomes a major value. Technologies to this end emerge or receive preference in a society where this value orientation prevails.

American readers should easily be able to identify the major value orientations of their society. They probably will find it more challenging to identify and appreciate the major value orientations of Mediterranean society. *Handbook of Biblical Social Values* aims to address that challenge.

THE NEW TESTAMENT WORLD

To give the reader a context or reading scenario for the entries that follow, here is a general overview of *value preferences* common in the world of the people we read about in the New Testament. This overview sketches the dominant values of the Bible. We note that Mediterranean culture, or the culture reflected in the Bible, favors:

(a) being over doing

(b) collateral relations over individualism

(c) present or past time orientation over future

(d) subordination to nature over mastery of it

(e) a view of human nature as a mixture of good and bad elements over a view of human nature as exclusively good or bad.

Knowing this complex of values, then, is essential if a reader wants to truly understand the people of the biblical world.

The following chart illustrates the range of value preferences available to all human beings but specifically as they are ordered in Mediterranean culture. The left column presents the first choice, the middle column the second choice, and the right column the last choice of value preferences in the Mediterranean world, generally speaking.

It should also be noted that these first, second, and third choices represent the dominant male choices. For females in this and every culture, the secondary male value preference tends to be the primary female value preference. Thus, in the United States, males generally are expected to achieve (doing), and only secondarily permit themselves to be spontaneous (being); women in general are primarily expected to be spontaneous, and only secondarily to be dedicated to achieving.

In Mediterranean society relative to this same area of concern, men are primarily socialized to spontaneity,

PROBLEM	RANGE OF SOLUTIONS		
Principal mode of HUMAN ACTIVITY	Being	Being-in-becoming	Doing
INTERPERSONAL RELATIONSHIPS	Collateral	Lineal	Individual
TIME ORIENTATION	Present	Past	Future
RELATIONSHIPS of humans TO NATURE	Be subject to it	Live in harmony with it	Master it
VIEW OF HUMAN NATURE	Mixture of good and evil	Evil	Good

This chart is taken from John J. Pilch, *Introducing the Cultural Context of the New Testament* (New York/Mahwah: Paulist Press, 1991), page 244, copyright © 1991 by John J. Pilch.

while women are primarily socialized to achievement, doing, "work."

The chart on p. xxv presents five major challenges to each culture and arranges the preferred order of responses (value orientations) in the circum-Mediterranean world in general, reading from left to right. It should be apparent that, reading from right to left, one can recognize the preferred order of responses in U.S. culture in general.

The following paragraphs further explain the chart with examples from the Gospel of Luke and other parts of the Bible.

Being: Like most people in his world, Luke viewed everything in dualistic terms. "Who is not with me is against me; who does not gather with me scatters" (Luke 11:23). Hence, people are divided into two groups: wheat or chaff (3:17) and bad or good soil (8:11–15). And the crowds are necessarily "divided" in the presence of Jesus into groups favorable to him and groups rejecting him; after all, "this child is set for the rise and fall of many" (2:34). All of Jesus' preaching serves to bring to light the *being* of people, where they stand and on which side of the line they are.

How vital it is in Luke's world to be in God's kingdom rather than in the kingdom of Satan, God's enemy. Luke's world, of course, is dualistically divided into two kingdoms, God's and Satan's. The role of Jesus is that of "savior" who liberates those in Satan's kingdom and brings them into God's kingdom, that is, into a different *state of being.* Hence, Jesus "saves" people from Satan's power by liberating them from misfortune and illness, sin and death (4:18–19; 7:11–15; 7:37–50; 13:16).

Collateral Relationships: The persons of Luke's world are invariably known not as individuals but in terms of relationships or embeddedness within a group. Personal identity derives primarily from group affiliation. People are "sons of so-and-so" or members of a certain family or clan. They are members of "parties" such as the Pharisees, Sadducees, or scribes. A major question may arise about "who is my neighbor?" (10:29) because the answer would clarify collateral relationships and hence appropriate duties.

Jesus seemingly attacks one set of collateral relationships, even as he replaces it with another. There is a considerable body of material in Luke which is highly critical of blood ties and kinship bonds. Jesus states that he has come not to bring "peace" but "division." He will set family members against one another (12:50–53). Later he states that those who do not "hate" family members cannot be his disciples (14:26–27). And he criticizes those who prize these family relationships but still want to be his disciples (9:57–62). Luke even indicates that Jesus was more dedicated to the affairs of his heavenly Father than to the concerns of his parents (2:48–50). Finally, he described his authentic family not as his blood relatives but as those who "hear the word of God and do it" (8:19–21). But even as he criticizes one set of collateral relations, the basic kinship group, Jesus proclaims its replacement by attachment to him and his new fictive kinship group. Disciples remain in relationship, only in different collateral ones. Disciples are subsequently identified as embedded in Jesus and his group by taking his name for their primary identification: "And in Antioch the disciples were for the first time called Christians" (Acts 11:26; see 26:28).

Present Time Orientation: Modern readers of Luke–Acts frequently identify as a major theme of his works the motif of "prophecy-fulfillment." The scenario needed for understanding this "prophecy-fulfillment" material is the present time orientation which Luke shares with his world. Now is the time to be alive, for God has remembered his promises to Abraham (Luke 1:54–55, 72–73) and to David (1:32–33). Now is the great day of salvation when the prophecies of redemption and salvation are fulfilled (Luke 2:25–26, 38).

Luke most dramatically expresses his present time orientation with the emphatic comment "Today!" Angels tell shepherds that *"Today* is born to you a savior" (2:11, author's trans.). Jesus himself proclaims that Isaiah's prophecies of gospel and liberation are fulfilled *"today* in your hearing" (4:21). To the tax collector Zacchaeus Jesus proclaims that *"Today* salvation has come to this house" (19:9), even as he tells the dying insurrectionist, *"Today* . . . you will be with me in paradise" (23:43). Therefore, do not expect much talk in Luke of Jesus' future coming. The basic time orientation is on "today" and not the distant future (see 12:28; 13:32–33).

This time orientation might lead a reader to examine again the statements about God's kingdom in Luke–Acts. If these reflections prove stimulating, a reader might well find a strong emphasis on what theologians call "realized eschatology," an emphasis on what is already achieved in Jesus. In Luke, one would look specifically at a passage such as 17:20–21 in which God's kingdom as a future or distant event is criticized in favor of a present orientation: "For behold, the kingdom of God is in the midst of you."

Relationships of Human Beings to Nature: With regard to *nature* it seems quite clear that first-century Palestinians felt there was little a human being could do to counteract the forces of nature. Their primary value orientation, like that of all peasants, was to suffer nature, to be *subject to it.* From this perspective Jesus' healings and miracles stand out as exceptional events in a world where humankind had no power over nature. When Jesus casts out a demon, the crowd is genuinely amazed: "With authority and power he commands the unclean spirits, and they come out" (Luke 4:36). When Jesus calms the storm, his disciples marvel: "Who then is this, that he commands even wind and water, and they obey him?" (Luke 8:24–25).

Assessment of Human Nature: The first-century Mediterranean assessment of human nature is that it is a mixture of good and evil propensities. Paul, for example, uses the words "flesh" and "spirit" to describe two different "drives" a human being experiences in nature and activity. To the Galatians, he writes that " . . . the works of the flesh are plain: fornication, impurity, licentiousness, idolatry, sorcery, enmity, strife, jealousy, anger, selfishness, dissension, party spirit, envy, drunkenness, carousing, and the like. . . . But the fruit of the Spirit is love, joy, peace, patience, kindness, goodness, faithfulness, gentleness, self-control" (Gal 5:19–23).

Jesus is even more to the point in his private discussions with his disciples after his confrontation with the Pharisees regarding support of one's parents (Mark 7). "What comes out of a [person] is what defiles a [person]. For from within, out of the heart of [the person], come evil thoughts, fornication, theft, murder, adultery, coveting, wickedness, deceit, licentiousness, [the evil eye] or envy, slander, pride, foolishness. All these evil things come from within, and they defile a person" (Mark 7:20–22, author's trans.). Here Jesus describes the wicked propensities of a human being.

In summary, not only must modern observers and interpreters clarify their own viewpoint and articulate their own values, they must strive as well to imagine and learn the viewpoint and values of those of another culture whom they would study. The model presented schematically here can be studied in greater detail elsewhere (see John J. Pilch, "Sickness and Healing in Luke–Acts," in *The Social World of Luke–Acts: Models for Interpretation* [ed. Jerome H. Neyrey, Peabody, Mass.: Hendrickson, 1991] pp. 181–209; and John J. Pilch, *Introducing the Cultural Context of the New Testament* [New York/Mahwah: Paulist, 1991]). Additional information about the United States based on this same model can be found in Edward C. Stewart and Milton J. Bennet, *American Cultural Patterns: A Cross-Cultural Perspective* (rev. ed.; Yarmouth, Maine: Intercultural, 1991). Such a study can prove to be of inestimable value in analyzing and comparing the U.S.

with the various groups that populated the first-century Mediterranean world. It can also assist in interpreting New Testament texts with sensitivity to the value preferences of the Mediterranean culture in which these texts originated.

The chart that follows was designed by Bruce J. Malina to illustrate how these various value preferences are arranged differently by different groups in the first-century Mediterranean world. Readers should be able to recognize the short-hand in the chart as it reflects the fuller statement of value preferences identified in the model above.

Key: "⇨" = is preferred to

Being-in-becoming characterizes that cultural preference whereby a person seeks to develop all aspects of personality at one time. Such a person often begins one activity and then turns to another, and yet another, prior to completing the first.

Note well the contrast between the value preferences of Jesus (along with Israelite peasants) and mainstream United States citizens. In contrast to prevailing American culture, the Mediterranean world in general places emphasis on:

1. *being and/or becoming* (that is, on *states*),
   not on *doing* (activity)

2. *collateral* (group) and *lineal (hierarchical) relationships*,
   not on *individualism*

3. *present* and *past* time orientation,
   not on the *future*

4. the *uncontrollable* factor of *nature*,
   not on its *manipulation* or *mastery*

5. *human nature* which is a mixture of both *good and bad*,
   not *neutral* or *correctable*.

VALUE ORIENTATION PROFILES

Italian Rural

Activity	Being ⇨ Being-in-becoming ⇨ Doing
Relational	Collateral ⇨ Lineal ⇨ Individual
Time	Present ⇨ Past ⇨ Future
People-Nature	Subordinate to ⇨ Live with ⇨ Rule over
Human nature	Mixed ⇨ Evil ⇨ Good

Israelite Peasant

Activity	Being ⇨ Being-in-becoming ⇨ Doing
Relational	Collateral ⇨ Lineal ⇨ Individual
Time	Present ⇨ Past ⇨ Future
People-Nature	Subordinate to ⇨ Live with ⇨ Rule over
Human nature	Mixed ⇨ Evil ⇨ Good

Jesus

Activity	Being-in-becoming ⇨ Being ⇨ Doing
Relational	Collateral ⇨ Individual ⇨ Lineal
Time	Present ⇨ Past ⇨ Future
People-Nature	Live with ⇨ Subordinate to ⇨ Rule over
Human nature	Mixed ⇨ Evil ⇨ Good

Roman

Activity	Being-in-becoming ⇨ Being ⇨ Doing
Relational	Lineal ⇨ Collateral ⇨ Individual
Time	Past ⇨ Present ⇨ Future
People-Nature	Rule over ⇨ Live with ⇨ Subordinate to
Human nature	Good ⇨ Mixed ⇨ Evil

Judean Elite

Activity	Being ⇨ Being-in-becoming ⇨ Doing
Relational	Lineal ⇨ Collateral ⇨ Individual
Time	Present ⇨ Past ⇨ Future
People-Nature	Rule over ⇨ Live with ⇨ Subordinate to
Human nature	Mixed ⇨ Evil ⇨ Good

Paul

Activity	Being-in-becoming ⇨ Being ⇨ Doing
Relational	Lineal ⇨ Collateral ⇨ Individual
Time	Present ⇨ Past ⇨ Future
People-Nature	Subordinate to ⇨ Live with ⇨ Rule over
Human nature	Evil ⇨ Mixed ⇨ Good

Greek

Activity	Being ⇨ Doing ⇨ Being-in-becoming
Relational	Lineal ⇨ Individual ⇨ Collateral
Time	Present ⇨ Past ⇨ Future
People-Nature	Subordinate to ⇨ Live with ⇨ Rule over
Human nature	Mixed ⇨ Evil ⇨ Good

Pharisees

Activity	Being ⇨ Doing ⇨ Being-in-becoming
Relational	Lineal ⇨ Individual ⇨ Collateral
Time	Past ⇨ Present ⇨ Future
People-Nature	Subordinate to ⇨ Live with ⇨ Rule over
Human nature	Mixed ⇨ Evil ⇨ Good

American

Activity	Doing ⇨ Being ⇨ Being-in-becoming
Relational	Individual ⇨ Collateral ⇨ Lineal
Time	Future ⇨ Present ⇨ Past
People-Nature	Rule over ⇨ Subordinate to ⇨ Live with
Human nature	Neutral ⇨ Evil ⇨ Good

To facilitate still deeper immersion into the world of the Bible in general and the New Testament in particular, consider the following chart of comparative features contrasting U.S. and Mediterranean societies. Familiarity with this chart will shed great light on the handbook entries.

Feature	U.S. Society	Mediterranean Society
Privacy	There is an unwillingness to enter the private lives of others or to have others enter one's own private life.	There is an unwillingness to leave alone the lives of others or to have others leave alone one's own life.
Communities	People have to freely join communities; they tend to have broad, shallow relationships rather than deep, long-term ones. Americans avoid obligations and indebtedness to others.	People have no choice but to fit into inherited communities; they have extremely few but deep relationships within those communities.
Primary reality	The basic belief is individualist realism. The individual is believed to be the primary reality, with society as a second order, artificial or derived construct.	The basic belief is group realism. Society (groups) is believed to be the primary reality, while the individual is a second order, artificial or derived construct.
Psychological development of the child	The focus in childhood psychological development is on separation, individuation, and leaving home in late adolescence (a sort of second birth). The prospect of the child never leaving	The focus in childhood psychological development is on co-dependence, on group embeddedness, "dyadization," and the son(s) and wife's fitting into the paternal home upon marriage

	home is a discomforting option for both parents and child.	rather early in adolescence. The prospect of a (male) child ever leaving home is a frightening thing for both parent and (male) child.
Moral imperative	The moral imperative is: be good because it makes sense, it is right, it works, it leads to competitive success.	The moral imperative is: be good to those in the group so that people in the group will continue to love/like/help you. The outside is important only insofar as it impacts the group.
Personal beliefs	One discovers one's personal beliefs in the isolation of one's private self. The self is seen as autonomous, imagined as existing independently, entirely outside any controlling tradition and community; individuals see themselves as actually free to choose their tradition and community.	One discovers one's deepest beliefs in and through the group, the community, and its traditions. There is rarely, if ever, an experience of an autonomous self; it is rather impossible to imagine a self acting independently, outside the inherited tradition and the community that upholds it.
Life	Life is like a game in which one joins teams for sociable problem solving, requiring respect for rules as much as love of competition. The good life offers achievement-oriented security within a fixed social order.	For elites, life is like a pilgrimage or quest, with a story line or narrative that links present to past, the individual to society, and both to a meaningful, ever unfolding cosmos.
		For the vast majority, the non-elites, life is a skirmish of

		ongoing conflicts in defense of the scarce acquisitions amassed by one's group and always desired by others. In these conflicts it seems that the immoral are ever victorious.
Personal features	Salient personal features are: self-reliance, individual happiness and success, self-realization, and psychological gratification.	Salient personal features are: strength of character, perseverance, concern for status, group well-being, and satisfaction from status and role performance.
Causality	Focus is on efficient cause (on how to produce effects, know-how, pragmatism). The focus is on future oriented potential (but without asking for what purpose, why?). There is achievement orientation assessed in terms of quantity (and often regardless of the quality of the achievement). The morality of a problem lies in the goodness or badness of strategies, means or techniques, hence on utilitarian concerns.	Focus is on final cause (for what purpose, on know-why, purposiveness). The focus is on present oriented selection of tasks in terms of purposes for pursuing them (but without concern for how these goals might in fact be realized; good facade and good intention suffice). The morality of a problem lies in the goodness or badness of principles concerning the ends pursued, hence on intentions.
Freedom	Concern is with a freer, more autonomous self; to be free of obstacles is a good in itself, with little concern about	Concern is with the primary goal of maintaining the status quo; to be free of constraints is a precarious

	asking "free for what?"	position, hence, little concern about asking, "how to get free?"
Focus or attentiveness	Constant attentiveness is given to what one does as individual agent. Total inattentiveness to what one has received from others or to one's obligations to those from whom one has received.	Constant attentiveness is given to what one has received from others and one's duties to those from whom one has received. Total inattentiveness to what one in fact has individually contributed to the realization of goals.
Nature of society	Society is individualist oriented; it is based on individual achievement orientation. Tenancy is temporary; no hereditary dependency. Obligation derives from individuals contracting to their own self-interest.	Society is kinship oriented: lineage and inherited status are decisive. Tenancy is permanent, serving as the basis of hereditary dependency. Obligation derives from group membership and serves the survival of the group.
Kinship relations	Since kinship relations are independent of individual choice and will, they can be dismissed to a considerable extent (unless elaborated on another basis, e.g., friendship).	Since kinship relations are independent of individual choice and will, they are perceived as God given, sacred. They couple with other imposed relations such as civic friendship in public solidarity (high grid) or in contending factions (low grid).
Relationships	Anything that creates more sensitive, more open, more intense, more	Anything that creates more obedient, more closed, more passive, more

	charitable relationships points to achievements of which group members may be proud. But anything that renders those same relationships fragile and vulnerable is seen to undermine those achievements (although free individual choice requires fragile and vulnerable relationships).	compliant relationships points to achievements of which group members may be proud. And anything that renders those same relationships permanent and unwaveringly impermeable is seen to further support those achievements.
True good	Since the only measure of good is what is good for the self, something that is really a burden to the self cannot be good.	Since the only measure of good is what is good for the group, something that is really a burden to the group cannot be good.
Meaning of life	The ultimate meaning of life stands quite apart from conforming to the purely procedural and institutionally variable rules and regulations that surround the individual in society; self-integration is what counts.	The ultimate meaning of life consists precisely in conforming to the purely procedural and institutionally variable rules and regulations that surround the individual in society; social integration is what counts.
Right to think	It is ethically and religiously wrong to violate the individual's right to: think for oneself, judge for oneself, make one's own decisions, or live life as one sees fit.	It is ethically and religiously wrong to violate the group's right to have its legitimate managers: think for its members, judge on their behalf, make decisions for them, or make sure that life is lived as those managers see fit.

Society and the individual	The individual is prior to society; society comes into existence only through the voluntary contract of individuals trying to maximize their own self-interests.	Society is prior to the individual; individuals come into existence as singular persons only through the societal recognition and legitimation of singular individual roles and statuses exercised by persons on behalf of their group(s) and trying to maximize the group's collective interests.
Success	Success is the outcome of free competition among individuals in an open market.	Success consists in living up to and maintaining one's inherited social status.
Achievement	Achievement is deserved only to the extent that individuals can claim to have succeeded through their own efforts. While others may have contributed, a successful person denies the moral relevance of those contributions.	Achievement is deserved only to the extent that individuals can claim to have succeeded through inherited status, kinship connections, and the group support that is one's due. A successful person is aware only of the moral relevance of the contribution of others to one's success.
Politics	Politics is viewed in terms of a consensual community of autonomous but essentially similar individuals.	For elites, politics is viewed in terms of the nation (or ethnic group) in which concerns of national (ethnic) interest and the best families that embody and represent those concerns

		transcend particular interests. For the vast majority, the non-elites, politics is viewed in terms of conflict among contending groups with differing utilitarian and expressive interests.
Illegitimacy and anomalous status	Non-autonomous individuals are illegitimate and anomalous.	For elites, families that represent non-elite and non-national interests are therefore illegitimate and anomalous.
		For the vast majority, the non-elites, groupless, unconnected individuals and families are therefore illegitimate and anomalous.
Wealth and power	Different levels and degrees of wealth and power derive from competition and achievement assessed as amoral.	For elites, different levels and degrees of wealth and power are what constitute the social body and have positive moral meaning (United States residents see this as due to exploitation and oppression, but Mediterraneans see it as deriving from some higher order norm ennobling and obliging high status people).
		For the vast majority, the non-elites, different levels and degrees of wealth

		and power are due to inequalities of moral probity, with the wealthier and more powerful perceived as more corrupt.
Religion	Religion, a free standing institution, is concerned with the moral order; religion is an individual concern operating through voluntary associations.	Religion, embedded in kinship and/or politics, is concerned with the moral order; domestic and/or political religion is a public concern, controlled by elites and operating to maintain the public order.
Attitudes and behaviors	Emphasis is on self-control, self-respect, and ethical commitments in a competitive world.	Emphasis is on deference and obedience to public authorities, on submission toward serving the stable harmony of an organic community.
Emphasis in religion	The emphasis in religion is on the individualistic, the self-affirming, the affective (e.g., on "God's" love or the equivalent, on sentiment and emotion, on acceptance of the self).	The emphasis in religion is on the collective, the group-affirming, the rational (e.g., on God's truth and commands, on doctrine and on objective ethical norms).

The Mediterranean world is a conflict-ridden world: it is agonistic (see **POWER**). But conflict is over practical means, not over ends. Conflict over practical means in no way implies doubts over ends. Conflict over the practical dimensions of realizing some goal or stage of behavior (e.g., how to leave home effectively, start a change group, choose a marriage partner) in no way means a conflict or even a doubt over the value of the goal or stage of behavior (e.g., to leave home at all, to work for change, to get married).

HOW TO USE THIS REFERENCE WORK

This handbook requires the reader's collaboration. Attend to whether the words and Mediterranean values described here are evidenced in all parts of the Bible. While the contributors are Bible scholars, not one of them believes that every occurrence of their assigned word and value has been identified and listed. The best way to use this Bible resource is to accept the words and values as presented at face value and to use them as a set of new lenses with which to read familiar Bible passages. The reader should strive to determine whether these new lenses make a difference in understanding and interpreting these familiar passages.

The question is not whether the entry is correct or incorrect. The question is whether it covers all cases. Can the definition and description offered in the entry be validated? Can the reader demonstrate that the explanation is valid or invalid? If the definition seems to work in a majority of cases, take careful note of the cases in which it doesn't seem to work and seek to explain why it does not work.

The editors and all the collaborators in *Handbook of Biblical Social Values* encourage readers to submit their comments and suggestions for improving subsequent editions of this pioneer publication.

John J. Pilch
Bruce J. Malina

Handbook of Biblical Social Values

ACTIVENESS/PASSIVENESS

As a value preference, "being" is favored over "doing" by people in the Bible, and living in harmony with or being in subjection to nature is preferred to seeking to master it. Consequently, it is no surprise to find that the group oriented (see **GROUP ORIENTATION**), dyadic personalities (see **DYADISM**) who people the pages of the Bible tend to deal with problem situations as follows: activeness is generally favored as a characteristic of affairs among human beings, whereas passiveness is favored in affairs having to do with God. Understood in this way, activeness and passiveness are secondary values since they are peculiar to specific arenas of human interaction.

Humanity: The people of Israel have the obligation to uphold the divinely instituted law and cultural traditions which govern their affairs. In this way, the holiness of Israel is assured (Exod 24:7–8; Deut 5:28–33). In the culture known to the Bible's authors, the ideally energetic pursuit of holiness demands constant vigilance in observing the law (Ps 119), avoiding impurity and pollution (Leviticus), and adhering to the requirements of one's social status (Sir 7:1–17). Considerable social energy is expended in the effort to keep boundaries (legal, religious, societal) obvious and to make crossing them dangerous (Lev 18; 20). Thus, the culture's resources are marshalled to maintain a relatively static equilibrium. This can be achieved only with the full and active cooperation of a society convinced of the rightness of its way of life (Ps 115).

God: God demands vigorous observance of the law and enthusiastic endorsement of the tradition from his people (Josh 24), but in his presence, i.e., in the face of his proclamations or great works, passiveness born of worship, i.e., awe and "fear of the Lord" (the *mysterium tremendum*), are the only legitimate responses (Ps 46:11; Isa 41:1, 47:5; Zech 2:17; Mark 16:8).

Indeed, the two attitudes, activeness and passiveness, are integrally interconnected and reciprocal—the first flowing from the second. That is, the self-revelation of God to Israel is the foundation of Israel's self-understanding as the people of the Covenant. Therefore, the law and the traditions which maintain the people's holiness as God's own must be upheld (activeness) lest God remove his presence, abrogate the covenant, and shatter the peace and security (passiveness) his presence affords (1 Sam 15:22–23; Ezek 10–11; 1 Cor 11:17–30).

In modern Western culture, ideas of activeness/passiveness are conceived along different lines. The relative autonomy of individuals is assumed, their obligations to the group are limited, and responsibilities to the self may legitimately transcend the group's demands. Furthermore, activeness in virtually every sphere of life (including the religious) is more generally favored in our culture than passiveness. (According to the model of value preferences presented in the Introduction, Western culture in general holds "doing" as a primary value, while "being," an occasionally more passive stance, is generally the third preference.) A pluralistic, technocratic society like the United States's encourages change, consciously tolerates a wide variety of religious and political expression, and prizes social mobility. In contrast, Mediterranean culture's stress on maintaining the status quo seems to a modern Western observer overbearing in its control of individual persons, overconfident of its knowledge of God's will, resistant to social evolution, and hence, outmoded. (Mark McVann)

Malina, Bruce J. 1994. " 'Let him deny himself' (Mark 8:34 & Par): A Social Psychological Model of Self-Denial." *Biblical Theology Bulletin* 24:106–19.

Malina, Bruce J., and Jerome H. Neyrey. 1991. "First-Century Personality: Dyadic, Not Individual." In *The Social World of Luke–Acts: Models for Interpretation.* Ed. Jerome H. Neyrey. Pp. 67–96. Peabody, Mass.: Hendrickson.

AGONISTIC SOCIETY—SEE POWER

AGRARIAN SOCIETY

The term "agrarian" does not refer simply to agriculture, for the agrarian world is not simply a world of farming and farmers. The term refers to the societies in which mass agriculture, made possible by the invention of the plow, wheel, and sail, the discovery of metallurgy, and the domestication of animals, replaced the small-scale hoe agriculture of earlier periods. The result was a rapid increase in agricultural production that created relatively large-scale economic surpluses for the first time in history, enabling an administrative category of persons to live off the surplus. The ripple effect produced coinage, alphabetic writing, standing armies, the spread of the pre-industrial city and the empire state. It was a world in which both city dweller and peasant farmer shared an outlook that was sharply different from that common in the industrial world.

The world of the New Testament was an agrarian world. It differed from modern society in ways that are easily overlooked. A random list can serve to remind us how great the transformation wrought by the industrial revolution really was:

1. In agrarian societies, 90 percent of the population was rural. In industrial societies 90 percent is urban.

2. In agrarian societies 90–95 percent of the population was engaged in so-called "primary" industries: farming and extracting raw materials. In the United States it is currently 4.9 percent.

3. In agrarian societies 2–3 percent of the population was literate. In industrial societies 2–3 percent are not.

4. The birthrate in agrarian societies was about 40 per thousand per year. In the U.S. it is less than half of that. Yet death rates have dropped even more dramatically than birthrates. We thus have the curious phenomenon of far fewer births and rising population.

5. Life expectancy in Rome in the first century BCE was 20 years at birth. If the perilous years of infancy were survived, it rose to

about 40 years—one-half of present expectations in the industrial world.

6. The U.S. Department of Labor lists in excess of 20,000 different occupations in this country, and hundreds are added annually. In an agrarian society for which we have records, the picture is somewhat different: the tax rolls for medieval (1313 CE) Paris list 157.

7. In agrarian societies 1–3 percent of the population usually owns one- to two-thirds of the arable land.

8. The size of the federal bureaucracy in the U.S. in 1816 (the period of transition to the industrial era) was 5, 000 employees. By 1971 it was 2,852,000 and still growing.

9. More than one-half of all families in agrarian societies were broken during the child-bearing and child-rearing years by the death of one or both parents. In India at the turn of the twentieth century it was 71 percent. Widows and orphans were thus an extremely widespread phenomenon.

10. In agrarian societies the family was the unit of production as well as consumption. Since the industrial revolution, family enterprise has nearly disappeared, and the individual has become the unit of production. The productive capacity of most industrial societies exceeds that of the most advanced agrarian societies by more than one hundredfold.

11. The largest "factories" in Roman antiquity did not exceed 50 workers; in the records of medieval London (pop. 35,000) the largest employed 18. The industrial corporation, a modern invention, did not exist in any agrarian society.

12. In 1850 the "prime movers" in the U.S. (i.e., steam engines in factories, sailing vessels, work animals, etc.) had a combined capacity of 8.5 million horsepower. By 1970 this had risen to 20 billion horsepower.

13. The cost of moving one ton of goods one mile (measured in U.S. dollars in China at the beginning of the industrial revolution) was:

Steamboat	2.4	Wheelbarrow	20.0
Rail	2.7	Pack donkey	24.0
Junk	12.0	Pack horse	30.0
Animal-drawn cart	13.0	Carrying by pole	48.0
Pack mule	17.0		

Obviously, land-based trade in agrarian societies was sharply limited in both distance and quantity.

14. Given the shock and consternation caused by the assassination of John F. Kennedy and the forced resignation of Richard M. Nixon, we sometimes forget that this sort of internal political upheaval is nothing like what it was in the agrarian world. Of the 79 Roman emperors, 31 were murdered, 6 were driven to suicide and 4 were deposed by force. Moreover, such upheavals in antiquity were frequently accompanied by civil war and the enslavement of thousands.

This list could extend much longer. Moreover, this list of information is random in nature. It may provide a feel, however, for the kind of change that has occurred as a result of the industrial revolution. It may also serve to alert the reader of the Bible to the fact that values in agrarian societies were sharply different from anything we know today.

For example, agrarian peasants favored a present orientation over future planning and subjection to or harmony with nature rather than attempts at controlling it. Peasants (the elite were a different matter) focused on "being" and surviving within a social system rather than on "doing," achieving, amassing surplus and hoarding it.

Such examples as these remind us that the outlook and value system of most persons living in the modern, industrialized, and information-oriented society is literally worlds apart from that of the agrarian society of the Bible. They make clear the need to reflect upon agrarian society and its values in order to empathize with the first audiences of the biblical books. (Richard Rohrbaugh)

Carney, Thomas F. 1975. *The Shape of the Past: Models and Antiquity.* Lawrence, Kans.: Coronado.

Finley, Moses I. 1985. *The Ancient Economy.* 2d ed. London: Hogarth.

Kautsky, J. H. 1982. *The Politics of Aristocratic Empires.* Chapel Hill: University of North Carolina Press.

Lenski, Gerhard. 1984. *Power and Privilege.* Chapel Hill: University of North Carolina Press.

Lenski, Gerhard, et al. 1995. *Human Societies: An Introduction to Macro-sociology.* 7th ed. New York: McGraw Hill.

Paige, Jeffrey M. 1975. *Agrarian Revolution.* New York: Free.

Sjoberg, Gideon. 1960. *The Preindustrial City.* New York: Macmillan.

Stavenhagen, Rodolfo. 1975. *Social Classes in Agrarian Societies.* Garden City: Doubleday.

Ste. Croix, G. E. M. de. 1981. *The Class Struggle in the Ancient Greek World from the Archaic Age to the Arab Conquests.* Ithaca: Cornell University Press.

Weber, Max. 1976. *The Agrarian Sociology of Ancient Civilizations.* Trans. R. I. Frank. Atlantic Highlands: Humanities.

ALMSGIVING—SEE ALTRUISM

ALLEGIANCE (PERSONAL AND GROUP)—SEE TRUST

ALTRUISM (ALMSGIVING)

This value urges those who have surplus goods or services to give to those who have little or nothing at all. It is part of the pattern of adaptation to the environment typical of subsistence societies, that is, societies which consume nearly all that they produce. Altruism is eminently interpersonal and invariably group specific. The "others" with whom one shares one's surplus, the "others" from whom one can ask for alms, are nearly always members of one's kinship group or ethnic group. The neighbor whom one is to love as oneself in Lev 19:18 is one's fellow Israelite. Altruism in antiquity never takes on universal scope, except perhaps in the ideal state envisioned by Stoic philosophers with their "Fatherhood of God and brotherhood of males."

"Ask and you shall receive" (Matt 7:7) is a cultural truism in such a context because altruism is an inescapable obligation incumbent upon more fortunate group members in a society which believes that all goods are limited in supply and already distributed (see LIMITED GOOD). Anyone with a personal surplus will normally feel shame and/or be considered greedy (Luke 12:15) or rapacious if that surplus is not shared with less fortunate "neighbors" (Luke 11:41). In Jesus' parable, the rich land-owner who intended to hoard his bumper crop rather than share it with less fortunate fellow citizens is called a "fool" by God (Luke 12:13–21).

The same value of altruism prompts a powerful person sometimes to forgo rights to goods so as to appear magnanimous. The king who forgave his peasant-servant exemplifies this altruism which nevertheless failed to impress that same peasant. When faced with a very similar challenge, this peasant was unable to see beyond his meager subsistence level of existence and was unwilling to forgive in kind (Matt 18:23–35).

In the final analysis, altruism is a means value that facilitates the realization of the core value of maintaining honor and avoiding shame. As such it is a key way of obtaining approval in the community, earning its respect, and increasing one's own self-respect. The Baptist urged his fellow Israelite with two coats or surplus food to share with the one who had none (Luke 3:11). Jesus proposed lending to one's fellow Israelite and expecting nothing in return (Luke 6:35) and inviting to the banquet those unable to reciprocate (Luke 14:13–14).

In mainstream United States culture, altruism (almsgiving) takes the form of impersonal and universally oriented generosity that operates in a highly organized context. Examples include riding a bus to a predetermined meeting place 200 miles from one's hometown to "hold hands across America" and pledge money to help the invisible and distant poor; dropping contributions to Jerry Lewis's Labor Day Telethon into a fishbowl located curbside at the local radio or television station without having to step out of the car; etc. All the while the economically poor are actually visible all around these "altruistic" people but are ignored or unobserved by them. (John J. Pilch)

Eisenstadt, Stuart N., and L. Roniger. 1980. "Patron Client Relations as a Model of Structuring Social Exchange." *Comparative Studies in Society and History* 22:42–77.

Foster, George. 1965. "Peasant Society and the Image of the Limited Good." *American Anthropologist* 67:293–315.

Gregory, James R. 1975. "Image of Limited Good, or Expectation of Reciprocity?" *Current Anthropology* 16:73–92.

Malina, Bruce J. 1988. "Patron and Client: The Analogy Behind Synoptic Theology." *Forum* 4/1:2–32.

Moxnes, Halvor. 1988. *The Economy of the Kingdom: Social Conflict and Economic Relations in Luke's Gospel.* Philadelphia: Fortress.

Oakman, Douglas E. 1986. *Jesus and the Economic Questions of His Day.* Lewiston, N.Y.: Mellen.

ASSERTIVENESS

The term embodies qualities related to boldness, openness, frankness, and self-confidence in speaking (Greek: *parrhēsia*). In classical and hellenistic Greek societies, assertiveness was practiced in political life which itself was limited to citizens: they alone had authority and responsibility to speak their mind and pursue their rights. Such liberty to speak was a right that enabled a citizen to proclaim truth before his fellows without fear. In the sphere of personal relations, assertiveness was the moral freedom manifested especially toward friends who valued openness in mutual dealings. It was the golden mean that preserved one from being impudent before equals and from fawning before superiors.

This quality appears in biblical writings only in those parts of Scripture written or translated under the influence of hellenistic Judaic writers and in the New Testament. The translator of Job states that the repentant sinner can pray before God with freedom to speak his mind (Job 22:26–27). Later, an unknown sage proclaimed that the just person will abide with God forever in self-confidence (Wis 5:1, 5). This quality therefore is a means value that assists or helps a person to maintain and preserve honor, the core value common to the entire Mediterranean world.

In the Synoptic Gospels Jesus' speech is designated as having assertiveness only once, when he boldly predicts to his disciples that he will be betrayed by the religious authorities (Mark 8:32). In contrast, frankness is a quality associated with the way Jesus speaks and acts in the Fourth Gospel both toward enemies (John 7:26; 18:20) and with his disciples (John 11:1–14; 16:25, 29). The crowd also demands openness of Jesus in asking him to reveal whether he is the Messiah (John 10:24).

Assertiveness emerges as a characteristic of believers. When Jesus is revealed as judge, his disciples will enjoy this freedom (1 John 2:28; 4:17). Yet they already have this freedom in that, even if their hearts trouble them, believers pray and function as totally open to God, who accepts them as gifted with the Holy Spirit and the love that casts out fear (1 John 3:19–21; 4:18; 5:14; Heb 10:19). The book of Acts esteems assertiveness as a value for Christian preachers. Peter, Paul, and other evangelists employ this freedom in the way they give public witness to the good news, thanks to the power of the Holy Spirit (Acts 2:29; 4:13, 29, 31; 9:27–28; 13:46; 14:3; 18:26; 19:8; 26:26; 28:31).

The Pauline corpus also employs assertiveness to describe the apostle's style of witness (2 Cor 3:12; 7:4; Eph 3:12; 6:19; Phil 1:20; 1 Thess 2:2; Phlm 8). Jesus displayed this freedom in his triumph over the principalities and powers at his resurrection (Col 2:15). The letter to the Hebrews reminds the recipients that they too have this freedom and urges them not to lose it (Heb 3:6; 4:16; 10:19, 35).

Parrhēsia was the mark of full participation in a free society in honest speech and courageous action. It was a means of pursuing the goals of that free society, and thus it is a means value. Christians, with their sense of being set apart from both Judaic and Roman agendas, applied this value to the exercise of their heavenly citizenship in proclamation, witness, and prayer. Martyrdom was and is the final witness of Christian assertiveness. The treason of apostasy meant betrayal of this quality.

Citizens of modern democracies value assertiveness as one of their most important rights. They do not look upon it as a guardian of traditional values but as a value that must be cultivated with creative vigilance. Contemporary Americans are committed to imaginative styles as the key to leadership in political, economic, and social spheres. Politicians sell their programs by assertiveness. But the intense competitiveness fostered by prevailing social standards drives a wedge between freedom of speech and honesty of action. Hence, liberal self-interest is different from the candor of truth. (†James M. Reese)

Fitzgerald, John T., ed. 1996. *Friendship, Flattery, and Frankness of Speech: Studies on Friendship in the New Testament World.* Leiden/New York/ Cologne: E. J. Brill.

Unnik, W. C. van. 1962. "The Christian's Freedom of Speech in the New Testament." *Bulletin of the John Ryland's Library* 44:466–88, reprinted in *Sparsa Collecta: The Collected Essays of W. C. van Unnik* (3 vols.; Novum Testamentum Supplements 29–31; Leiden: Brill, 1973–1983) 2:269–89.

ATTACHMENT (PERSONAL AND GROUP)—SEE LOVE

AUTHORITARIANISM—SEE ALSO DOMINATION ORIENTATION; POWER

This is a value-set rather than a simple, single value. The cluster of values that comprise authoritarianism is rooted in the social experience of authority nearly always sanctioned by force. "Authority" refers to the socially recognized and approved ability to control the behavior of others. For example, parents have authority over their minor children, the police have authority over the citizenry in disorderly or problem situations, physicians over persons committed to hospitals, and the like. Authority is common to all human societies. But what is not common is the nature of sanction(s) involved for not complying with the directions or commands of authority. Such sanctions can be fines, property confiscation, public service, required study, return to parents or family, beatings, imprisonment, and the like. When the prevailing, if not exclusive, sanction is *force* (i.e., physical arrest and imprisonment, the inflicting of physical and psycho-physical pain ranging from beating and bombing to torture and death), there is good reason to believe that the society in question is authoritarian.

Authoritarian societies repeat and reinforce the focus on force as sanction with a number of values. These values include the expectation of: (1) total submissiveness (see **OBEDIENCE**) to authority; (2) the tendency to exercise power for its own sake (see **POWER**); (3) admiration for the application of physical force (see **PARENTING**); and (4) high regard for a person's ability to endure pain. Further, these force-related values are often clustered with the following features: (5) a tendency to be very conventional (see **COMPLIANCE**); (6) great sensitivity to group pressure (see **GROUP ORIENTATION**); (7) anti-introspective personality; (8) a preference for thinking in terms of either/or, black or white; (9) a tendency to shift responsibility from the individual onto outside forces, human and non-human, and to project one's unacceptable impulses onto others, particularly "out-groups"; and (10) a preference for stereotypical thinking.

It would seem that the whole of the ancient Mediterranean world was a world of authoritarianism, characterized by the foregoing features. Any perusal of the Bible will readily reveal how the God of Israel requires total submissiveness. The *Shema* requires total and unvarying attachment to God alone to the exclusion of all other deities (see **LOVE**): "You will love the Lord your God with all your heart, and all your soul and all your might" (Deut 6:5, author's trans.; see Mark 12:30 and parallels). This God is essentially a powerful and mighty God. Aside from the awesome power involved in creation, after the expulsion of the first couple, "the cherubim, and a flaming sword which turned every way" (Gen 3:24) henceforth keep humans out of the garden. The story of God's freeing a people to serve him begins with God's sending all his plagues that all may know "there is none like me in all the earth" (Exod 9:14). Such acts of power result in

God's receiving "glory over Pharaoh and all his host" (Exod 14:4). The Deuteronomistic theologian, for example, saw all of this as the work of God's power and "outstretched arm" (Deut 4:34; 5:15; 7:19; 9:29; 11:2; 26:8; 1 Kgs 8:42; 2 Kgs 17:36; 2 Chron 6:32; Ps 136:12; Jer 27:5; Ezek 20:33, 34). The point is clearly expressed by Jeremiah: "Ah Lord GOD! It is you who made the heavens and the earth by your great power and by your outstretched arm! Nothing is too hard for you. . . . You brought your people Israel out of the land of Egypt with signs and wonders, with a strong hand and outstretched arm, and with great terror" (Jer 32:17, 21, NRSV). The point is that God essentially wields Power, and in the tradition of Israel everyone is subject to God's Power. In fact, "Power" is even another name for God (Mark 14:62; Matt 26:64; Luke 22:69 has "power of God"). His word of command is power. He speaks and it is done. He does not attempt to convince or argue; he does not offer promises or rewards apart from not employing his power negatively. The same is true with kings; their essential glory was to command total submissiveness (consult the ideal picture of regal power in 1 Sam 8:11–18).

On the other hand, God also wields "steadfast love" (see **STEADFAST LOVE**) or "mercy" (see **GRACE/FAVOR; GRATITUDE; STEADFAST LOVE**) toward those with whom he is in covenant. He is one "who shows steadfast love to thousands, but requites the guilt of fathers to their children after them, O great and mighty God whose name is the LORD of hosts" (Jer 32:18, RSV adapted). "Steadfast love" is a technical term referring to the debt of interpersonal obligation one has due to having entered a covenant; it is a form of solidarity between covenant members. The "hosts" of which God is Lord are heavenly armies numbering countless warriors (Matt 26:53 mentions an immediately available force of "twelve legions of angels"; the title "Lord of hosts" occurs 248 times beginning with 1 Sam 1 and following). This warrior Lord is in solidarity with his own, yet uses force as sanction against them as well as outsiders.

Such focus on power and its sanction, force, moves attention as well to those who have to bear such sanction, specifically those who suffer punishment and torture. The classic biblical example of such a person, of course, is Job. The cultural question is not *why* Job suffers, but *how*, the style in which he endures. The ability to endure harsh pain without uttering a sound is considered quite admirable. For example, take the heroic person described in the songs of Isaiah: "He was oppressed, and he was afflicted, yet he opened not his mouth; like a lamb that is led to the slaughter, and like a sheep that before its shearers is dumb, so he opened not his mouth" (Isa 53:7). Similarly, the centurion, observing how Jesus suffered the horrendous Roman torture of crucifixion in silence from the third hour to the ninth hour before he shrieked and died, was prompted to exclaim: "Truly, this man was a son of God!" (Mark 15:39, NEB; Matt 27:54; see also the pain-witness in 2 Macc 6:28–31; 7:1–42). High interest in enjoying the death struggle of living beings, in bull-fighting, animal sacrifice, gladiatorial combat, torture, crucifixion, and the like, all point to the authoritarian personality. Thus, the ability to wield force, to inflict pain, and to endure it are part of the value cluster called authoritarianism (see also **PARENTING**).

Another value in the authoritarian cluster is anti-introspection. Persons who are not at all psychologically minded interact in standardized and conventional ways almost all the time. Such behavioral interaction is replicated linguistically in the use of proverbs and cliches as explanatory devices: "No prophet is acceptable in his own country" (Luke 4:24; also Matt 13:57; Mark 6:4; John 4:44); "Do not be anxious about tomorrow, for tomorrow will be anxious for itself" (Matt 6:34); "Let the day's own trouble be sufficient for the day" (Matt 6:34); "A disciple is not above his teacher" (Matt 10:24); The "first will be last and the last first" (Matt 19:30; see

20:16). There are countless proverbs of this sort in the gospel story alone. Similarly, the use of Scriptural quotations as standardized and conventional ways of explaining indicates the same anti-introspective approach (e.g., "Scripture says . . . [followed by a quote]" in Matt 4:4, 7, 10; 11:10; 21:13, 42; 22:29; 26:24, 31, 54, 56; similarly in Mark and Luke–Acts; even more frequently in John and in Paul, e.g., Rom 1:17; 2:24; 3:4, 10; 4:3, 17, 23; 8:36; 9:13, 17, 33; 10:5, 11, 15; 11:2, 8, 26; 12:19; 14:11; 15:3, 9, 21; 16:26).

There is constant concern about what outsiders might think and do. Jesus' concern with "who do people say that I am" (Mark 8:27; Matt 16:13; Luke 9:18) is echoed in early Christian writings. Even though God is to judge outsiders (1 Cor 5:12–13), Paul tells Christians to behave properly "so that you are seen to be respectable by those outside the church" (1 Thess 4:12). Hence, Christians must "be tactful to those who are outside" (Col 4:5). In their choice of community leaders, "It is also necessary that people outside the church should speak well of him" (1 Tim 3:7).

Authoritarianism is further indicated by total concern with orthopraxy (proper behavior) and full absorption with questions of the dimensions of orthopraxy. Such a personality will develop a view of orthodoxy (proper belief) that is unambiguous, rigid, and clear. We find evidence of this value in the Roman proverb: "*Dura lex, sed lex*" (It is a severe law, but it is the law) and well known Roman legalism (e.g., see Acts 25:24–27 of Festus dealing with Paul). All the accusations put against Jesus in the gospel story are about orthopraxy: sabbath observance several times, fasting, eating with "sinners," eating with unwashed hands, authorization to teach in the temple area, and the like. The reason for this is that authoritarian personalities, being anti-introspective, fear the very existence of their individual, own, internal self. They take their life's cues from the outside rather than from within themselves. There are human persons and non-human spirits to blame for the evil that befalls them. They wish these external cues to be clear enough and loud enough for the message to ring through and dominate the inner psyche. Concrete behavior which deviates from their own causes dissonance. And it is the dissonance among the various factions in the "house of Israel" (Pharisees, Sadducees, Essenes, John the Baptist's group, Jesus' group) that required greater group adherence; hence the need to define "neighbor" as "the sons of your own people" (Lev 19:18). Jesus' message was for "the lost sheep of the house of Israel," and this explicitly excluded Samaritans and non-Israelites (Matt 10:5–6); yet in the end, "all nations" are included (Matt 28:19). Similarly, in Luke, Samaritans are included (Luke 10:33), while in Acts God brings in Gentiles as well (Acts 10:34–35). Yet obviously the Christian groups of the first century remained extremely small and were confined to a group of "brothers," the main term for Christian group members (e.g., Matt 5:22, 23, 24, 47 etc., especially Matt 18:15, 21, 35; and frequently in early Christian letters; the title indicates that they considered themselves a fictive kinship group over against other such groups).

The preference for thinking in terms of either/or is clear in the common proverb found throughout the gospel narrative in various forms: "For he that is not against us is for us" (Mark 9:40); "For he that is not against you is for you" (Luke 9:50); "He who is not with me is against me and he who does not gather with me scatters" (Matt 12:30; Luke 11:23). There are either blessings (Deut 33:2–29) or curses (Deut 27:15–26); blesseds ("truly honorable or esteemed" Matt 5:3–11) or woes ("truly shameful" Matt 23:13–34); left hand and right hand, sheep and goats (Matt 25:31–46). There is no room for a compromising middle ground, for as the oracle in Revelation declares: "So because you are lukewarm, and neither cold nor hot, I will spew you out of my mouth" (Rev 3:16). (See also EMOTION/DEMONSTRATION OF FEELINGS.)

Authoritarian persons seem to be highly controlled personality types, quite suspicious and fearful of those who do not belong to their groups. Every group possesses negative information concerning people who are not of their group, even those never met before. Of course such information is group-specific and stereotypical rather than individualistic and psychological. As a rule, other ethnic groups are characterized by their own geographical location, that allows for geographically rooted ethnic stereotypes. For example, "Can anything good come out of Nazareth?" (John 1:46); Tiberians have "a passion for war" (Josephus, *Life* 352); Scythians "delight in murdering people and are little better than wild beasts" (Josephus, *Against Apion* 269); "Cretans are always liars, evil beasts, lazy gluttons" (Titus 1:12); in "the seamanship of its people . . . the Phoenicians in general have been superior to all peoples of all times" (Strabo, *Geography* 16. 2. 23); "this is a trait common to all the Arabian kings" that they do "not care much about public affairs and particularly military affairs" (Strabo, *Geography* 16. 4. 24).

In the prevailing culture of the United States, authoritarianism is a second order value, that is, it occurs only in certain social locations (the military, the practice of medicine, some parts of the corporate business world) and in certain circumstances (war, medical emergencies). The primary value orientation is egalitarianism which accompanies the high value placed on individualism. In the United States, even parents are eager to move their offspring away from levels of authoritarian-style discipline to a discipline rooted in respect for individual freedom, mutual dialogue and persuasion. Such outlooks also characterize the political and religious spheres. The clear, primary preference is for the values of democracy and congregationalism and a rejection of authoritarianism and hierarchic structures. (Bruce J. Malina)

Arendt, Hannah. 1958. "What Was Authority?" In *Nomos I: Authority.* Ed. Carl J. Friedrich. Pp. 81–112. Cambridge: Harvard University Press.

Malina, Bruce J. 1992. "Is There a Circum-Mediterranean Person: Looking for Stereotypes." *Biblical Theology Bulletin* 22:66–87.

Seland, Torrey. 1995. *Establishment Violence in Philo and Luke: A Study of Non-Conformity to Torah and Jewish Vigilante Reactions.* Biblical Interpetation Series 15; Leiden: Brill.

Stone, William F., Gerda Lederer, Richard Christie, eds. 1993. *Strength and Weakness: The Authoritarian Personality Today.* New York: Springer.

BELIEF—SEE FAITH/FAITHFULNESS

CHANGE/NOVELTY ORIENTATION

The seeking of change or novelty is normally disapproved of throughout the Bible. Indeed, the general orientation is precisely to the opposite, i.e., to stability and constancy (Deut 6:4–9; Ps 105:44–45). Because cultural and religious traditions provide the grounds for social values and the standards against which anything new is measured, change and novelty are usually met with hostility: change is fraught with fear of the unknown, bringing pollution and chaos in its wake; novelty doubts the value of tradition by manifesting disloyalty toward it (1 Sam 8, cf. Hos 8:1–4; 9:15; 1 Kgs 14:7–16; Ps 119:9–10, 35–37; Prov 28:9; Sir 1:21–24 Jer 6:18–21, 11:1–13; Mark 3:23–24, 13:21–23; 2 Cor 11:1–5; Gal 5:7–12).

Change or novelty in traditional religion or religious doctrine and practice meet with especially violent rejection. In situations where the tradition and its values are believed to be seriously at risk, compromise is categorically rejected, and a struggle is waged to reassert the ascendancy of, or to remain faithful to, the tradition, no matter the personal or social cost (1 Macc 2; 2 Macc 6:18–7:41; Ezra 10:9–14, 44, cf. Neh 13:23–31; Matt 5:10–12; Mark 13:9–13; 2 Cor 11:22–31, 12:10, cf. Acts 19:23–40). In Mediterranean culture, therefore, change or novelty is a means value which serves to innovate or subvert core and secondary values.

An example related to the disapproval of change and novelty may be found in the cultural and religious tradition's ancient and unambiguous definition of the role of women: they are subject to men (Exod 20:14, 17, 21:7–11; Sir 7:26, 9:2). Attempts to change the role of women or to introduce novelty into established roles are spurned (Eccl 7:26–29; Sir 25:12–26:18; 1 Cor 11:2–16; Eph 5:22–24).

Religious doctrine and practice as well as the role of women are regarded as having been divinely mandated. Therefore, tampering with them is tantamount to a rejection of God and an expression of contempt for the people who belong to him (Lev 24:10–16; John 4:27).

As is the case with curiosity (see CURIOSITY), however, there is a biblically advocated form of change: conversion, which is always a call to return wholeheartedly to the demands of the covenant, and therefore, to a right relationship with God (Jer 7:1–7; Hos 14:2–10; Matt 3:7–12, 4:17). Indeed, it is axiomatic that right relationship to God is the foundation and source of all good (Deut 6:1–3; Matt 6:9–13), and sin (i.e., rejection of God) is the foundation and source of all evil (Deut 6:12–15; Rom 6:12–14). Consequently, change and novelty assessed in this covenantal light, the only authentic one (Hos 5:6–7; Mark 7:6–13), are means values that would support the core value of honor as defined in this specific context.

Conformity to the requirements of God's changeless law upon which biblical society believes itself to be erected is at the core of its resistance to change and disapproval of novelty (Deut 32–33, cf. Sir 8:9; Matt 24:35). It must be stressed, therefore, that the theological proposition of rightness of relationship to God is not a weightless idea to which merely intellectual assent is given in biblical culture. On the contrary, it is concretely embedded in cultural ideology and societal structure as loyalty to tradition and is embodied by keeping the law (Exod 22:17–19; Ps 119).

Loyalty to the tradition and law is supposed to make life uncomplicated and straightforward: the pious are praised, sinners shunned (Sir 10:20–22), assertive women ridiculed (Prov 11:22), devoted wife and mother extolled (Prov 31:10–31); rebellious son castigated, obedient lauded (e.g., Sir 3:1–16); lawbreakers reviled, upholders of the law reverenced (Ps 37), covenanted people (Jews and Christians) have light; outsiders live in darkness (e.g., Mark 4:11), etc. Even so, life is very hard (especially for the wicked: Sir 40:1–11), and much about it is painfully unintelligible or deeply mysterious (Jer 12:1–4; Job 38–42:6; 1 Cor 1:26–28). God alone is the master of life and the world, and he is utterly beyond human understanding (Isa 40:13–14, 55:8–9; Wis 9:13; Mark 10:27). Since this is the case, curiosity is either frivolous or perilous because it questions the time-tested communal wisdom which rejects it.

Clearly, we in the modern Western world do not share this view of change and novelty. While we acknowledge the painfulness of change, it is so much a fact of modern Western life and popular culture, and its benefits are so often believed to be abundantly obvious (especially scientific, medical, technological, and economic "advances"), that hostility to change is regarded as more dangerous than change itself. The same is true of novelty: not only are we extremely tolerant of it, but we seek it out on a consistent basis. This is why change and novelty are indeed salient characteristics of contemporary Western culture. (Mark McVann)

Gulick, J. 1976. "The Ethos of Insecurity of Middle Eastern Culture." In *Responses to Change: Society, Culture, and Personality.* Ed. G. DeVos. New York: Van Nostrand.

CHARITY—SEE LOVE

CLOTHING

Ancient Israelites ordinarily wore a linen tunic over some form of underwear, a woolen cloak, a belt around the chest, and sandals. Felt made of goats' hair was used for hats and socks. For special occasions they wore festal

(Gen 45:22; Judg 14:12–13) and wedding garments (Matt 22:11–14), which were noteworthy for their fine cloth, rich coloring, and embroidery. The prodigal son was clothed in just such a garment: "Bring the best robe!" (Luke 15:22). He was honored as well with "a ring on his finger and shoes on his feet." Clothing of any sort was valuable, hence, executioners competed for the garments of a crucified man (Mark 15:24); thieves took the clothing of the man they robbed (Luke 10:30; see also 2 Tim 4:13).

Clothing was not mere body covering, but indicated one's role and status, and so it is best viewed in terms of the values of honor and shame (see **HONOR/SHAME**). As such, clothing is a means value serving to express the core value of honor. Cultures structured according to honor and shame divide the world in terms of male and female (see Introduction). Since clothing signals gender, we read: "A woman shall not wear anything that pertains to a man, nor shall a man put on a woman's garment" (Deut 22:5; see 1 Cor 11:14–15 for different hair styles for men and women). Clothing could indicate nationality: Romans wore togas and Persians, peaked caps; Hellenized Jews signalled this by the wearing of "the Greek hat" (2 Macc 4:12). Clothing might signal trade and social position, for soldiers' dress would differ from merchants' robes, and peasants' garments from priests' vesture: helmet, breastplate and greaves indicate battle dress (Eph 6:14–17; see Isa 59:17).

In a context of conspicuous display, the rich signalled their wealthy status by wearing "fine linen and purple" (Luke 16:19); those who wore soft raiment and were gorgeously appareled lived in kings' courts (Luke 7:25). Cotton from Egypt (Isa 19:9) and silk from the orient (Ezek 16:10, 13; Rev 18:12) were available for the rich. The clothing of the elite would be dyed in blue, scarlet, and purple (Exod 28:5–6; Jer 10:9; 1 Macc 4:23; Rev 18:12). We can imagine Herod's splendor when "he put on his royal robes" to take his seat on his throne (Acts 12:21). On the other end of the scale, the dishonored poor are known in terms of their nakedness (see Jas 2:2; Matt 25:36).

The honorable part of the body, the head, is honored by the wearing of appropriate gear. Crowns indicate royal status; a conquering monarch might assume the wearing of the crown of a king he conquered to signal his acquisition of this new honor (2 Sam 12:30); he might signal the extent of his empire by wearing simultaneously two regional crowns, as Ptolemy wore both the crown of Asia and that of Egypt (1 Macc 11:13). Other nobles (Esth 8:15) as well as elders (Rev 4:4) might be honored with crowns.

Women traditionally heralded the wealth of the family by the jewelry they wore, thus signaling their status to prospective husbands (see Esth 2:17; Ezek 16:11–12; 23:42). We read in Luke of the distress of a woman of modest means who lost one of the coins from her jewelry/dowry. She lost not only one-tenth of her dowry, but a comparable proportion of her social status as well (Luke 15:8). The temptation to claim higher status by virtue of clothing and jewelry seems to have been irresistible: "Let not yours be the outward adorning with braiding of hair, decoration of gold, and wearing of fine clothing" (1 Pet 3:3).

Clothing signalled religious status as well. Observant Jews wore tassels and phylacteries (Matt 23:5); the Essenes at Qumran symbolized their pursuit of radical purity by wearing the "white robe" (Josephus, *War* 2.129; Philo, *Contemplative Life* 66). And prophets like John the Baptizer identified their roles on the margins of society by wearing garments of skin, not cloth woven in households (Mark 1:6; see Heb 11:37–38; Zech 13:4; Josephus, *Life* 11). Those who preached repentance might dress in sackcloth (Rev 11:3), as well as those who sought repentance (Matt 11:21).

But the role and status of the Jerusalem priests was most clearly replicated by their special clothing. "The High Priest ministers in eight pieces of raiment, and common priest in four: in tunic, drawers, turban and girdle.

To these the High Priest adds the breastplate, the apron, the upper garment and the frontlet" (*m. Yoma* 7:5). While officiating, ordinary priests wore breeches made of linen, which were snug to the loins to prevent any exposure of the privy parts (Exod 28:42); over this they wore a checkered linen tunic which reached their feet; they girded their chests with a linen girdle and crowned their heads with a turban cap of wound linen bands; of course they went barefoot (see Exod 3:5). For special feasts such as Yom Kippur, the high priest wore even more distinctive clothing. It consisted of the articles mentioned above for ordinary priests plus the following pieces: over the breeches and tunic he wore another tunic of blue linen, girded with a sash of blue, purple, and scarlet hues. From the hem of this tunic hung an alternating pattern of gold bells and tassels like pomegranates. Over this he wore an ephod (waistcoat), in the center of which was a breast pouch to hold the Urim and Thummim (the lots). The breast pouch was studded with twelve precious stones. The ordinary priest's cap was covered with blue embroidery and encircled with a tiered crown of gold (Exod 28; Josephus, *Antiquities* 3.151–158). Thus, clothing signals a claim to honor in terms of gender, role, and status, and therefore, it is clearly a means value.

Clothing can also be viewed from the perspective of purity and pollution. Since purity has to do with "wholeness," kashrut rules prescribe that the garments of the high priest be made wholly of one kind of material, linen or wool, not a mixture of both: "You shall not wear a mingled stuff, wool and linen together" (Deut 22:11; see 22:10 and Lev 19:19). The outer tunic of this holiest of persons is whole in another sense: "The tunic is not composed of two pieces, to be stitched at the shoulders and at the sides: it is one long woven cloth" (Josephus, *Antiquities* 3.161).

Clothing eventually required laundering. But most of the "washing of clothes" we read about in the Bible has more to do with purity concerns than with hygiene.

In preparation to meet God on Sinai, the people were told to wash their clothes (Exod 19:10, 14); they must be pure to encounter the Pure One. After performing parts of the Yom Kippur ritual, the various priests must wash their clothes (Lev 16:26; Num 19:7–10); likewise soldiers after battle in a holy war (Num 31:24). The washing of clothes, then, symbolizes proper entrance into and exit from the space of the Holy One.

If washing is appropriate for commerce with the holy, it is also necessary after contact with uncleanness. Those declared clean of skin diseases washed not only their bodies but their clothes (Lev 13:6, 34; 14:8–9); those who have the merest contact with uncleanness must also wash their clothes (Lev 15:5–8), especially those who touch something dead (Lev 11:40; 17:15). Such washings symbolize separation from uncleanness rather than concern for germs, about which the ancients knew nothing. Total purity was expressed by the complete separation from the corruption of the past by the following ritual demands: "He shall shave all his hair off his head; he shall shave off his beard and his eyebrows, all his hair. Then he shall wash his clothes, and bathe his body in water" (Lev 14:9).

Wealth and royal status were symbolized by the wearing of purple, blue, and scarlet. Yet bleached, white clothing was deemed appropriate for a heavenly encounter or a heavenly liturgy. At his transfiguration, Jesus' inclusion in the world of the Holy God was expressed by the remark about his clothes: "His garments . . . glistening, intensely white, as no fuller on earth could bleach them" (Mark 9:3). In the book of Revelation, the saints before the throne of the Lamb wore "white robes," which they had washed after being stained, presumably with blood from suffering. Yet their washing was done paradoxically in the blood of the Lamb (Rev 7:14). Spotlessness and total purity are required of both persons and their clothing. In this context we are reminded of baptismal exhortations to keep the new garment "spotless" (see Eph 4:24).

In the contemporary Western world, clothing also is a means value serving to express values peculiar to mainstream United States culture. Given the cultural emphasis on equality, styles are very important. Everyone strives to be in style by purchasing and wearing what the designers or manufacturers suggest each season. Nearly everyone dresses alike within a limited range of choices. The value of equality between the genders in the United States is similarly expressed by the fact that some types of clothing, e.g., trousers, suits, or male-style shirts, are worn by men and women alike.

The elite express the high priority placed on economics as a social institution in the United States. Among the elite, clothing symbolizes status and expresses a personal level of wealth. Elite women make no secret of their favorite designer whose clothes often cost more than the ordinary citizen's daily or weekly wages. Photographs of the elite attending their social functions are published weekly (sometimes more often) on the society pages of newspapers in larger cities. In smaller, especially rural towns, clothing as a status indicator would be too jarring, hence, status is more often expressed by reports in articles or a special "gossip" column describing the travels (domestic and foreign) of the local elite. Thus, while clothing in the Mediterranean world is linked with honor (and nakedness with shame), clothing in the Western world is linked with equality and economics among other values, but not necessarily with honor. (Jerome H. Neyrey)

Bonfante, Larissa, and Eva Jaunzems. 1988. "Clothing and Ornament." In *Civilization of the Ancient Mediterranean*. Vol. 3. Ed. Michael Grant and Rachel Kitizinger. Pp. 1385–414. New York: Scribners.

Hamal, Gildas. 1990. "Poverty in Clothing." In *Poverty and Charity in Roman Palestine, First Three Centuries C.E.* Pp. 57–93. Berkeley: University of California Press.

Milgrom, Jacob. 1983. "Of Hems and Tassels." *Biblical Archaeology Review* 9:61–65.

Reinhold, Meyer. 1970. *Purple as a Status Symbol in Antiquity.* Brussels: Latomus.

Schneider, Jane. 1987. "The Anthropology of Cloth." *Annual Review of Anthropology* 16:409–48.

Schwarz, Ronald A. 1979. "Uncovering the Secret Vice: Toward an Anthropology of Clothing." In *The Fabrics of Culture: The Anthropology of Clothing and Adornment.* Ed. Justine Cordwell and Ronald Schwarz. Pp. 23–45. The Hague: Mouton.

Weiner, Annette B., and Jane Schneider. 1989. *Cloth and the Human Experience.* Washington: Smithsonian Institution Press.

COMMUNICATIVENESS (MOUTH-EARS)—SEE ALSO EQUIVOCATION

Communication in the ancient Mediterranean region is generally reflected in the concrete images of mouth and ears. Anthropologically, these orifices are viewed as boundaries of the human body. In the eastern Mediterranean culture of biblical times, in which purity concerns are intense, these boundaries are tightly regulated and subject to continuous and close scrutiny. The purity of the mouth is guarded in two ways: by censuring that which comes in (food), and that which goes out (speech). Dietary regulations serve principally to buttress cultural cosmology, understood to have been divinely ordained (e.g., Lev 11:1–43; cf. Mark 7:18–19; Acts 10:9–16). Thus, these regulations help delineate the (ritual) purity and uniqueness of Judaic ethnicity, as well as Christian anti-ethnicity, both equally understood as having been divinely ordained (e.g., Lev 11:44–45; Acts 11:1–18). Therefore, speech that issues from the mouth should, by way of analogy to what enters it, be clean, i.e., should indicate both acceptance of and compliance with the divinely ordained cosmos. This is bedrock in both Israelite and Christian tradition, since speech is singled out in two commandments in the decalogue (Exod 20:7, 16; Deut 5:11, 20), and in the Sermon on the Mount (Matt 5:33–37). Ideally, what goes out of the mouth, like what comes in, should be determined by God's will as expressed in his law and institutionalized in the culture of his people.

Communicativeness, therefore, serves as a means value in the Mediterranean world. Communicativeness is a key strategy for establishing, maintaining and defending honor. It can also serve as a strategy for attempting to shame others.

In addition to the literal reference of mouth to eating and drinking, and the figurative reference to the ethics of speaking, mouth and ears are also metonyms for persons who may be rebellious and wicked (e.g., Jer 9:2, 7), wise and steadfast (e.g., Sir 5:11–13; 6:5; Job 12:11–12); trustworthy and truthful (e.g., Prov 8:7), foolish and dangerous (e.g., Prov 22:14, 30:20, 32–33; 1 Cor 12:16; 2 Tim 4:3–5), humble and obedient (e.g., Isa 1:10; Prov 5:7), deceitful and cunning (e.g., Prov 10:18; 11:9), clean or unclean (e.g., Ps 50:16–21; Ezek 4:12–15; Mark 7:18–23; the examples are legion), all illustrated by the employment of mouth and/or ears as figures of human attitudes and behaviors.

Ears are analogous to mouth in that what one permits to enter should also be consonant with the established cosmology, i.e., pure and undefiled (e.g., Prov 2:1–2; 5:1; 18:15; Acts 7:57). In this sense, the numerous appeals to God to incline his ear (e.g., Isa 37:17; Ps 5:1; 88:2) are based on the purity and righteousness of the supplicant's mouth (speech) and hands (actions) (e.g., Ps 24:3–6), recognition of the need for purity (e.g., Ps 51), or faith in Jesus as Lord (e.g., Acts 2:21). The supplicant acknowledges God's and/or Jesus' power to save (e.g., Ps 18; 86; Rom 10:12–13), restore (e.g., Ps 102; Rom 6:3–11), and forgive sins (i.e., remove or cover uncleanness, e.g., Ps 32; Rom 6:12–23). That is, the supplicant acknowledges God as the source of cleanness, and hence, as the foundation of the cosmos, its Creator and Savior, as exemplified particularly in such psalms as 96 and 89, and the hymns found in such passages as Philippians 2:6–11 and Revelation 5:9–13. In the ideal, this understanding of God is the premise upon which the culture reflected in the Bible is erected and maintained, and which determines the standards of acceptable communicativeness. Blasphemy, then, represents the ultimate rejection of Israelite first principles, and the death penalty for blasphemers is the community's ultimate rejection of them (Lev 24:14–16). Thus, insults and taunts are appropriately directed at those whose behavior indicates their rejection of established wisdom and tradition (e.g., Ps 22:8; 109:17–19; cf. Prov 18:6–7; Mark 14:60–65; 15:29–32).

In the Bible, then, communicativeness is effective, valued, and prized if it endorses and explicates the world view and ethos held by the culture in general, i.e., if it upholds and defends the tradition. It is inadequate, untrustworthy, or contemptible if it challenges, denies, or repudiates the culture's core values. The world view and its values are structured and informed by what is understood to be God's revealed law, in both Israelite tradition and Christianity (Deut 5:28–32; Matt 5:17–48). The degree to which communicativeness conforms with the ethical requirements of observance of the law is the degree to which it may be understood as authentically communicative. Anything less is nonsense or anathema (Prov 15:2; Gal 1:1–9).

The notion that communicativeness should be assessed from the standpoint of its conformity to the requirements of religious purity and cleanness makes little sense to contemporary westerners, especially Americans, who live largely in an "information culture," and for whom the value of communicativeness is increased by its capacity to expand or improve the established and routine. Progress and innovativeness are highly regarded and form the basis of the technological culture in which we live. Communicativeness in our context, therefore, is valuable especially if it helps us keep abreast of new developments. It is untrustworthy if it attempts to perpetuate the status quo. Thus, the biblical estimate of the value of communicativeness is virtually inverted in modern, Western society where change, progress, and originality clearly take precedence over cultural constancy, fidelity to tradition, and maintenance of social class distinctions. (Mark McVann)

Malina, Bruce J. 1993. "The First Century Personality: The Individual and the Group." In *The New Testament World.* Rev. Ed. Pp. 63–89. Louisville, Ky.: Westminster John Knox.

COMPASSION

In the Mediterranean biblical world, compassion is a value rooted primarily in kinship obligations, whether natural or fictive. The Hebrew word for compassion derives from the word for womb (*rhm*), but this etymology does not designate the value as peculiar to women so much as it reflects the cultural belief that children of the same mother, that is, from the same womb, are the most closely bonded of all kin and ought to be most considerate of one another. See Deuteronomy 13:6: "If your brother, the son of your mother . . . "; and contrast this with Genesis 20:12: "She (Sarah, says Abraham) is my sister, the daughter of my father but not the daughter of my mother; and she became my wife."

From this perspective, compassion is a peripheral value, that is, it is specific to given interactions, namely those guided and governed by kinship considerations. Compassion would thus be defined as the caring concern that ought to be felt and acted upon between real or fictive kin, specifically between brothers since the basic connotation of *rhm* was brotherhood or brotherly feeling.

Zechariah (7:9–10) reports: "Thus says the LORD of hosts, Render true judgments, show kindness and mercy each to his brother (=one another), do not oppress the widow, the fatherless, the sojourner, or the poor; and let none of you devise evil against his brother (=one another) in your heart." Similarly, Amos (1:11, NRSV adapted) notes: "Thus says the LORD: For three transgressions of Edom, and four, I will not revoke the punishment. Because he pursued his brother [Judah] with the sword and cast off

all compassion, and he kept his anger perpetually, and
he kept his wrath forever."

In spite of this observation, in the Hebrew Bible God
and not a human being is the most common subject of
the verb "to show compassion." He is free to show compassion to whomever and whenever he wills (Exod 33:19;
see also Deut 13:18; 30:3) but in many of these occurrences the word compassion is linked with mercy (Hebrew: *hen*) and situated in the context of God's covenant
promises: "The Lord had compassion on Israel . . . because of his covenant with Abraham, Isaac, and Jacob" (2
Kgs 13:23) which reflects a [fictive] kinship context (see
also Isa 49:13; 54:8–10; Jer 33:26).

But since all theology is analogy, that is, everything
said about God is based on human experience, the primary analogue for compassion is indeed the parent: "As
a father has compassion for his children, so the LORD has
compassion for those who fear him" (Ps 103:13, NRSV). Or
again: "Can a woman forget her sucking child that she
should have no compassion on the son of her womb?
Even though these may forget, yet I will not forget you
[says the Lord]" (Isa 49:15).

The latter comment indicates that many human beings neglected or refused to show compassion. King
David's wish is most revealing. When given a choice of
"divine punishments" for taking a census, David opts
for one directly from God rather than an indirect one
through an enemy: "Let me fall into the hand of the LORD,
for his compassion is great; but let me not fall into the
hand of man" (2 Sam 24:14, RSV adapted). This experience at the hand of other human beings must have been
common, for in the Hebrew Bible compassion is most
commonly ascribed to or desired from conquerors or
other powerful figures. Solomon prays: "Grant your people
mercy before their captors, so that these will be compassionate to them" (1 Kgs 8:50; see also Neh 1:11; Dan 1:9;
Jer 42:12; Ps 106:46; 2 Chron 30:9; in contrast see Jer
6:23; 21:7; 50:42). Culturally, compassion is related to

almsgiving or altruism (see **ALTRUISM**), whereby a strong man who does not insist on his rights is perceived as magnanimous. Jacob/Israel instructs his sons: "May God Almighty grant you compassion before the man [Joseph], that he may send back your other brother and Benjamin" (Gen 43:14).

In the New Testament, two Greek words correspond to the Hebrew word *rhm*. One (*oiktirō* and derivatives) occurs but once in the Gospels! Luke (6:36) refashions the traditional "You shall be holy as your Lord is Holy" (Lev 11:44–45 and elsewhere) into "You shall be compassionate as your Father is compassionate." The other (*splanchnizesthai*) occurs more frequently (thirteen times). It describes the feeling which motivated Jesus to heal petitioners (Mark 9:22; Matt 14:14//Mark 6:34; Matt 20:34), to raise the deceased and only son of the widow of Nain (Luke 7:13), and to interact with the crowds (Matt 9:36; 15:32//Mark 8:2).

In Jesus' parables, the father of the prodigal son is moved with compassion to readmit his errant offspring into the family circle (Luke 15:20), the Good Samaritan shows compassion to his wounded "enemy" which this enemy's own fictive kin failed to demonstrate (Luke 10:33), and a powerful ruler displays appropriate cultural magnanimity by forgiving his servant a huge debt "out of compassion" (Matt 18:27), which apparently made no impression on that servant as he behaved quite uncompassionately toward a fellow-debtor. These three instances epitomize the role of compassion in Mediterranean biblical society: it is a kinship-rooted value which ought to be shown to real or fictive kin, and ought also to characterize powerful people's dealings with underlings. For Christians, compassion is rooted in love and modelled in Christ (Col 3:12–14).

In mainstream United States culture, compassion is an aspect of pity which implies sorrow for another's suffering or misfortune and sometimes connotes mild contempt because the object of pity is regarded as weak or inferior. Compassion is pity which is accompanied by an urge to help or spare, but it is limited chiefly to one in need "through no personal fault." Thus, victims of floods, fires, or other natural disasters (usually called "acts of God" by insurance companies) are unquestioned recipients of American compassion. Not so the needy on welfare or other forms of public assistance, since these are presumed to have fallen into this predicament by their own fault and therefore should be able to help themselves out of it by their own efforts. (John J. Pilch)

Hatfield, Elaine, and Richard Rapson. 1993. "Love and Attachment Processes." In *Handbook of Emotions*. Ed. Michael Lewis and Jeannette M. Haviland. Pp. 605–16. New York: Guilford.

COMPLIANCE

An attitude of compliance, i.e., of a willingness to conform one's actions to the wishes or desires of another or to cultural standards, is a value highly regarded in the Bible (e.g., Sir 41:14–42:8; Prov 4:1–4, 10–12; Matt 23:2; John 2:4–5; 1 Cor 7:17–24). Compliance is closely related to the virtues of humility (see **HUMILITY**), meekness (see **MEEKNESS**), obedience (see **OBEDIENCE**), and loyalty (see **FAITH/FAITHFULNESS**) in a culture which commends persons for recognizing and accepting the social rank in which they find themselves (e.g., Luke 12:42–48; Col 3:22–4:1) and disapproves of jumping class, ethnic, or other group boundaries (e.g., Neh 13:1–2, 23–31; Mark 10:35–41). Thus, compliance can be construed as a means value.

Compliance is an integral aspect of cultural cohesion in societies in which strict adherence to social codes and patterns of living is demanded, enforced, and rewarded, and resistance is punished (e.g., Deut 25:5–10; Matt 24:43–51). Compliance also figures significantly in the code of honor and shame. Adherence to the law, custom, and tradition is a matter of honor (e.g., 2 Macc 8:18–31; Sir 35; 1 Tim 2:1–15); disregard for or defiance of them is cause for shame (e.g., Prov 6:16–19; 1 Cor 11:1–16). Thus, compliance should not be mistaken for passivity (see ACTIVENESS/PASSIVENESS), for it represents the active upholding of and participation in a culture's value system which centers on respect for authority and tradition.

An important aspect of compliance is manifested religiously in the elaborate ritual apparatus (reflected most completely in the Hebrew Bible in Leviticus, Numbers, and Deuteronomy and pertaining to priests, prophets, Levites, Pharisees, Sadducees, shrines, altars, temple, sacrifices, etc.) which was instituted to regulate and administer cultic life (e.g., Lev 10:8–11), assign cultural and ethnic boundaries (e.g., Deut 7), determine purity (e.g., Lev 5:1–13; 13–15), certify status (e.g., Deut 15:12–18), and define communal membership (e.g., Deut 23:2–9). Its purpose, in short, was to map the cosmos, guide one's passage through it, and institute sanctions against those who did not comply with its vision of reality (e.g., Deut 21:18–21). This system of ritual has remained intact in its basic outline throughout the many centuries of the biblical era, and it persists in many respects into the modern age in peasant Mediterranean societies.

Indications of biblical culture's stringent demands for conformity to its requirements may be seen in the Decalogue (Exod 20:1–17; Deut 5:6–21; cf. Mark 7:1–6; Matt 5:18–19; 18:15–17); defiance of any of these laws is a capital offense. The first four commandments identify superiors, i.e., God and parents, and unambiguously disclose the proper attitude toward them: unquestioning compliance with their commands. Thus, maintenance of social balance and cultural continuity are assured.

Compliance, then, occupies a place of central importance in the culture of the people of the Bible, because the compliant person, by his or her actions and behavior, demonstrates conviction regarding the system of cultural and religious values which constitute and order the society of which he or she is a member.

The reverence for authority and tradition implied in compliance is considered a liability in contemporary Western culture. We inculcate, encourage, and praise initiative, inventiveness, and efficiency. From our point of view, compliance is virtually equivalent to passive acquiescence to the way things are, and it betrays a lack of imagination, energy, and aspiration to improve one's lot, or that of one's family, neighborhood, etc. Compliance becomes a primary value in United States culture in areas of life where free individual choice could be counterproductive, as in the military, in medical care, and in corporate structures (see AUTHORITARIANISM). Model soldiers, good patients, and praiseworthy climbers on the corporate ladder are characterized by compliance. But freed from these roles and returned to their lives as private citizens, these same people will eschew compliance as a value. (Mark McVann)

Eickelman, Dale F. 1981. "Change in Practical Ideologies: Self, Sexuality, and Ethnicity." In *The Middle East: An Anthropological Approach*. Pp. 135–74. Englewood Cliffs, N.J.: Prentice Hall.

CONVERSION—SEE CHANGE/NOVELTY ORIENTATION

COOPERATIVENESS

Family-centeredness (see FAMILY-CENTEREDNESS) is the Mediterranean cultural value that governs the value of cooperativeness, which is best interpreted as "help" rendered to those in need of it. Thus, cooperativeness is a value that serves as a means to the goal of maintaining honor. Primarily, it contributes to and strengthens the tight-knit family structure characteristic of the Mediterranean world. Stephen matter-of-factly reports the behavior of Moses helping one of "his relatives, the Israelites" who was being wronged by an Egyptian: Moses took revenge by striking down the Egyptian (Acts 7:24–25; Exod 2:11–12). Clearly, in this instance Moses rendered "help" to a member of his extended kin, a member of his ethnic group, and not narrowly to an immediate family member. This latter kind of help is taken for granted and falls not under the rubric of cooperativeness but rather under family obligation or family-centeredness.

Extending help toward members of one's ethnic group lies at the heart of Jesus' story about the Good Samaritan (Luke 10:29–37). The Samaritan, a despised person of mixed breed, extended help to an Israelite in need, while the priest and Levite deliberately ignored this needy member of their "pure breed" ethnic group.

How is cooperativeness or helpfulness shown to those outside the extended kinship group, or the ethnic group? Here the rules of dyadic contract (see **DYADISM**) and related notions come into play. In this culture where all goods are considered finite in quantity and already distributed to everyone (an idea known as **LIMITED GOOD**), it is shameful to accept a gift or favor without repaying it. That would be equivalent to depriving another of the person's just due. For this reason Paul urges the recipients of his letter to the Romans to welcome and help Phoebe into their midst, "for she has been a benefactor of many [believers, our extended, fictive kin group] and of myself [Paul] as well" (Rom 16:2). Paul calls into play the cooperativeness and spirit of help which ought to govern relationships among members of the early Christian community, an extended, fictive kinship group. Paul himself confidently expected to receive similar help from the Roman Christians during his brief visit with them on his way to Spain (Rom 15:24).

Though incumbent upon all members of the kinship group (real or fictive), the duty to help others appears to have been expected especially for widows. It is significant that children or grandchildren of widows are expected to "first learn their religious duty to their own family and make some repayment to their parents" (1 Tim 5:3–4). In order to be recognized as a member of the order of widows, a candidate must be well attested for having helped the oppressed (1 Tim 5:10).

When the resources of real and fictive kin groups cannot meet a person's needs, that person can have recourse to yet another cultural institution: patronage (see **PATRONAGE**). Relationships in patronage involve a superior and an inferior, or one who has or has access to an abundance of resources and one whose access is rather restricted. A patron is one who either can obtain for a client something that client could not obtain personally or can obtain it under better terms than the client might be able to. The needy person can seek and court a patron, but ultimately the decision to be a patron lies with the patron alone. The patron chooses to meet the needs of or acquiesce to the requests of the client. In return the client sings the praises and enhances the honor of the patron far and wide.

Another way of viewing the client-patron relationship is that the patron chooses to treat clients "as if" they were family. In Jesus' parable of the workers in the vineyard (Matt 20:1–16), those who worked from early morning on and received the same remuneration as those who were hired late in the day made the painful discovery that the vineyard owner freely chose to become a patron to the last-hired workers. He freely chose to treat them "as if" they were family. The first hired were treated strictly in accord with the contractual agreement; those hired last, who needed a full day's wage, succeeded in finding a patron who could help them in their need.

The strong kinship basis that undergirds the cooperativeness or help that characterizes Mediterranean culture is much weaker and often lacking in Western culture. Children in the West are raised as strong individualists and urged to learn how to "stand on their own two feet" as quickly as possible. Aged parents proudly proclaim that they do not want to be a burden to their adult children. Western culture encourages self-reliance and self-sufficiency; the popularity and abundance of "self-help" literature in Western culture bears powerful witness to these individualistic values.

In the culture that prevails in the United States, "apparent" cooperativeness is usually based on self-interest. Help and cooperativeness are readily extended in team-efforts toward winning, because each individual member of the winning team gains something (ring, money, trophy, letter, promotion, raise, better contract, etc.). Limited help and cooperativeness are extended to the unemployed and victims of a disaster who are temporarily bereft of the resources needed to achieve, to gain, to win, to behave self-sufficiently—resources they must strive to regain as quickly as possible. In each of these instances, cooperativeness and help have a definite limit. This is radically different from the ever available help and cooperativeness in the Mediterranean world. (John J. Pilch)

Eisenstadt, Shlomo N., and Louis Roniger. 1984. *Patrons, Clients and Friends: Interpersonal Relations and the Structure of Trust in Society.* Cambridge: Cambridge University Press.

CURIOSITY

In Mediterranean culture, curiosity is usually regarded as the vice of a fool which leads to distraction from responsibilities and therefore potentiates disaster (Deut 5:32–33; Prov 4:25–27; 7:21–27; 9:1–6, 11; 15:21). The society described in the Bible is generally characterized by its preoccupation with ritual purity, resolute observance of religious laws, and firm maintenance of class and social boundaries. Singly and together, purity, law, and rank are thought of as divinely instituted aspects of Israel's holiness (Deut 6:4–9; Neh 10). In such a cultural context, curiosity would betray impatience with the status quo (by implying illegitimate aspirations) and/ or interest in illicit pleasures. Both are regarded as sinful consequences of idle, "good for nothing" curiosity (Prov 17:24; 21:17; cf. Ps 131; Sir 8:15; Col 2:8; 1 John 2:15–17).

There is, however, a specific kind of curiosity of which the Bible approves, namely, the seeking of wisdom

(Prov 3:13–18; Wis 6:12–21). It is not accidental that, given the traditional culture of the biblical authors, wisdom here means obeying the law and accepting the responsibilities of one's station in life by seeing that they are honorably, and thus fully, discharged (Prov 6:35; 22:1; 23:12; 28:4; Eccl 12:13–14; Sir 1:24–29; 11:20–21; 37:12–15). Even so, due in large measure to the influence of Hellenistic speculative philosophy on Judaic thought (Philo), a limited tolerance for curiosity develops before and during the New Testament era. This was the case not only for elites and missionaries, to whom the *Pax Romana* afforded previously unparalleled opportunities for trade and travel (witness Acts), but for many ordinary people as well (especially those in cities and towns): the effects of international trade, travel, and Roman military presence were felt nearly everywhere. The widespread curiosity about new religions in the empire (e.g., worship of Isis and Mithras, not to mention Jesus), shows this conclusively.

Nevertheless, during the historical period in which responsibilities of church membership superseded all other social obligations (see **FAMILY-CENTEREDNESS**), the early Christian movement (which was at least partly a revolt against traditional Judaism and the religion of the empire) soon developed its own accommodated form of the prohibition against curiosity, seeing it as impatience with the status quo or interest in illicit pleasures—the sinful qualities of idle curiosity (Matt 5:27–30; 1 Tim 6:9–10; 1 John 2:15–17; Jude 10–19). As would be expected, Christian wisdom, concerned in the main with the requirements of honorable discipleship, also quickly emerged as an approved form of curiosity (John 1:35–51; 4:21–24; 1 Tim 5; 2 Tim 3:15–17; 1 Pet 4:2–5). Thus, in both Judaic and Christian contexts, the Mediterranean cultural constant of disapproval of curiosity remained in force. It is easy to see, therefore, that curiosity could be identified as a negatively esteemed means value because of its potential for damage to the core value of honor. Such curiosity stimulates the development of cultural strategies of secrecy and deception (see **DECEPTION**) as a means of protecting honor.

The Bible frowns upon curiosity because it typically leads, not to wisdom, but to dissipation and shame. Likewise, the modern West acknowledges a distinction between "sick" and "healthy" curiosity, although we tend to see the distinction from a psychological rather than cultural viewpoint (e.g., appreciation of the nude in art is not voyeurism).

Another difference is that Americans tend to relate curiosity with knowledge or information rather than wisdom. This is the case because "wisdom" often carries with it connotations of a tradition-bound conservatism. In a rapidly changing, information- and image-driven U.S. culture, "knowledge" and "information" bear connotations of progress and advancement. We assume, in contrast to the biblical authors, that social and cultural forms evolve more or less naturally. Geographical, social, and educational mobility are taken for granted as facts of modern life. For us, then, curiosity (despite its having killed the cat), is generally regarded as a positive trait because we see it as the impetus for the discovery of useful information and new knowledge. (Mark McVann)

Tefft, Stanton K., ed. 1980. *Secrecy: A Cross-Cultural Perspective.* New York: Human Sciences Press.
Walsh, P. G. 1988. "The Rights and Wrongs of Curiosity (Plutarch to Augustine)." *Greece and Rome* 35:73–85.

DECEPTION—SEE ALSO EYES-HEART

In the world of the Gospels, one cannot tell a book by its cover or a man by the company he keeps. People are warned against judging by appearances (John 7:24; 8:15) because appearances are unreliable. People carefully distinguish between outer and inner, appearances and reality. They know that the world is ambiguous, even deceptive. Ambiguity surrounds Jesus and often characterizes his teaching. He himself proclaims that the expected way of the world is reversed; for in his order of things, low is high, humbled is exalted, poor is rich, weak is strong, master serves, last is first, unclean is clean, and dishonor is honor (see Luke 13:30; 14:7–11; 18:14; 22:26).

Appearances, then, are deceptive; exteriors do not match interiors. Concerning Jesus himself, the crucified Christ appears foolish and weak to the Jew and the Greek, but in truth he is God's wisdom and strength (1 Cor 1:23–25). Comparably, when Paul first came to the Galatians, he did not appear as one risen with Christ and full of power; he had a "bodily ailment" which was a trial to them (Gal 4:13–14), but they took him for an angel! Therefore, what outwardly appears to be weak, foolish, and even sinful may inwardly be wise, powerful, and holy; conversely what appears outwardly to be holy and honorable may inwardly be corrupt.

In addition to this, people sense that others actually deceive them by a facade of probity and mask what is within. Deceit, not just ambiguity, plagues the world of the Gospels. But deceit invites revelation of the truth and the unveiling of secrets hidden. For example, Jesus relentlessly exposes the "hypocrisy" of the scribes, Pharisees, and Sadducees, people credited with knowledge of the Law and boastful of their observance of it. They appear orthodox, observant, and holy, yet in his eyes they preach what they themselves do not practice (Matt 23:3). Worse, they cleanse the outside of cup and vessel, but "inside they are full of extortion and rapacity" (23:25); they are like whitewashed tombs, which outwardly appear beautiful, but "within are full of dead men's bones and all uncleanness" (23:27). The outer clearly does not match the inner. And from Jesus' perspective they are not just ambiguous but deceptive: they disguise the evil within. Jesus resolves the problem of their ambiguity by penetrating their disguise and revealing their hidden corruption.

Yet they act the same way toward him. He claims to be God's agent, even a prophet, but his actions belie this. And by exposing his external failures, they call constant attention to what they consider deception on his part. In their eyes, his external actions do not match his claims to internal holiness and righteousness. Jesus violates one of the oldest and most obvious of God's commandments, "Keep holy the Lord's Day" (Matt 12:1–12; Luke 13:10–17; John 5:9–16; 9:14–16). As a holy man, he should keep separate from all uncleanness, but he enlists public sinners as his associates (Mark 2:13–14); he regularly eats with tax collectors and sinners (Matt 11:19; Mark 2:15; Luke 19:6–7); he profanes God's temple (Mark 11:15–16) and regularly speaks of its destruction (Mark 13:1–2). Despite Jesus' claims to be holy, his actions are those of a sinner; the outer does not match the inner. In their eyes he is not merely ambiguous but deceptive (John 7:12). He is a false prophet, a false christ. And they claim the ability to penetrate his disguise.

Granted that outer does not match inner, it happens that people disguise what is in their hearts and what is genuine about them with exterior masks. The people of the Gospels regularly deceive others and expect to be deceived. For example, Jesus speaks critically about "hypocrisy," the deliberate cover of a corrupt interior with an exterior mask of piety (Matt 23:28; Mark 7:6; Luke 12:1; 13:15; Gal 2:13). While Jesus criticizes hypocritical piety done in public to win honor (Matt 6:2, 5, 16), he curiously tells his disciples to hide their good actions and do them "in secret," masking their behavior from others. He says, moreover, that they are actually to deceive others: "For when you fast, anoint your head and wash your face, that your fasting may not be seen by men" (Matt 6:17–18).

Hypocrisy and deception are no innocent matters, for people begin to follow Jesus "who pretend to be sincere" but are spies who try to catch him in his words (Luke 20:20). And one of the Twelve proves to be the greatest of hypocrites, pretending loyalty to Jesus but plotting his betrayal (John 13:27–30). The presumption arises that one's world is full of disguised enemies; it is difficult to tell friends from foes and the stakes are high: loss of honor and even bodily harm and death.

Deception is thus a means value in the Mediterranean world. It is a strategy for establishing and protecting honor, as well as for bringing shame upon one's enemies.

Yet the expectation of deception is not restricted to the conflict between Jesus and rival synagogue leaders. Within the circle of Jesus' followers one hears constant warnings about "false prophets" and "false christs." The Synoptic Gospels' record of the final address by Jesus concerning future crises for the disciples is illustrative. It begins with warnings about deception (Matt 24:4–5); it predicts "false prophets who will lead many astray" (24:11) as well as "false prophets and false christs" who will try to lead astray even the elect (24:23–24). Paul too fears deception, for he claims that just as Satan disguised himself as an angel of light to deceive Eve, so Satan's disciples are disguising themselves to seduce the Corinthian church (2 Cor 11:14–15). A fuller explanation of remarks such as these would invite examination of them as sorcery accusations, accusations that evil masquerades as good and seeks to seduce, corrupt and destroy what is pure and holy. The deceptive world is intensely hostile.

Where ambiguity and deception abound, claims will be made to penetrate disguises and to read hearts. Like his mentor John the Baptizer (Matt 3:7–10), Jesus knows what is in the heart of man (John 2:24–25). He reads secret criticism of himself (Mark 2:8); he ferrets out the lies and deceptions in the false allegiance of certain disciples (John 8:31–58). And Jesus can identify the demonic power which possesses certain people, both outsiders (Matt 12:43–45; John 8:44) and disciples (John 6:70). But it is especially God who has the ability to read hearts (1 Thess 2:4; Rev 2:23) and whose final judgment will be a revealing of secrets (1 Cor 4:5). For nothing is hidden which shall not be revealed (Matt 10:26).

New Testament people, then, experienced a world of masquerade and deception, in which people both deceived others and expected to be deceived in turn. It was a world of flatterers, spies, hypocrites, and disguised demons. "Do not be deceived" was a serious, but common, watchword, even for members of the church (Matt 24:4; Mark 13:5; Luke 21:8; 1 Cor 6:9; Jas 1:16).

Modern Western culture, of course, has effective safeguards against deception: polygraph tests, regulatory governmental agencies, legal penalties for perjury, and the like. Yet there are some major differences between Western and Mediterranean culture. In the Mediterranean world, deception is a legitimate strategy at the service of honor; it is a means value. Those who excel in deception are cheered by the crowd, even as those they have "taken in" smart from the shame and plot retaliation.

In the West, deception is not a value at all, except perhaps in games (the "fake," the "bluff"). People who resort to it are viewed as fools, for they will always be found out. Unlike the Mediterranean world, deception has no connection with honor. In Western culture, people firmly believe that they can know or find out what others are thinking, feeling, planning, scheming, or doing by such means as psychological tests, sophisticated surveillance technology, and investigative reporting. An American proverb reminds us that "honesty is the best policy." (Jerome H. Neyrey)

Bolle, Kees W. 1987. *Secrecy in Religions*. Leiden: Brill.

Du Boulay, Juliet. 1976. "Lies, Mockery and Family Integrity." In *Mediterranean Family Structures*. Ed. J. G. Peristiany. Pp. 389–406. Cambridge: Cambridge University Press.

Kippenberg, Hans G., and Guy G. Strousma. 1995. *Secrecy and Concealment: Studies in the History of the Mediterranean and Near Eastern Religion*. Leiden: Brill.

Pilch, John J. 1992. "Lying and Deceit in the Letters to the Seven Churches: Perspectives from Cultural Anthropology." *Biblical Theology Bulletin* 22:126–35.

_____. 1994. "Secrecy in the Mediterranean World: An Anthropological Perspective." *Biblical Theology Bulletin* 24:151–57.

Simmel, Georg. 1950. "The Sociology of Secrecy and of Secret Societies." In *The Sociology of Georg Simmel.* Ed. Kurt H. Wolff. Pp. 305–76. Glencoe, Ill.: Free. First published in *American Journal of Sociology* 11 (1906): 441–98.

Tefft, Stanton K. 1980. *Secrecy: A Cross-Cultural Perspective.* New York: Human Sciences Press.

DEFEAT

The whole concept of defeat (Greek: *hypotassō*) must be seen against the backdrop of the Mediterranean idea of honor and shame, for the one who defeats another gains or enhances honor. It is therefore a secondary value. Relative to the person or nation defeated, defeat means shame pure and simple.

Defeat (syn. conquest) may be individual, that is, a personal feeling of failure, e.g., "we are unworthy servants" (Luke 17:10) but, much more commonly, it is social in aspect, that is, one party is conquered by another. This may arise when that party fails to make a riposte to a challenge with regard to honor or when that party fails to defend successfully his or her honor. Thus, to be defeated is to be dishonored, to be reduced to shame, to become a nonentity, and therefore to be in the condition of life most despicable in the eyes of the vast majority of Mediterranean peoples.

Defeat is graphically depicted by certain actions perpetrated by the conqueror who seeks to shame the individual, group, or nation, often reducing them to a status below that of a human being. What the conqueror attempts to create is a reversal of status. This is shown in a number of ways which are closely associated with the physical body and all that it symbolizes. The conqueror seeks to eliminate all order and classification in the life of the victim and seeks to reduce the social and religious status of the person(s) by exile or deportation, that is, to destroy the familial and fictive kinship boundaries and the spaces sacred to the defeated one.

The victim is often obliged to live in a state of ritual impurity; sometimes (but not often) the victim is imprisoned, fettered, or placed in stocks to restrict social space. Prison deprives him/her of light, and the prisoner is surrounded by darkness which is often associated with malicious powers. Victims may be stripped, thus being subjected to extreme shame by bodily exposure, or be provided with garments unbecoming to their former status (2 Kgs 25:27, 29). Clothing (see CLOTHING) in the ancient world is part of one's personality as are possessions, so that the withdrawal of both decreases the honor of the individual. Frequently the head, which is the symbol of authority, is shaven, thus denoting abdication of all authority and honor. The diet normally provided to the victim is meager rations designed to decrease his bodily beauty. This nourishment usually defies the dietary laws which had been observed by the victim in his free state.

In addition to physical shame the conqueror often seeks to torment the victim with mockery, gloating, and malicious glee. This verbal abuse is important to the Mediterranean person because a word is dynamic, creating what it names. The victor may also curse the victim, and the curse is seen as a withdrawal of divine vitality. The victim may also endure physical violence, such as scourging, a ring in the nose, etc. (cf. Amos 4:2–3).

Two examples may be taken from the New Testament. In the Apocalypse of John, the prostitute (symbolizing the enemy of the righteous) is conquered by divine power. Her status corresponds dramatically to the defeated person in the ancient world. The angel proclaims that Babylon has fallen (Rev 18:2); she becomes a dwelling place of demons, unclean spirits, carrion birds, and unclean animals. She experiences death, mourning, and famine (Rev 18:8). Her former associates stand far from her (Rev 18:10, 15); her luxurious commerce has come to an end (Rev 18:12–13); her clothing of pure linen and gold has been stripped away; festivities are removed (Rev 18:21–22); she is deprived of light (Rev 18:23).

The other example may be found in the Passion of Christ. He becomes the defeated one and allows people to treat him shamefully, for he does not respond in kind, as the core cultural value of honor would dictate in this situation. This is seen particularly in the Passion narratives, where each evangelist contributes a personal interpretation of Jesus' "dishonorable" comportment. A few examples may be given. Mark portrays Jesus in the garden as "coming to pieces at the seams" (*ekthambeisthai kai adēmonein*) and groveling on the ground to pray (Mark 14:33–35). The fictive group of which he is the leader deserts him (Mark 14:50): one of them is shamed by nudity in his eagerness to escape (Mark 14:51–52). One Lukan text describes Jesus as sweating, as if with drops of blood, trembling like an athlete before a contest (Luke 22:44). All the Gospels describe a mockery both before and during the crucifixion (Matt 27:27–30; Mark 15:16–20; John 19:2–3; Luke 22:63–65 and 23:11). In this scene Jesus' head and body are dishonored by a status reversal ceremony which includes spitting, buffeting, crowning with thorns, and ridicule; all this is the lot of a defeated person. All the Gospels report his presence in the praetorium, an unclean space for the Jews (cf. John 18:28), but it is John's Gospel which dramatizes above all the whole Passion as the defeat of a kingly figure: there is a mock investiture and homage (John 19:2–3); mock proclamation (19:5) and acclamation (19:3); mock enthronement (19:18) and naming (19:19). This means that Jesus' Passion completely reverses the worldly concept of sovereignty and honor. But Jesus' defeat is most graphically shown in that he is condemned to a death normally imposed upon slaves, the lowest social stratum. Lastly, he is physically and publicly exposed on the cross, which is the extreme denial of honor, he is closely ranked with criminals, given vinegar to drink, and his clothing (which is an extension of personhood) is divided by lot among the soldiers (John 19:23–24). Mark (15:34) and Matthew (27:46) report the last climax of defeat, Jesus' cry: "My God, my God, why have you abandoned me?" (author's trans.).

In the United States, popular culture generally believes that "winning isn't everything; it's the only thing!" For this reason, defeat is not suffered easily. Yet within the wider cultural context of fair play, the victor strives to behave tactfully so as not to aggravate the sense of loss experienced by the one defeated and the loser is encouraged to be a gracious loser in defeat. Even so, the shame of defeat experienced in the United States is nowhere near as devastating and calamitous as the shame experienced in the Mediterranean world. In the United States, shame is only temporary, that is, only until the next opportunity of fair play when the defeated person can possibly gain a victory. In the Mediterranean world, defeat can often have devastating consequences. (Josephine Massyngbaerde Ford)

Ford, Josephine Massyngbaerde. 1993. "BTB Readers Guide: Prostitution in the Ancient World." *Biblical Theology Bulletin* 23:128–34.
———. 1995. "Jesus as Sovereign in the Passion According to John." *Biblical Theology Bulletin* 25:110–17.
Howard, M. 1983. *The Causes of War.* 2d enl. ed. Cambridge: Harvard University Press.

DOMINATION ORIENTATION—SEE ALSO POWER

This value forms part of the authoritarian value cluster (see **AUTHORITARIANISM**). It is a value that imposes sanctions of power in order to gain honor. Such sanctions of power include physical force, pain, violent expulsion, and death. Domination sanctioned by God is the theme of the book of Joshua, a sort of reward for the Egyptian domination of the Israelites. Thus, domination orientation is a value that serves as a means to gaining honor.

What people seek in dominion over others is to be "lord," to "lord it over" others. A "lord" is a person with the right to control other persons totally and at will, with the right of life and death over another, with full rights to the property and being of another. As a title of respect (e.g., Matt 21:3), it denotes great deference. In the hymn cited by Paul (Phil 2:5ff.), lordship describes the highest conceivable role in terms of legitimate power and precedence. A slave, of course, is the other social extreme: a person that is another's property with no rights at all, not even "human" rights.

This value is realized by subjecting others. One common context in which this theme appears is passages which exhort a person to "be subject to." A review of such passages would flesh out the details of this theme (see **HANDS-FEET**).

While "lording it over" others and "being subject to" others in the Mediterranean world are means by which honor is gained and shame is imposed, the prevailing culture in the United States generally pursues these values not among its citizens but among other nations of the world, whether by violence (war or other aggression) or by economic means (high tariffs, boycotts, etc.). The central importance of freedom and equality in the United States makes domestic domination repulsive to a majority of citizens. Historically, the United States has tended to validate its domination of other nations by declaring them uncivilized or less than human. Ethnic slurs against enemies of the United States or descriptive phrases such as "the evil empire" facilitate the acceptance of a domination orientation over other nations by citizens otherwise committed to the values of democracy and respect for freedom. Often is it these latter values that underpin the domination orientation in this country. (John J. Pilch)

Gilmore, David D. 1987. *Aggression and Community: Paradoxes of Andalusian Culture.* New Haven: Yale University Press.

Goldstein, A. P., and Marshall H. Segall, eds. 1983. *Aggression in Global Perspective*. Elmsford, N.Y.: Pergamon.

Segall, Marshall H. 1988. "Psychocultural Antecedents of Male Aggression: Some Implications Involving Gender, Parenting, and Adolescence." In *Health and Cross-Cultural Psychology: Toward Applications*. Ed. P. R. Dasen, J.W. Berry, and N. Sartrorius. Pp. 71–92. Newbury Park, Calif.: Sage.

Dramatic Orientation (exaggeration, over-assertion)

This is a means value for maintaining and enhancing the Mediterranean core values of honor and shame. Dramatic orientation finds expression in word (language, eloquence, hyperbole, boasting) and deed (heroic gestures, speaking as if the deed already took place). These are some of the means available to a Mediterranean person to gain, maintain, and enhance personal and group honor.

Luke describes his Gospel as a presentation of "all that Jesus began to do and teach" (Acts 1:1). This is a tip-off that he presents Jesus as an honorable Mediterranean person who demonstrates this very fact by his deeds and words. The heroic gesture, for example, is viewed in itself as fitting an occasion and hardly ever perceived as a possible link in a chain of cause and effect. Jesus undoubtedly viewed his heroic gesture of cleansing the temple (Luke 19:45) as precisely such an action fitting the occasion with no thought at all that it was also one more link in a chain of causes stirring "the chief priests and the scribes and the principal men of the people" (20:47) to seek to destroy him. On the other hand there apparently were times when Jesus knew he was being watched, as when he healed the man with the withered hand (6:6–11). The scribes and Pharisees became "filled with fury" and discussed what they might do to Jesus.

Matthew depicts dramatic orientation gone totally awry in his presentation of Jesus' assessment of the Pharisees as "hypocrites." Literally, the word in Greek (*hypokritēs*) means "actor." Jesus notes the dramatic exaggeration of the Pharisees in their fasting (applying special make-up), almsgiving (making a big show of it), and other behaviors. It is not the dramatic orientation Jesus challenges. Rather, it is the groundless "play-acting" or "role-playing" he takes to task. The Pharisees deliver lines and play roles like actors seeking applause. Their behavior is not an authentic life-style. They may quote the Torah, but that is not the script by which they live.

What interpreters have traditionally called "realized eschatology" (the belief that at least certain elements of the end-time already exist) may well be instead part of the typical Mediterranean inclination to behave as if spoken words are deeds-already-come-to-pass. Thus, in Luke's Gospel, after Jesus reads from Isaiah in the synagogue, yet before he is reported to have done anything else, Jesus says: "Today this scripture has been fulfilled in your hearing" (Luke 4:21). A more mundane example would be the son who tells his father he will go work in the fields but does not (Matt 21:28–31). Mediterranean culture has a proclivity for substituting words for actions.

Words and language are very important in Mediterranean culture, for they are related to manliness. The man who is eloquent and capable of strong rhetoric is viewed as a strong man. Jesus most certainly fits this description, beginning with his visit to the temple as an adolescent (Luke 2:46–47) when all who heard him were astonished and amazed.

Eloquence involves the skill of verbal exaggeration and over-assertion. The most familiar instance of Jesus' use of hyperbole is his comparison of a rich man's chances of entering the kingdom with a camel's ability to pass through the eye of a needle (Matt 19:24 and parallels). Another is the suggestion to cut off a scandalizing hand or pluck out a scandalizing eye (Matt 5:29–30). Exaggeration is quite common in the culture. Recall Jesus' report of popular opinion concerning the Baptist and himself: "John came neither eating nor drinking, and they say,

'He has a demon'; the Son of man came eating and drinking, and they say, 'Behold, a glutton and a drunkard, a friend of tax collectors and sinners' " (Matt 11:18–19). Such exaggerated statements are not intended to be taken seriously but are made solely for effect and are heartily appreciated and applauded by an audience that enjoys such eloquence when it hears it.

Jesus' principal formula for expressing emphatic-assertion or over-assertion is "amen . . ." or "truly I say to you" (e.g., Matt 5:18; 6:2). This is a very necessary strategy in a culture wherein deception (see **DECEPTION**) of all kinds is also a routine strategy for establishing and maintaining honor, but perhaps more particularly for heading off shame.

Raphael Patai has noted that dramatic exaggeration is a cultural phenomenon with socio-economic foundations. A peasant who is essentially "self-employed" (tends his own fields or flocks or plies his trade) decides how to use his time and how much leisure to take in a very independent and free fashion. Exaggeration and imagination make a person more free. One can fill time with florid greetings, lengthy discussions, and other occasions to develop the skill of exaggeration.

A technological society like mainstream United States culture is tied to precision. It conceives of time as a scarce commodity to be used efficiently and productively and not to be wasted. Dramatic orientation, exaggeration, and over-assertion waste precious time by not getting directly to the point. A modern proverb claims "time is money." Creativity, imagination, and boasting are activities that waste precious time. They have no place in a society driven by productivity; machines will tolerate no exaggeration, imprecision, or tardiness. Dramatic orientation is suitable for the theater but not for real life. (John J. Pilch)

Batey, R. 1984. "Jesus and the Theatre." *New Testament Studies* 30:563–74.

Eickelman, Dale F. 1989. *The Middle East: An Anthropological Approach.* Rev. ed. Englewood Cliffs, N.J.: Prentice Hall.

Pilch, John J. 1992. "Lying and Deceit in the Letters to the Seven Churches: Perspectives from Cultural Anthropology." *Biblical Theology Bulletin* 22:126–35.

Stock, Augustine. 1986. "Jesus, Hypocrites, and Herodians." *Biblical Theology Bulletin* 16:3–7.

DYADISM

When we examine the information given about individual people in the New Testament, we learn about them in terms of their relationship to someone or something else.

Place: Simon is the man from Cyrene (Mark 15:21); Naaman is a Syrian (Luke 4:27); the woman who begs Jesus for her daughter is a Canaanite (Matt 15:22). Paul and others are known in terms of their city of birth (Acts 22:3; 18:24).

Nation: Appropriate to a given audience, Paul insists that he is an Israelite, a Hebrew born of Hebrews (Phil 3:5) and that he holds Roman citizenship (Acts 22:27). Jesus ought not to talk to the woman at the well because he is a Judean who has no dealing with Samaritans (John 4:9). This type of thinking begets ethnic slurs, such as "Cretans are liars" (Titus 1:12).

Clan: It matters to which of the tribes of Israel one belongs. We repeatedly learn that Mary is of the house of David (Luke 1:27), and that among her cousins, Zechariah belongs to the division of Abijah and Elizabeth is a daughter of Aaron (Luke 1:5). Paul boasts of being of the tribe of Benjamin (Phil 3:5). It would matter greatly to Gentile converts to be known as offspring of Abraham. Connected with this is the importance given to a genealogy, which establishes one's exact pedigree (Matt 1:1–18; Luke 3:23–38).

Family: Individual men and women are known in terms of their family relations. Simon is son of Jonah (Matt 16:17), and James and John are known as the sons of Zebedee (Mark 1:19). Joanna is known to us as the wife of Chuza, who in turn is known as Herod's steward (Luke 8:3). Jesus, of course, is the son of Mary (Mark 6:3) or the carpenter's son (Matt 13:55); more significantly, he is the son of God (Mark 1:11; 9:7; 15:39). One of the James mentioned in the New Testament is known to us as the brother of John (Acts 12:2) and son of Zebedee, while another James is identified as the brother of the Lord (Gal 1:19).

School: Students are known in terms of their teacher; hence, Paul is a student of Gamaliel (Acts 22:3); a debate in John 9 distinguishes the disciples of Moses from those of Jesus (9:28).

Individual people are not known or valued because of their uniqueness, but in terms of their dyad, that is, some other person or thing. Dyadism, therefore, is a means value by which one's honor can be continually checked, affirmed, or challenged. And individual people would describe themselves in this way, as a servant of God, as a priest of God's temple, and as a centurion of the Italian cohort. Personal identity and knowledge of this sort belong in a cultural world which is highly ordered and carefully classified, so that there is a place for everyone and everyone in his place. The source of this system is God, who "arranged the organs of the body, each one as God chose" (1 Cor 12:18). It follows that such people tend to think of themselves and others in stereotypes which tell of their role and status: as fishermen and carpenters, as scribes and lawyers, as governors and kings.

From this way of knowing and being known flow many issues and social strategies. Christian preachers describe a new dyadic identity for the disciples of Jesus: they become brothers and sisters of his family. They assume a new identity, as members of Christ's body (1 Cor 12:12), as adopted offspring of God (Gal 4:4–6), and as citizens of God's kingdom (Phil 3:20). As members of a new family, moreover, people allow their personal identity and desires to be shaped by others; and so one learns from others to have a "conscience," to share their evaluations, and to determine one's duties from that collective description (1 Cor 8:7–13). Paul can instruct all, even slaves, to remain in the state in which they were called (1 Cor 7:20). Paul can instruct people through traditional lists of virtues and vices about commonly held values (Gal 5:19–23; 1 Cor 6:9–10). He articulates "conscience," that is, knowledge known in common (*cum-scientia*) among a group of people. In such a world, moral aphorisms find a special place. Third, individuals do not tend to make claims about their identity so much as to listen to what others say of them: "Who do men say that I am? Who do you say that I am?" (Mark 8:27–29). Jesus, for example, claims never to speak "of myself," but as the one whom God sent, as God's agent (John 7:16; 14:10). And so the question of one's authority to speak or act remains a key question, for individuals always need legitimacy from another, from God, the governor, the high priest, etc. (see Acts 22:5). This will be most clearly realized in the way people seek patrons. One can advance one's cause by seeking the patronage, protection, authorization and favor of another. Students seek teachers; farmers seek landlords; the pious seek God. Finally, in this context one finds great value placed on obedience (see **OBEDIENCE**), faithfulness (see **FAITH/FAITHFULNESS**), and loyalty to tradition. Children should obey their parents by accepting their definition of one's role and status (Col 3:20), just as slaves should obey their masters (Eph 6:5–8). Wives should be loyal to their husband's family and its interests (Eph 5:22). It is not surprising then, that Jesus' great virtue was his faithfulness (*pistis*) to God (Heb 3:2–6) and his loyal obedience to God's will (Mark 8:31; 14:36).

Thus, dyadism, or an other-directed orientation, is a value which serves as a means of learning about and pursuing one's honor. Since honor is a public claim to worth *and* a public acknowledgment of that claim by others, the opinions of others hold central importance in this culture.

In contrast to this Mediterranean, other-directed orientation, the culture of the United States favors unique and distinctive individualism. It applauds the person who "marches to the beat of a different drummer" and who knows how to stand on his or her own two feet. American individuals care little about what others think or say of them: "sticks and stones will break my bones, but names will never hurt me." In the U.S., individuals cherish the right to be "captain of one's soul and master of one's fate" quite independently of the assistance or opinions of others. The preference in this culture is to be "inner-directed." (Jerome H. Neyrey)

Hui, C. Harry, and Harry C. Triandis. 1986. "Individualism-Collectivism—A Study of Cross-Cultural Researchers." *Journal of Cross-Cultural Psychology* 17:225–48.

Malina, Bruce J. 1979. "The Individual and Community—Personality in the Social World of Early Christianity." *Biblical Theology Bulletin* 9:126–38.

Malina, Bruce J., and Jerome H. Neyrey. 1991. "First-Century Personality: Dyadic, Not Individualistic." In *The Social World of Luke–Acts: Models for Interpretation.* Ed. Jerome H. Neyrey. Pp. 67–96. Peabody, Mass.: Hendrickson.

———. 1996. *Portraits of Paul: An Archaeology of Ancient Personality.* Louisville, Ky.: Westminster John Knox.

Triandis, Harry C. 1990. "Cross-Cultural Studies of Individualism and Collectivism." In *Nebraska Symposium on Motivation 1989: Cross-Cultural Perspectives.* Ed. Richard A. Diensbier and John J. Berman. Pp. 41–133. Lincoln: University of Nebraska Press.

EMOTION/DEMONSTRATION OF FEELINGS

The Mediterranean cultural preference for "being" more than "doing" (see Introduction) involves an emphasis on those human activities which express the basic qualities or endowments of the human personality. Hence, the spontaneous expression of impulses, desires, and feelings or emotions flows from this preference. Such behavior is normal, acceptable, and in fact expected in daily Mediterranean life. Thus, the free and unrestrained expression of emotions in all human interactions is a core value in Mediterranean culture since it marks a person as authentically human from a Mediterranean perspective.

Mediterranean emotions invariably come in paired extremes, a trait which may well reflect desert experience where the scorching heat of the day can be succeeded by an icy cold night (see **AUTHORITARIANISM**). Since a Mediterranean person believes that nature cannot be controlled by human beings and considers human life to be subject to nature, spontaneous emotional outbursts are considered difficult to restrain. They simply happen. Thus, the same Jesus who says: "Learn from me; for I am gentle and lowly in heart" (Matt 11:29) later makes a whip of cords and drives the merchants and money-changers out of the temple, pours out the coins and overturns the tables (John 2:13–15 and parallels). Quite likely after the event, he was contrite, baffled, and totally amazed at what he did and how he managed to do it, a common reaction in this culture.

Related to the expression of emotions in paired extremes is the tendency to polarize all of reality and perceive it in extremes: black and white, good and bad, chivalrous generosity alternating with savage ferocity. The final (last) judgment will separate sheep from goats on a very clear-cut, good and bad basis (Matt 25:31–46). The Lukan Jesus' woes and beatitudes pitch people into two quite radically distinct camps with no possibility of a middle ground (6:20–26). The Laodicean problem was that it was neither hot nor cold but lukewarm (Rev 3:14–21). The owner of the house who returns to find a faithful servant will be generous to him but will punish severely the one he finds unprepared (Matt 24:43–51).

Men and women express emotions differently: men tend to sigh and call upon God as when Jesus looked up to heaven and sighed before restoring hearing to the deaf man in Mark 7:34 (for other instances of sighing see also Rom 8:23, 26; Acts 7:34; 2 Cor 5:2, 4). Women are permitted piercing cries and shrieks as when Rachel cried for her children (Matt 2:18) or the women cried at Jesus' Passion (Luke 23:27). Still, though self-control is an ideal, it is not considered unmanly to demonstrate one's feelings under heavy affliction. Jesus wept over the city of Jerusalem (Luke 19:41) and was deeply moved by friend Lazarus' death (John 11:33, 38). Peter wept (Mark 14:72) bitterly (Matt 26:75//Luke 22:62) when he realized he had betrayed Jesus. As he dies, Jesus cries out with a loud voice (Matt 27:46, 50 and parallels).

The powerful king Herod is troubled at news of a new king's birth (Matt 2:3) and enraged when he learns the astrologers disobeyed him (Matt 2:16). Zechariah is likewise disturbed to see an angel in the Holy of Holies (Luke 1:12). The disciples are terrified at the sight of Jesus coming to them walking on the sea (Matt 14:26//Mark 6:50) and again upon seeing the Risen Jesus in their midst (Luke 24:37).

Consciously aware of the value of emotional response, speakers make a direct effort to stir emotions. Jesus' sermon in the synagogue at Nazareth so [intentionally?] enraged the listeners that they wanted to kill him (Luke 4:28–30). Matthew's Jesus in particular seems fond of the phrase "wailing and gnashing of teeth," sometimes balanced with a picture of halcyon reward for the faithful—phrases undoubtedly intended to elicit an emotional response in the listeners (Matt 8:12; 13:42, 50; 24:51; 25:30; Luke 13:28). Demetrius the silversmith was quite successful in enraging the crowd (Acts 19:28) and stirring up a riot in Ephesus even though "most of [the crowd] did not know why they had come together" (Acts 19:32). Even in ordinary daily life people converse in loud, animated voices.

In contrast, mainstream United States culture allows women to be openly demonstrative of affection and emotion, but men are expected to demonstrate equanimity in every situation. Men are never to display anger or excessive joy. It is best to appear unmoved, to bear pain stoically, and endure hardships without any show of emotion.

Some years ago, crying in public cost former Maine Senator Edmund Muskie a clear shot at being nominated a presidential candidate of the Democratic party. The preferable image is that of Massachusetts Senator Ted Kennedy striving to retain composure as he delivered the eulogy during his assassinated brother John's funeral service.

The difference between Mediterranean and mainstream United States culture on emotion and demonstration of feelings hinges on control. Mediterranean people approve spontaneous expression of emotions by both men and women; in the United States, men are expected to control their emotions while women are permitted to express them uncontrollably. (John J. Pilch)

Lewis, Michael, and Jeannette M. Haviland, eds. 1993. *Handbook of Emotions.* New York: Guilford.

Pilch, John J. 1996. "A Window on the Biblical World: Slow to Anger and Long of Nose." *The Bible Today* 34/5:305–10.

Schweder, Richard A. 1993. "The Cultural Psychology of Emotions." In *Handbook of Emotions.* Ed. Michael Lewis and Jeannette M. Haviland. Pp. 417–31. New York: Guilford.

Wierzbicka, A. 1992. *Semantics, Culture, and Cognition.* New York: Oxford University Press.

END ORIENTATION—SEE PURPOSIVENESS/END ORIENTATION

ENVY—SEE ALSO FATE

This is a value which directs one to begrudge another the possession of some singular quality, object, or relationship. It is the limited nature of the quality, object, or relationship in question and the social status of the possessor that trigger envy. The social deviance involved in possessing something perceived as singular is that the one possessing the unique item stands out or stands above his or her proper social status and/or the group in general. The one who is envious becomes negatively disposed toward the person with the singular possession and is often seized by the desire to deprive the other person of that possession—often in the name of the group. The person possessing the singular quality, object, or relationship can defend himself or herself from envy in various ways. The most common and generalized way is some device that would keep envy at bay, such as tattoos, seals, and signet rings, incantations and the like (see Judg 8:21, 26; Isa 3:20). The purple tassels at the bottom of one's cloak served this purpose (Luke 8:44). The pregnant Mary could travel alone to visit her cousin—a very unusual behavior in Mediterranean culture—since the child in her womb served to defend and protect her from all harm. The leaping of Elizabeth's own foetus in her womb can be interpreted as a recognition of Jesus' apotropaic (evil thwarting) powers and abilities (Luke 1:39–41). Another way to deal with envy is to confront envious persons and accuse them of harboring the "evil eye" (see below in this entry, and see also EYES-HEART).

Jealousy, in contrast to envy, refers to attachment to and concern for what is exclusively one's own: one's child, spouse, house, fields, town. A "jealous God" (Exod 20:5; 34:14; Deut 4:24; 6:15; Josh 24:19) is attached to and concerned for his status and his clients (see PATRON-AGE); a "jealous husband" is attached to and concerned for his social standing and for his wife (Num 5:14, 30). Jealousy is a form of protectiveness that would ward off the envious and their machinations. It should not be confused with envy.

Envy clearly presupposes the perception of limited good (see LIMITED GOOD). The perception of limited good is the socially shared conviction that the resources enabling a community to support itself are in finite supply and that any disruption of the social equilibrium can be only detrimental to community survival. Persons believe that in their social, economic, and natural universe—in sum, in their total environment—all goods exist in finite, limited quantity and are always in short supply. This literally includes all desired goods in life: land, wealth, prestige, blood, health, semen, manliness, honor, friendship and love, respect and status, power and influence, security and safety. It is equally apparent to all that there is no way directly within a person's power to increase the available quantities. It is much like applying the obvious fact of land shortage and/or housing opportunity in a densely populated area to all other desired things in life: there simply is not enough to go around. The good things constituting life, like land, are seen as inherent in nature, there to be divided and redivided, if possible and necessary, but never to be increased.

Since all that is good exists in limited amounts which cannot be increased or expanded, it follows that an individual, alone or with his family, can improve his social position only at the expense of others. Hence, any apparent relative improvement in someone's position with respect to any good in life is viewed as a threat to the entire community—obviously someone is being deprived and denied something that is his, whether he knows it or not. And since there is often uncertainty as to who is losing—it may be me and my family—any significant improvement is perceived not simply as a threat to other single individuals or families alone, but as a threat to all individuals and families within the community, be it village or city quarter. Community stability and harmony among individuals and families can develop and be maintained only by keeping to the existing arrangements of statuses. Thus, most people would be interested in maintaining things just the way they are. It is this perspective in which envy is rooted.

In the Bible envy manifests itself on both the tribal (Gen 26:14; Isa 11:13) and familial levels (Gen 30:1; 37:11). As noted previously, it is associated with the world view that prosperity occurs only at the expense of others, hence, the few who prosper are "wicked." Their prosperity must necessarily have been obtained by social oppression and will be punished by Yahweh in the end, so envy is warned against (Job 5:2; Ps 37:1; 73:3; Prov 3:31; 23:17; 24:1, 19; 27:4).

In the Gospel story, Jesus is handed over to Pilate to be crucified because of envy. Both Matthew and Mark assert that Pilate was fully aware of this motive: "For he knew that is was out of envy that they had delivered him up" (Matt 27:18; Mark 15:10). What this means, of course, is that there surely was something singular about Jesus that his enemies perceived as threatening to their social well-being. In the epistolary admonitions against factionalism and divisions in the Christian community, envy is an undesirable quality (Rom 1:29; 13:13; Gal 5:21, 26; Phil 1:15; 1 Tim 6:4; Titus 3:3; 1 Pet 2:1).

On the other hand, its presence is well attested to, given the references to the evil eye (Deut 15:9; 28:54, 56; Prov 23:6; 28:22; Tob 4:7, 16; Sir 14:3, 6, 8, 9, 10; 18:18; 31:13; 37:10; Wis 4:12). The New Testament has its share of evil eye accusations. Four such accusations are attributed to Jesus in the Gospel story (Matt 6:22–23//Luke 11:34; Matt 20:15; Mark 7:22). Paul sees the opposition he finds in the groups to which his letter to the Galatians is directed as rooted in the evil eye: "O foolish Galatians, who has afflicted you with the evil eye?" (Gal 3:1, author's trans.). Finally, the association of eyes-heart with desire or envy likewise reflects the influence of the evil eye concept (1 John 2:16; Jas 4:1–10).

Twentieth-century U.S. society is one of "limitless goods." Hence, the meaning of envy has changed from that attested to in the Bible. In this culture, envy usually describes polite rivalry or competition between individuals. The limited good application of envy would work only for the possession of truly singular and unique qualities, objects, or relationships, e.g., a marriage partner, a unique corporate or government possession, etc. Yet in a U.S. context the perceived detriment would usually be not to community well-being and solidarity, but to individual advantage and gain. And in United States society, envy rarely entails a wish for the destruction of the goods of another as in the Mediterranean. One wishes only to have a good like that of another. (Bruce J. Malina, Chris Seeman)

Foster, George M. 1972. "The Anatomy of Envy: A Study in Symbolic Behaviour." *Current Anthropology* 13:163–203.
Ghosh, Amitav. 1983. "The Relations of Envy in an Egyptian Village." *Ethnology* 32:211–23.
Malina, Bruce J. 1993. *The New Testament World: Insights from Cultural Anthropology.* 2d rev. ed. Louisville, Ky.: Westminster John Knox.
Plutarch. 1959. "On Envy and Hate." In *Moralia* VII (523C–612B). Trans. Phillip H. DeLacy and Benedict Einarson. Pp. 94–107. Loeb Classical Library. Cambridge: Harvard University Press.
_____. 1959. "On the Delays of the Divine Vengeance." In *Moralia* VII (523C–612B). Trans. Phillip H. DeLacy and Benedict Einarson. Pp. 170–299. Loeb Classical Library. Cambridge: Harvard University Press.
Schoeck, Helmut. 1970. *Envy: A Theory of Social Behavior.* New York: Harcourt, Brace & World.
Walcott, Peter. 1978. *Envy and the Greeks: A Study in Human Behavior.* Warminster, England: Aris & Phillips.

EQUALITY—SEE PATRONAGE; AUTHORITARIANISM

EQUIVOCATION (SAYING ONE THING, DOING ANOTHER)— SEE ALSO DECEPTION; COMMUNICATIVENESS

Considerable attention is given to the control of the mouth in the cultures reflected in the Bible. James declares that perfection lies in correct governance of speech (3:1–6); oaths are taken to affirm the truth of one's assertion. On the other hand, the NT always condemns: a) hypocrisy, which is speech used to mask the true situation in the mind and heart, and b) deception (see DECEPTION), which is a particular but all too common evil. Yet it is quite another thing to say one thing and do another; while Westerners might consider this a vice, that is not clearly the case in the NT literature.

Great importance is put on public utterances. Because public, they are imbued with the honor of the speaker. A man is as good as his word. But the biblical

world contains elaborate rituals of etiquette, one of which
is not to give public offense; so it may be that a person
agrees to what is being publicly discussed to avoid conflict. Besides, it may be that those in the public discussion
have no right to know one's private thoughts; speaking
candidly may betray family interests, which have a prior
claim on an individual's loyalty. Etiquette may dictate
saying one thing publicly and doing another thing pri-
vately, or simply not following up what was publicly
stated.

A regular pattern can be noted in John's Gospel in
which Jesus: (1) is asked to do something, (2) refuses, and
(3) then acts contrary to his first statement. His mother
asks for a wedding favor (2:3); an official asks a healing
for an ill son (4:47); his brothers ask Jesus to go up to the
festival (7:3–4). Jesus publicly says "no" to these urgings
and requests (2:4; 4:48; 7:6–8), yet he later changes
water into wine (2:7–9), cures the sick son (4:50) and
goes up to the feast (7:10). His public "no" allows him to
act on terms favorable to his interests, not those of others. Obviously Jesus is not criticized for saying one thing,
yet doing another.

Moreover, Matthew records a parable about a father
and two sons: both sons said one thing publicly, but did
the opposite later. In the context, the son who ultimately
did the father's will is praised, and all people like him
(21:28–32). Yet the surprise in the parable lies in the rejection of the son who said "yes" publicly, but did not
act. It is shameful for a son to say "no" in public to a father's request; the son who said "yes" did the socially
correct thing by not shaming his father. Ironically, his
failure to go the vineyard later is far less shameful, if at
all, than the public "no" which the other son said to his
father, thus shaming his parent. The parable shocks precisely because it upsets the expected custom of saying the
correct thing in public, even if action never follows (see
Matt 7:21). The surprise, then, only confirms that there is
an expected pattern.

Paul's letters offer many examples of a person who was less than consistent about the relationship of his speech to his actions. He cites the public description of himself, "His letters are weighty and strong, but his bodily presence is weak, and his speech is of no account" (2 Cor 10:10). When present, he is "gentle as a nurse"; but when absent, he sends powerful letters. He maintains that he is thoroughly consistent in speech and action (10:11), yet even in his speech, he is not consistent. Although he constantly makes travel plans to visit his churches, he seems not to have acted upon them; this necessitated an apologetic response at the very beginning of 2 Corinthians, "Do I make plans like a worldly man, ready to say 'Yes' and 'No' at once?" (1:17). Evidently just saying that there is no problem is expected to excuse the behavior which follows. This discrepancy between word and action crops up in a number of issues. Paul boasts that he acts in accord with kosher rules when among Judaic Christians (1 Cor 9:19–23) but is publicly outraged when others do the same (Gal 2:11–14). Although critical of others who "boast" and recommend themselves, he does the same (2 Cor 3:1–3; 11:21ff.), although he claims that it is not really boasting (2 Cor 5:12). He is accused of valuing circumcision, although he inveighs against it (Gal 5:11; 1:10). On one occasion, he says that he did not regret a harsh letter sent to Corinth, although in the same breath he admits that he did regret it (2 Cor 7:8).

Saying one thing and doing another is most evident in the manner in which Paul presents himself. He often states that public criteria for status, such as blood and education, count for nothing, although he clearly states that he excels in these very criteria (Phil 3:3–4; 2 Cor 11:22). Paul would base his authority on God's ascription to him of the role of apostle, servant, and steward; but in dealing with those who legitimate their authority by achievement, Paul claims to equal them in achievements (1 Cor 2:6; 14:18; 15:51–57). Paul certainly sees nothing wrong in saying one thing and doing another; he obviously thinks others agree with his evaluation.

In line with this, even as Jesus inveighs against hypocritical piety in Matthew 6:1–18, he tells his followers to wash their faces and not flaunt their fasting. He is being inconsistent by criticizing hypocrisy while urging disguise. Yet his followers would not criticize this.

In the Hebrew Scriptures, the term *dabar* can mean what is said as well as what is done; it can refer to speech, action, and things. For example, in Chronicles one reads of "the 'acts' (*dbr*) of David," yet the very book is called "the 'words' (*dbr*) of the times"; words-acts are equal to chronicled history. God's word is powerful: by just saying "Let there be . . ." God caused action to occur, and the world was made (Gen 1). Of the word which goes forth from God's mouth, Isaiah says: "It accomplishes that which I purpose" (Isa 55:11). God's word must come true; history unfolds "according to the word of the Lord" (1 Kgs 13:26). Just by God's speaking, action must follow. Perhaps mortals treat their words similarly; having said it, they must act, but not with action that one must worry about. In God there is no saying one thing and doing another, for God must be faithful (1 Cor 1:9; 1 Thess 5:24), but this is not the case with mortals.

The all powerful God has but to say something and it occurs. This might explain why attention is given to beginnings. Luke reports a remark from Jesus about discipleship, comparing would-be disciples with people who start to build a tower or wage a war. They must begin by assessing whether they are able to complete what they begin (14:28–33). At stake here is public honor; a person intending to do some public thing must at least state at the beginning wise and provident intentions and plans. No concern is noted for ultimate failure to achieve the tasks, which might fail for a host of reasons, but will not be perceived as dishonorable because the failure will not be the fault of the actor who begins with care. Beginnings, then, are important, especially those that are public. Stating a plan to achieve something is what counts, irrespective of failure to follow through or of doing something other than what one stated.

Westerners may never be further from understanding ancient biblical culture than in understanding the dynamic about saying one thing and doing another. Western culture values consistency very highly. Political candidates are keenly aware of the damage inconsistent statements can do to their aspirations.

But in the Mediterranean world, much importance is given to "the word," such as rhetoricism and verbal exaggeration. One finds a proneness to make a verbal statement in which the desired event is represented as an already accomplished fact. And on occasion words are substitutes for actions. More important is the intention of doing something or the plan of doing, which can serve as a substitute for achievement. Hence, beginnings are all important, for one does not expect long process, much less actual accomplishment. Things are stated as fact, when in reality they are but a wish. Ancient Arabs and Jews would see nothing wrong in this, although Westerners might call it "facade-ism," placing importance only on the initial, stated intentions without planning to follow through on how to achieve what was stated.

Westerners place a high value on consistency between word and deed and hence take lying very seriously. The Middle-Eastern understanding of equivocation, however, is not, strictly speaking, a lie. Saying one thing and doing another has parallels in American politics with "trial balloons," that is, statements released in order to test public opinion. If the public approves, the statement will be carried out. If the public disapproves, the statement will be changed and refined until assent is forthcoming. Even so, Americans are ever suspicious of this strategy. People who become adept at equivocation, saying one thing and doing another, are frequently described as "slick," which is not an honorable designation in the United States. (Jerome H. Neyrey).

Gilsenan, Michael. 1976. "Lying, Honor and Contradiction." In *Transaction and Meaning: Directions in the Anthropology of Exchange and Symbolic Behavior*. Pp. 191–219. Philadelphia: Institute for the Study of Human Issues.

Malina, Bruce J. 1993. "VII. Common Values." In *Windows on the World of Jesus: Time Travel to Ancient Judea*. Pp. 113–20, 137–42, 151–43. Louisville, Ky.: Westminster John Knox.

Pilch, John J. 1992. "Lying and Deceit in the Letters to the Seven Churches: Perspectives from Cultural Anthropology." *Biblical Theology Bulletin* 22:126–35.

_____. 1994. "Secrecy in the Mediterranean World: An Anthropological Perspective." *Biblical Theology Bulletin* 24:151–57.

EVIL EYE—SEE ENVY

EXAGGERATION—SEE DRAMATIC ORIENTATION

EXORCISM—SEE POWER

EYES-HEART—SEE ALSO DECEPTION

These are correlative terms that refer to the human capabilities of thinking, judging, evaluating and the like, and doing all of these with feeling. Briefly, the "eyes-heart" area of human capability refers to emotion-fused thinking and its outcome, emotion-fused thought.

The "eyes-heart" zone is one of the three interrelated zones that comprise distinctively human behavior. Just as society consists of a number of interpenetrating and yet distinct groups comprised of interpenetrating and yet distinct individuals, so too the individual is perceived to consist of interpenetrating yet distinct zones of activity. These zones of activity proceed from some inner, dynamic source, the individual's very life (often called "soul" in the Bible). Yet the existence and function of these zones is verified and validated on the basis of outward, external, concrete observations chunked in terms of three areas: eyes-heart, mouth-ears (see COMMUNICATIVENESS; DECEPTION; EQUIVOCATION), and hands-feet (see HANDS-FEET). In more abstract terms, eyes-heart is the zone of emotion-fused thought; mouth-ears is the zone of self-expressive speech; and hands-feet is the zone of purposeful activity.

People think by "saying in their heart" (Gen 24:45; Deut 7:17; 8:17; 9:4; 18:21; 29:19; Ps 10:13; 14:1; 53:1; Isa 47:8; 49:21; Jer 13:22; Obad 1:3; Mark 2:8; Luke 5:22; Rom 10:6; Rev 18:7). Hence, there are "thoughts of the heart" (Gen 6:5; Deut 15:9). And people remember by "laying it to one's heart" or "laying it up in one's heart" (Exod 7:23; Deut 4:39; 11:18; 32:46; 1 Kgs 8:47; 2 Chron 6:37; Job 22:22; Ps 119:11; Isa 47:7; 57:1; Jer 12:11; Mal 2:2) or "keeping it in one's heart" (Prov 4:21; Luke 2:19, 51). Furthermore, the heart can be hardened, resulting in a total inability to think and/or feel, to judge and evaluate, to remember and know what to do, to learn and relate to others (Exod 4:21; 7:3, 13, 14, 22; 8:15, 19, 32; 9:7, 12, 34, 35; 10:1, 20, 27; 11:10; 14:4, 8; Deut 2:30; 15:7; 2 Chron 36:13; Mark 3:5; 10:5; Matt 19:8; Rom 2:5; 9:18). The hard heart results from not fearing the Lord (Prov 28:14; Isa 63:17) and results in ignorance about God (Eph 4:18). The extreme case is the heart of stone, as hard as the lower millstone (Job 41:24). The hard heart is a non-functioning heart.

To underscore the need to have the heart function as it should, the image of the circumcised heart was used. "Circumcise therefore the foreskin of your heart, and be no longer stubborn" (Deut 10:16; see Lev 26:41). Circumcision of adolescent males symbolized publicly the acknowledged ability of the organ in question to function in its intended way, hence, endowing the circumcised person with the status of maturity and adulthood along with the ability to marry and have offspring. The circumcised heart would symbolize a similar ability of the organ in question to function in its intended way. The properly functioning heart would work in the way God intended people to behave in interpersonal relations. Hence, the need for "the LORD your God" to "circumcise your heart and the heart of your offspring, so that you will love the

LORD your God with all your heart and with all your soul,
that you may live" (Deut 30:6). Yet the prophets say that
while the nations might be uncircumcised, the problem
is that "the house of Israel is uncircumcised in heart"
(Jer 9:26).

Paul insists that "he is a Jew who is one inwardly,
and real circumcision is a matter of the heart, spiritual
and not literal" (Rom 2:29; see Acts 7:51). Such "circumcision of heart" marks the demise of the heart of stone:
"A new heart I will give you, and a new spirit I will put
within you; and I will take out of your flesh the heart of
stone and give you a heart of flesh" (Ezek 36:26).

The "fat" heart is equally dysfunctional. In the passage from Isaiah 6:10 quoted in Matthew 13:15, we find:
"Make the heart of this people fat, and their ears heavy,
and shut their eyes; lest they see with their eyes, and
hear with their ears, and understand with their hearts,
and turn and be healed" (Isa 6:10; 32:3; 43:8; see also
Acts 28:27; John 12:40 removes the "ears," leaving it
"heart-eyes" only).

The double heart, too, is a problem since it is deceitful and lying: "Every one utters lies to his neighbor; with
flattering lips and a double heart they speak" (Ps 12:2).
Thus, the need for singleness of heart (Eph 6:5; Col 3:22),
i.e., a pure heart (mentioned in contexts of lying and deceit: Ps 24:4; Prov 22:11; see Matt 5:8; 1 Tim 1:5; 2 Tim
2:22; see EQUIVOCATION). The pure heart is much like the
"whole heart," "all one's heart" required in dedication to
God (basic to the *Shema*, Deut 6:5; see Mark 12:30; Matt
22:37; Luke 10:27; the phrase is quite common).

The heart receives its input from the eyes; the heart
goes after the eyes (Job 31:7). One walks "in the ways of
your heart and the sight of your eyes" (Eccl 11:9). "The
light of the eyes rejoices the heart" (Prov 15:30), just as
the heart rejoices from the enlightened eye (Ps 19:8). And
negatively, "but you have eyes and heart only for your
dishonest gain, for shedding innocent blood, and for
practicing oppression and violence" (Jer 22:17). Conse-

quently both eyes and heart are often described as functioning in tandem (Num 15:39; Deut 4:9; 28:65, 67; 1 Sam 2:33; 1 Kgs 9:3; 14:8; 2 Kgs 10:30; 2 Chron 7:16; 16:9; 25:2; Job 15:12; Ps 36:1; 131:1; Prov 21:2, 4; 23:26; Eccl 2:10; Lam 5:17; Ezek 6:9; 21:6).

To say people have "eyes to see" indicates that they know from experience (Deut 3:21; 4:3; 7:19; 10:21; Josh 24:7; etc.) much like "to have one's eyes opened" is to learn from experience, since the eyes are the vehicle of desiring, delighting in (and their negatives), as well as judging (Gen 3:5–7; 21:19; Num 24:3). On the other hand, "to open the eyes" usually means "to pay attention" (clearly stated in Neh 1:6). The frequent phrase "in one's eyes" means "in one's estimation," just as the common phrase "before one's eyes" means "with firsthand knowledge."

It is insulting to "raise your voice and haughtily lift your eyes" (2 Kgs 19:22). The proverb had it that "the eye is the lamp of the body" (Matt 6:22) because light in some way shines out of the eyes (from the heart) to enable one to see because "the Lord gives light" to the eyes (Prov 29:13). Given this understanding of the light source, "haughty eyes and a proud heart" are "the lamp of the wicked" (Prov 21:4). On the other hand, the non-functioning eyes of the blind person represent darkness and gloom (Isa 29:18). Hence, the disgrace of putting out the eyes of the king of Judah (2 Kgs 25:7), and the willingness of the Galatians to endure disgrace for Paul's sake expressed in his praise of them: "you would have plucked out your eyes and given them to me" (Gal 4:15). Similarly, to gouge out a person's "right eye" is to dishonor a person (1 Sam 11:2; cf. Matt 5:29 where the "right eye" is involved).

In sum, the zone of emotion-fused thought is referred to with the following words: eyes, heart, eyelid, pupil, and the activities of these organs: to see, know, understand, think, remember, choose, feel, consider, look at. The following representative nouns and adjectives pertain to this zone as well: thought, intelligence, mind, wisdom, folly, intention, plan, will, affection, love, hate, sight, regard, blindness, look; intelligent, loving, wise, foolish, hateful, joyous, sad, and the like.

In our culture, this zone would cover the areas we refer to as intellect, will, judgment, conscience, personality thrust, core personality, affection, and so forth. While the operations are similar, the ways of explaining and describing the operations are quite different. (Bruce J. Malina)

Borhek, James T., and Richard F. Curtis. 1975. *A Sociology of Belief.* New York: Wiley.

Elliott, John H. 1994. "The Evil Eye and the Sermon on the Mount: Contours of a Pevasive Belief in Social Scientific Perspective." *Biblical Interpretation* 2:51–84.

Géradon, Bernard de. 1958. "L'homme à l'image de Dieu." *La nouvelle revue théologique* 80:683–95.

Malina, Bruce J. 1993. *The New Testament World: Insights from Cultural Anthropology.* 2d rev. ed. Louisville, Ky.: Westminster John Knox, pp. 73–81.

FAITH/FAITHFULNESS

These terms refer to the value of reliability. The value is ascribed to persons as well as to objects and qualities. Relative to persons, faith is reliability in interpersonal relations; it thus takes on the value of enduring personal loyalty, of personal faithfulness. The nouns "faith," "belief," "fidelity," "faithfulness," as well as the verbs "to have faith" and "to believe," refer to the social glue that binds one person to another. This bond is the social, externally manifested, emotionally rooted behavior of loyalty, commitment, and solidarity. As a social bond, it works along with the value of (personal and group) attachment (translated "love") and the value of (personal and group) allegiance or trust (translated "hope").

In the Hebrew Bible, God is rarely called "faithful" (only in Deut 7:9 and Isa 49:7). In the New Testament,

Paul uses this quality of God to encourage his churches in their new Christian behavior (1 Cor 1:9; 10:13; 2 Cor 1:18; 1 Thess 5:24; see 2 Tim 2:13; Heb 11:11). And as any New Testament reader will readily attest, faith is a topic found throughout early Christian writings. For example, as founder of a faction dedicated to the renewal of Israel, Jesus required loyalty and commitment to himself and his project (Mark 9:42//Matt 18:6; see also Matt 11:28–29; Mark 15:32; Matt 27:42). And even if the word "faith" is not used, concern for loyalty to Jesus and his project is paramount. "Whoever is ashamed of me and of my words in this adulterous and sinful generation, of him will the Son of man also be ashamed, when he comes in the glory of his Father with the holy angels" (Mark 8:38//Matt 16:27//Luke 9:26). Such loyalty was expected even in the face of family opposition: "If any one comes to me and does not hate his own father and brothers and mother and sisters, yes, even his own life, he cannot be my disciple" (Luke 14:26, RSV adapted//Matt 10:37–38). The Johannine community, with its distinctive "believing into" Jesus (used 34 times in John), underscored the need for such enduring loyalty (see also the Johannine synonyms for "believe into": to come to, abide with, follow, love, keep the words of, receive, have, see).

Loyalty too was expected by that other prophet and faction founder, John the Baptist. Jesus expected the people of Israel to give him loyalty and commitment (Matt 21:32). However, as a rule, this loyalty is to be directed to the God of Israel: in the midst of a storm (Mark 4:40//Matt 8:26//Luke 8:25); in the face of anxiety about daily needs (Matt 6:30//Luke 12:28); when seeking a healing from God's prophet, Jesus (Matt 8:10//Luke 7:9; Mark 5:34//Matt 9:22//Luke 8:48; Mark 10:52//Matt 9:29// Luke 18:42); by the disciples in their encounter with Jesus walking on the water (Matt 14:31); by the Syrophoenician woman in her encounter with Jesus (Matt 15:28); by the disciples' misunderstanding of Jesus' feeding (Mark 8:17//Matt 16:8); by the Pharisees (Matt 23:23).

Such loyalty can be equally manifested in solidarity with others bent on obedience to the God of Israel (Mark 2:5; Matt 9:2; Luke 5:20). Even Jesus is praised for his faithfulness to God (Heb 3:1–3) and his obedience to him (Heb 5:8; Rom 5:14–21).

As for faith in the impersonal, one can seek reliability in objects as well as in statements. For example, in the social system which controls our English language usage, faith or belief usually mean the psychological, internal, cognitive, and affective assent of the mind to truths. This assent is given because the truths make sense in themselves (e.g., most people believe if A = C and if B = C, then A = B). Similarly, assent is given because the person speaking is credible, has credibility (e.g., most college students believe the authors of their chemistry and physics textbooks as to the outcome of 99 percent of the experiments mentioned since there is no time in college to carry them out for themselves). This dimension of the word "faith," or "belief," looks to the reliability of the impersonal. It is the acknowledgement of the reliability of what one believes in, hence, the assent to something or to something somebody says. This usage is found in Matthew 9:28: "do you believe that I am able to do this?"; or in 24:23, 26: "do not believe it." It seems Mark 11:24 belongs here also.

However, Matthew 21:21 is translated in the RSV as follows: "have faith and never doubt." This translation puts the phrase into the first category above, assent of the mind. But this is not the normal use of the words in Matthew. They are better translated: "stay loyal (to God) and do not hesitate (in your fidelity or loyalty)." Similarly, in the next verse, the obvious meaning is: "Whatever you ask in prayer, you will receive if you remain loyal (to God)."

In sum, "faith" primarily means personal loyalty, personal commitment to another person, fidelity and the solidarity that comes from such faithfulness. Secondarily, the word can mean credence as in phrases such as: to give credence, or to find believable.

In American culture, faith has a strong intellectual character. It is an act of the mind. Because this culture is so strongly rational, faith takes on the further nuance that a person believes something or someone merely on a word of authority, even—perhaps even especially—when the evidence doesn't necessarily add up. Thus, in medicine, the placebo is effective because the person receiving it strongly believes that the person in the white jacket administering it is qualified (even though that person may be an impostor or an actor). (Bruce J. Malina)

Hatfield, Elaine, and Richard Rapson. 1993. "Love and Attachment Processes." In *Handbook of Emotions*. Ed. Michael Lewis and Jeannette M. Haviland. Pp. 605–16. New York: Guilford.

Sakenfeld, Katharine Doob. 1985. *Faithfulness in Action: Loyalty in Biblical Perspective*. Philadelphia: Fortress.

Schaar, John H. 1968. "Loyalty." In *International Encyclopedia of the Social Sciences*. Ed. D. L. Sills. 9:484–87. New York: Macmillan.

FAMILY-CENTEREDNESS

This term is an aspect of kinship and is perhaps the main pillar of the culture reflected in the Bible. Staunch loyalty to the family and obedience to family authorities are constant features of the culture reflected in the Bible. The value of family-centeredness derives from three distinct but closely related components: honor/shame, tradition, and land. Family-centeredness or kinship is thus part of honor, the core value of Mediterranean culture.

Honor/Shame: Social standing, i.e., worth in the community, is of inestimable value in cultural contexts where the well-being of the collective is of paramount importance (see Introduction). The idea of the autonomy of the individual, a development of the modern West, is entirely absent from the societies and cultures reflected in the Bible or those known to its authors. Hence, family-centeredness should be understood in a directly literal sense: the family *is* the *center*, not only of the social interaction of its members, but of the system of meaning out of which such cultures arose. The individuals responsible for the procurement (honor:male) and maintenance (shame:female) of the family's social standing are the patriarch and matriarch of the extended family (clan or tribe patriarch and matriarch), or the husband and wife of the nuclear family. They command uncompromised respect and obedience (e.g., Exod 20:12; Deut 5:16; 21:18–21; Prov 30:17). Although father and mother are frequently mentioned together, male authority is clearly preeminent in this strongly patriarchal society (Num 1:2–3, 17–19; 27:8; Eph 5:22; Col 3:18). Attacks on family honor are serious matters and likely to result in acts of vengeance (e.g., Gen 34; Deut 22:13–23:1) or strong censure (Gen 9:20–27; 2 Sam 12:1–12).

Tradition: The honor paid to father and mother by their children is their due not only because they have given them life (Sir 7:27–28) but because they convey the tradition to them. Tradition here refers to the handing down of established and time-tested communal wisdom, a wisdom which simultaneously grounds and encompasses identification with the culture (e.g., Exod 10:2; 12:26; 13:8; Deut 4:9; 6:7, 20–25; 32:7, 46). Thus, a circular movement of societal formation is established: tradition grounds and informs family structure, and family structure perpetuates tradition. From these two interlocking aspects of the culture reflected in the Bible arise the attitudes of respect for authority, and exclusiveness, i.e., suspicion of outsiders. Exclusiveness is a hallmark of the culture reflected in the Bible (e.g., Exod 19:2–8; 20:2–6; Deut 5:6–10; 7:1–6), and it forms the basis of the view of the nation of Israel as a family (descended from Abraham, Isaac, and Jacob: Gen 48:15–49:27) which commands the same respect and obedience paid to parents (e.g., Josh 24:14–18; Ps 103:7; 105:4–11, 23–25, 42–45; 147:19–20). Thus, the common religious and cultural traditions of Israel are reflected both in the individual family and in the nation as a whole, i.e., the nation is thought to replicate the family on a large scale. Authority in the larger segments of the society (e.g., tribal area, royal province, or whole kingdom) is shaped on the model provided by the *pater familias* (e.g., Deut 8:1–6; Isa 9:2–5). Tradition is thus viewed as analogous to parents, i.e., it gives life (e.g., Deut 30:15–20; Ps 119:17, 25, 50, 88, 92; 2 Macc 7; Prov 3:1–2, 7:1–4). Those outside the tradition (e.g., Ps 129), or those who remove themselves from it (e.g., Deut 13:6; 19:11; 1 Sam 18:15–17; Matt 18:15–17) are cut off from life, i.e., from meaning, since meaning is conceived of as belonging to the chosen people and having some standing among them (honor/shame) (Ps 128; cf. Jer 35; Matt 3:9). Thus, adherence to tradition is an extremely important aspect of family-centeredness since tradition itself is derived from the central importance of family in the culture.

Land: The land where the people of the tradition dwell in families provides the framework in which honor/shame and tradition are knitted together with the land into a single whole (e.g., Lev 25:18; Deut 30:15–20). The land is a gift from God, and therefore sacred (e.g., Deut 5:28–33; Prov 2:20–22). Other lands and the peoples who live in them are unclean (e.g., Lev 18:24–25; Deut 20:15–18). Control and maintenance of the land (family property and national borders) are not simply matters of survival, but are questions of honor/shame and tradition as well (e.g., Deut 19:14; Isa 5:8). Expulsion from the land is a catastrophe because it necessarily seems to mean the destruction of tradition and the families who live by it (e.g., Ps 137). Restoration of the land is cause for rejoicing (e.g., Ps 126).

Family-centeredness, then, is a complex cultural phenomenon which receives expression at every level and in all times of society as reflected in the Bible, and which provides the foundation for the society itself. This explains why family-centeredness is part of the core cultural value of Mediterranean society.

Undoubtedly, Christianity was regarded with hostility because it threw foundational values of Judaic tradition radically into question by reversing them. Authority in the Christian community is determined on the basis of service rather than rank (e.g., Matt 10:37; Mark 10:42–45), membership in the church takes precedence over family or ethnic membership (e.g., Mark 3:31–35), dietary traditions are rejected (e.g., Mark 7:19), the value of land and property is redefined (e.g., Mark 10:28–30; Acts 2:45), exclusiveness is repudiated (e.g., Gal 2:1–10; Col 3:11), and obedience to the authority of tradition is relativized to meet the requirements of the gospel (e.g., Matt 5:10–12; Mark 13:9–13; Gal 3:10–14).

What struck the opponents of Christianity as chaos and anarchy, however, quickly developed its own culture, i.e., its own standards of honor/shame, tradition, and attitudes toward land and property. The Pastoral Epistles give ample evidence of this evolution in Christianity. The practical effect of the early Christian movement was to replace family-centeredness with a church membership-centeredness, and to create the church as the new family, or the community of the new age (e.g., Acts 2:42–46).

Such close identification with the family and the concomitant unquestioning obedience to family authorities is alien to modern Western and especially United States experience where social and geographic mobility and the fluidity of the modern family are regular features of contemporary life. Our standard cultural myth involves the desire that children will have a life better than their parents. The standard cultural myth assumed in the Bible is that children should aspire to maintain the same social standing in the community their parents enjoy. Thus, the biblical understanding of family-centeredness is seen as dysfunctional in the modern West, where adaptability, flexibility, and independence are regarded as virtues. (Mark McVann)

Eickelman, Dale. 1981. "Personal and Family Relationships." In *The Middle East: An Anthropological Approach*. Pp. 105–34. Englewood Cliffs, N.J.: Prentice Hall.

Fernea, Elizabeth Warnock. 1985. *Women and the Family in the Middle East: New Voices of Change*. Austin: University of Texas Press.

Geertz, Hildred. 1979. "The Meanings of Family Ties." In *Meaning and Order in Moroccan Society*. Ed. Clifford Geertz, et al. Cambridge Studies in Cultural Systems. Pp. 315–91. Cambridge: Cambridge University Press.

Peristiany, Julian G. 1974. Visiting Patterns and Social Dynamics in Eastern Mediterranean Communities. *Anthropological Quarterly* 12 (January): entire issue.

_____. 1976. *Mediterranean Family Structures*. Cambridge Studies in Social Anthropology 23. New York: Cambridge University Press.

FATE

The term refers to the value of perceiving the events in one's life as somehow fixed or determined. This perception is closely related to the primary value orientation of viewing human beings as controlled by and subject to nature. And it is further underscored by the common belief of the agrarian world that all goods are in fact limited (see COOPERATIVENESS; ENVY; LIMITED GOOD; PURPOSIVENESS/ END ORIENTATION). The world of the Bible is a world of limited good; everything that exists is perceived to exist in limited and fixed amounts that simply cannot be increased by either more hard work or greater intelligence and diligence. In fact, any augmentation can take place only by depriving others.

For Israel, fate was in the control of the God of Israel: "Have you not heard that I determined it long ago? I planned from days of old what now I bring to pass" (Isa 37:26); "This is your lot, the portion I have measured out to you, says the Lord . . ." (Jer 13:25). He was the God of Israel because "Israel is the Lord's own portion" (Sir 17:17); "The Lord's portion is his people, Jacob his allotted heritage" (Deut 32:9). The one who controls the destinies of other peoples is indirectly specified in references where Israel looks to other deities to discern its fate: "But you who forsake the Lord, who forget my holy mountain, who set a table for Fortune and fill cups of mixed wine for Destiny; I will destine you to the sword . . ." (Isa 65:11–12). Yet it was quite apparent that group and individual fate and fortune were quite fixed.

The existence of a fixed and determined destiny for persons and groups is further evidenced by the custom of drawing lots to divine God's choice. "The lot is cast into the lap, but the decision is wholly from the Lord" (Prov 16:33). By lot, then, God himself has determined the tribal apportionments (see Num 26:55–56; 33:54; 34:13; 36:2–3; Josh 14–21; Ezek 48). So, too, God determines what portion belongs to each person. In Jonah, lots are cast to find out who is the cause of the evil fate of the seafarers (Jonah 1:7); temple service was determined by lot (Luke 1:9) as was the choice of person to fill the number of the Twelve (Acts 1:26).

Why draw lots? Popular wisdom had it that: "The lot puts an end to disputes and decides between powerful contenders" (Prov 18:18). Christians are fairly certain that affliction is their lot in Thessalonica (1 Thess 3:3).

One's fate, indicated by one's allotment and apportionment in life, was likewise symbolized by means of the cup. "The Lord is my chosen portion and my cup; thou holdest my lot" (Ps 16:5). As a container, the cup holds a limited and fixed amount of liquid for individual consumption. One's lot can run from penury to luxury, just as cups are made of varying materials, from clay to precious metal (cups: Gen 44:1–34; Jer 51:7; Rev 17:4; the cup-like oil holder of the temple lamp: Exod 25:31–35). In this perspective, all people can be said to have their "cup," i.e., the limited and fixed amount of whatever God has to offer them in life, either in entirety, such as a lifetime of devotedness to God (Ps 16:5), a life of abundance (overflowing cup, Ps 23:5), or in part: such as rescue (cup of salvation, Ps 116:13); of consolation (Jer 16:7), or punishment (cup of wrath, Isa 51:17; Hab 2:15; cf. Ps 11:6); of staggering or reeling (Isa 51:22; Zech 12:2). The cup then symbolizes the lot, life-portion, or fate of a group or an individual person (Jer 49:12; Ezek 23:31–33; Mark 10:38–39 and parallels; 14:36 and parallels). And a cup of wine served as prophetic symbol of the significance of one's fate (Jer 25:15–28; at the Lord's Supper, Mark 14:23–25 and parallels; 1 Cor 11:25–29).

Americans for the most part share a belief in limitless goods. They believe in an open universe, endless in its reaches and not unlike the planets, as well as resources that are endlessly available to the individual. Fate is usually what one makes of one's life by means of choices typical of psychological individualism. Industrialization, space exploration, and the various "miracles" of modern medicine offer proof enough that human beings are masters of nature (see Introduction). These perspectives (and there are others) provide indication of how the belief in fate typical of the world of the Bible will not find full resonance in the adult experience of United States citizens. (Bruce J. Malina)

Aalders, G. J. D. 1979. "The Hellenistic Concept of the Enviousness of Fate." In *Studies in Hellenistic Religions.* Ed. M. J. Vermaseren. Pp. 1–8. Etudes prelim aux religions orientales dans l'Empire Romain 78. Leiden: Brill.
Greene, William C. 1944. *Moira: Fate, Good, and Evil in Greek Thought.* Cambridge: Harvard University Press.

FAVOR—SEE GRACE/FAVOR

FEAST

This formal, elaborate meal is often called a banquet. The name "feast" is also applied to the day(s) during which such elaborate meals are consumed. People all over the world use food and drink both as nourishment and as ways of saying something to each other. A meal to which others are invited is a form of communication, with important social messages being exchanged between the host and those invited, those who should/might have been invited but were not, and those who decline the invitation. Just as the material used for communication in speech is language, so the material used for communication in a festive meal is food and drink and their setting. Thus, the type of food and drink chosen, their mode of preparation, the method of service, and the seating or reclining arrangements, all say something about the host's assessment of those invited. A festive meal differs from simply sharing a meal much like a formal speech differs from casual conversation. A festive meal is formal communication, usually with messages of great significance.

From the point of view of the types of messages involved, there are two general types of banquets: ceremonial and ritual. A ceremonial feast is a banquet in which the inviter and the invited celebrate their mutual solidarity, their belonging to each other, their oneness. The festive meals of Israel's appointed feasts (see Lev 23:2–44), much like the national and personal celebrations in the story of Esther (banquet for Persian elites, non-elites and women [Esth 1:3–9], in honor of Esther [Esth 2:18], and of the king and, by ruse, of Mordecai [Esth 5:1–7:10]), are examples of such ceremonial festive meals. The same is true of the gathering of Christians described by Paul in 1 Corinthians 11:17–33; the problem noted by Paul, of "each one [going] ahead with his own meal, and one is hungry and another is drunk" (v. 21) points to wrong meanings being communicated. Instead of mutual solidarity and oneness, the behavior communicated "factions" (v. 19).

A ritual festive meal is one that marks some individual or group transition or transformation, held to give honor to those undergoing the important social change. As a ritual feature of hospitality, festive meals indicate the transformation of a stranger into a guest (Gen 19:3–14; Luke 5:29), of an enemy into a covenant partner (Gen 26:26–31; 2 Sam 3:20). Feasts mark important transitional points in a person's life, e.g., Isaac's weaning day (Gen 21:8); the weddings of Jacob (Gen

29:22), Samson (Judg 14:10), the Lamb (Rev 19:9), and in the parable of Matthew 22:2–10; the birthdays of the Pharaoh (Gen 40:20), and Herod (Mark 6:21); or the victory banquet hosted by God (Rev 19:17).

At his final meal with his disciples, Jesus changes the ceremonial banquet of the Israelite Passover into a ritual banquet effectively symboling the meaning of his impending death (Mark 14:12–25 and parallels). Since Judeans adopted the Greco-Roman elite practice of reclining "like free men" for the Passover, it should be useful to take a look at the Roman main meal customs.

The Roman workday ran from dawn until noon— for everyone. The *cena* (supper) took place in mid-afternoon, lasting until dark. The custom of reclining on a couch (*accumbere*) with the elbow on a cushion (*pulvinar*) was introduced among elites at the end of the second century BCE. It probably imitates Eastern behavior (and it was perhaps the officers of Scipio Africanus who were the first to adopt it). As for the ordinary people, they never adopted the custom.

On the couches were straw mats and more often mattresses filled with feathers (*culcita*). One reclined only for the supper. The minimum number of guests for a supper was three (the number of the Graces in Greco-Roman mythology. Graces were three sister goddesses: Brilliance, Joy, and Bloom, who had control over pleasure, charm and beauty in human life and in nature) and the maximum number was nine (the number of Muses in Greco-Roman mythology: Calliope, Clio, Euterpe, Melpomene, Terpsichore, Erato, Polyhymnia, Urania, and Thalia. They presided over literature, the arts, and the sciences). When there were more than nine persons, several tables were used. Around a square table were three reclining couches (hence, the term *triclinium*) with three places each (a dining room with two couches was called a *biclinium*).

The couches and places had fixed designations. The place of honor is the first place of the *medius lectus* (middle couch). It was called the *locus consularis* because the consul would take that place if invited. The host takes the third place of the *imus lectus* (lowest couch).

Having removed their outer garments and city clothes and having been crowned with flowers and perfumed, the guests are served by slaves and eat with their fingers, i.e., without knives or forks. Hand washings are frequent, with slaves carrying about the washing bowls. Each guest brings his own napkin. Invocations with a libation (the first pieces of each course are put into the fire) are directed to the gods at the beginning of the meal or before the dessert. Women as a rule were excluded from the cena. But about the first century BCE married women were admitted. This kind of cultural information is helpful in understanding and interpreting biblical and other texts which originated in the Mediterranean world, particularly in the Greco-Roman period.

Meal-taking and feasting in the contemporary Western world is considerably different. The foods we eat and the way in which we eat reflect our goals and values. Fast foods create the illusion of home-cooked meals and are intended to replace traditional family meals. The truth is, the speed with which foods can be prepared eliminates the necessity of a family eating together, or even eating the same food. These modern practices are definitely changing the nearly three-centuries old Western "tradition" of a time-consuming, elaborate, manifestly hierarchical and communal meal partaken around a dining room table. (Bruce J. Malina)

Braun, W. 1995. *Feasting and Social Rhetoric in Luke 14.* Society for New Testament Study Monograph Series 85. Cambridge: Cambridge University Press.

Gil Calvo, Enrique. 1991. *Estado de Fiesta.* Madrid: Espasa Calpe.

FIDELITY—SEE FAITH/FAITHFULNESS

FIRST-LAST—SEE PROMINENCE

FREEDOM

This enables one to choose to be free of obstacles in order to attain some end or goal. Freedom in the Bible is synonymous with liberty, specifically the freedom of a group and its members not to be under the dominion of any other group and directed to the service of God. This is political freedom maintained by and in the service of God. It is articulated most clearly in the Exodus ("bringing out") story where a group of Hebrews are in Egyptian bondage (Exod 2:23; 6:5–9) and an ancestral God decides to deliver them. This God sends a message to the Pharaoh through his spokesmen, Moses and Aaron: "Let my people go, that they may hold a feast to me in the wilderness" (Exod 5:1); or more usually, Moses alone: "The LORD, the God of the Hebrews, sent me to you, saying, 'Let my people go, that they may serve me in the wilderness' " (Exod 7:16 and repeatedly thereafter: 8:1, 20, 21; 9:1, 13; 10:3). The group is subsequently "brought out" by its ancestral God from bondage for the service of this God. This "bringing out" is called a "redemption" (Deut 7:8; 13:5), i.e., an action that restores the honor of a group by restoring its proper social status.

Thanks to the Exodus story, freedom as depicted in that story comes to be the core value in the Bible. It is a group freedom without submission to alien peoples yet with limits. The limits are defined by the goal of this group freedom, the service of God. Abstractly, one might say that the core value in the Bible is the quality of a group's being finite (limited) and free. Of course the individual group representatives in the society, specifically adult males who head households, replicate the same freedom. As symbolic bearers of the large group's core value, such individual male householders are expected to be finite and free, not subject to any other man, not unlike city-state elites in antiquity. The Ten Commandments spell out the rights of the ancestral God to exclusiveness, and the rights of adult male householders to an honorable and feud-free existence (Exod 20:1–17; Deut 5:6–21).

A careful reading of the Bible will indicate that for Israel the value of being finite and free functions in the same way as instrumental mastery does in the United States (see Introduction). The word "finite" covers the category of the group's being of service to God, hence, limited by God's rights and God's honor. As the group, so the individual replicating the group's central value. In other words, any attempt by Israel as a group or by individuals in the group to disobey God deviates from the quality of being "finite" or "limited" or "bounded" by the requirements of the service of God. Such deviation covers the category of "sin," from idolatry to theft. Further, the word "free" entails political and social non-subjection and non-submission of Israel as a group and of individuals who replicate the group's values, i.e., the individual adult male.

With the monarchy and subsequent imperial occupation, the practice of slavery emerges. It was always an anomaly in Israel. Under Zedekiah, a mechanism for the release of persons from slavery was introduced (see Jer 34:8). It was a mechanism introduced into the Mosaic law by the Exilic Priestly tradition. This is the practice of jubilee entailing the return of slaves and lands to their families and release from debt: "And you shall hallow the fiftieth year, and proclaim liberty throughout the land to all its inhabitants; it shall be a jubilee for you, when each of you shall return to his property and each of you shall return to his family" (Lev 25:10). Such a practice would indeed reaffirm the core value of the finite and free Israelite householder. But such jubilee was never practiced. Jeremiah had harsh words about it: "Therefore, thus says the LORD: You have not obeyed me by proclaiming liberty, every one to his brother and to his neighbor; behold, I proclaim to you liberty to the sword, to pestilence, and to famine, says the LORD. I will make you a horror to all the kingdoms of the earth" (Jer 34:17). Similarly, conquests and exile by alien nations caused as much difficulty for the core value as does lack of energy for a culture focused on instrumental mastery.

The Christian story begins in a situation requiring the revitalization of Israel. The proclamation of God's patronage ("the kingdom of heaven"; see PATRONAGE) by John (Matt 3:2), and then by Jesus (Matt 4:17; Mark 1:15), points to a prior situation of alienation from God and his benefaction, a situation called "sin." Such lack of well-being pointed to the practical non-realization of the traditional core value. "The lost sheep of the house of Israel" were once again "in bondage" in some way (Matt 10:6). Luke has Jesus proclaiming the jubilee year with the onset of his ministry, citing Isaiah (61:1) on the same subject: "The Spirit of the Lord is upon me, because he has anointed me to preach good news to the poor. He has sent me to proclaim release to the captives and recovering of sight to the blind, to set at liberty those who are oppressed, to proclaim the acceptable year of the Lord" (Luke 4:18–19). And Jesus' death is viewed as "a ransom for many" (Matt 20:28; Mark 10:45; 1 Tim 2:5–6; 1 Pet 1:18), involving "blood of the covenant, which is poured out for many for the forgiveness of sins" (Matt 26:28). He gave himself for us to redeem us and to make us a people of God's own (Titus 2:14). With terms like "acceptable year" indicating a new jubilee, "blood of the covenant," "redeem," and "ransom" recalling the Exodus, the career, death, and resurrection of Jesus are all placed within the framework of Israel's traditional core value—life of peace with God, with finite and free householders bent on the proper service of the Lord. Consequently, one now loyal to God through what happened in Jesus' death-resurrection has new freedom: "by him every one that believes is freed from everything from which you could not be freed by the law of Moses" (Acts 13:39).

As with the Exodus, the final goal of this freedom is the proper service of God: "But now that you have been set free from sin and have become slaves of God, the return you get is sanctification and its end, eternal life" (Rom 6:22). Since the freedom involved pertains to the group, the group now forms God's sacred place, the temple of God's power: "your (plural) body is a temple of the Holy Spirit within you (plural) which you (plural) have from God" (1 Cor 6:19). For group members "were bought with a price" (1 Cor 6:20), an idiom meaning "paid in full," and are henceforth freed for the service of God.

The Exodus of the Hebrews led to political freedom and the establishment of a tribal confederation under God. Early Christians expected the new Exodus in Christ to lead to a similar political freedom, with God soon to send "the Christ appointed for you, Jesus" (see Acts 3:20). But instead, this freedom was confined "in Christ," that is within the small Christian groups: "There is neither Jew nor Greek, there is neither slave nor free, there is neither male nor female; for you are all one in Christ Jesus" (Gal 3:28); "Here there cannot be Greek and Jew, circumcised and uncircumcised, barbarian, Scythian, slave, free man, but Christ is all, and in all" (Col 3:11). These groups were fictive kin groups consisting of "brothers" and "sisters" in Christ. Males could readily find the finite freedom characteristic of the "sons of God," but even with this "household of the faith," there remained a problem of whether meeting together in a city house was a family affair, where women and men could freely interact, or a public affair with the proper separation of the sexes lest males be dishonored, and God likewise (see 1 Cor 11:2–16). The political realization of the finite freedom wrought by Jesus had to await Emperor Constantine and the eventual founding of Christendom, yet without God's Messiah, Jesus, "whom heaven must receive until the time for establishing all that God spoke by the mouth of his holy prophets from of old" (Acts 3:21).

The American understanding of freedom contrasts starkly with the Mediterranean understanding reflected in the Bible. For Americans, this value is viewed as "freedom from obstacles," or freedom from external forces. Thus the American tendency in religion is to produce a God symbol that would limit God so that Americans might be totally unlimited, which we believe to be our symbolic birthright.

In the American context, the New Testament understanding of freedom would require a choice to live under the right set of both internal and external restraints with particular emphasis on duty to neighbor as demanded by subjection to God in Christ. (Bruce J. Malina)

Kopytoff, Igor. 1982. "Slavery." *Annual Review of Anthropology* 11:207–30.
Malina, Bruce J. 1978. "Freedom: The Theological Dimensions of a Symbol." *Biblical Theology Bulletin* 8:62–76.
Oppenheim, John H. 1968. "Freedom." In *International Encyclopedia of the Social Sciences*. Ed. D. L. Sills. 5:554–59. New York: Macmillan.
Schlier, Heinrich. 1964. "ἐλεύθερος." In *Theological Dictionary of the New Testament*. Ed. G. Kittel and G. Friedrich. Trans. G. Bromiley. 10 vols. Grand Rapids: Eerdmans, 1964–1976. 2:487–502.

GRACE/FAVOR

This term refers to the outcomes of the value process called patronage (see **PATRONAGE**). What clients seek of patrons is favor, and grace is favor. Favor might be defined as receiving something, either that could not otherwise be obtained at all, or on terms more advantageous than could otherwise be obtained. Favoritism is the main quality of patron-client relationships.

The frequent phrase in the Hebrew Bible, "to find favor in the eyes (sight) of" means to have a person treat one with all the benefactions of a client (e.g., Gen 6:8; 18:3; 31:5; 32:5; 33:8, 10, 15; 34:11; 39:4; 47:29; 50:4; Exod 33:12–13; 34:9; Num 11:11, 15; Deut 24:1; 28:50). God shows his favoritism toward Israel by causing the Egyptians to show favor to them (Exod 3:21; 11:3; 12:36). The patron-client mooring of this behavior is clearest in passages like Exodus 33:16–17: "For how shall it be known that I have found favor in thy sight, I and thy people? Is

it not in thy going with us, so that we are distinct, I and
thy people, from all other people that are upon the face of
the earth?" And the LORD said to Moses, "This very thing
that you have spoken I will do; for you have found favor
in my sight, and I know you by name."

The New Testament is heavily sprinkled with the
vocabulary of favoritism, such as reward, gift, grace (a
word occurring only in Luke 1 and 2, Acts, Paul, and
John's prologue: 1:14, 16–17) and the like. Perhaps due to
Paul, the most obvious terms for the favoritism of God's
patronage and its outcomes are the vocabulary of "grace."

> (1) "grace" (*charis*) is a shorthand way of referring to the
> patron-client relationship, to enjoying patronage, while
> when referring to God, it is his willingness to be patron, to
> give patronage. The Christian gospel, in short, is "the
> gospel of the grace of God" (Acts 20:24). And the "grace of
> God" or "grace given . . ." is God's patronage and its
> outcomes (Acts 11:23; 14:26; 15:40; Rom 1:7; 5:15; 12:3, 6;
> 15:15; 1 Cor 1:4; 3:10; 15:10; 2 Cor 1:2, 12; 6:1; 8:1; Gal 2:9,
> 21; Eph 3:2, 7, 8; 4:7; Col 1:6; Titus 2:11; Heb 2:9; 12:15).

> (2) "to give-in; to yield to someone; bestow freely"
> (*charizomai*) refers to acting like a patron, to showing
> patronage by giving or forgiving a debt (by giving: Luke
> 7:21; Acts 27:24; Rom 8:32; 1 Cor 2:12; Gal 3:18; Phil 1:29;
> 2:9; by forgiving a debt: Luke 7:42, 43; 2 Cor 2:7, 10; 12:13;
> Eph 4:32; Col 2:13; 3:13).

> (3) "gift" (*charisma*) is the outcome of patronage, favor (Rom
> 1:11; 5:15, 16; 11:29; 12:6; 1 Cor 1:7; 7:7; 12:4, 9, 28, 30, 31;
> 2 Cor 1:11; 1 Tim 4:14; 2 Tim 1:6; 1 Pet 4:10).

Considering the cultural presuppositions of "all goods
are limited" (see **ALTRUISM; COOPERATIVENESS; ENVY; FATE;
LIMITED GOOD; PURPOSIVENESS/END ORIENTATION**) and the
"debt of gratitude" involved in giving, it would seem there
really were no "free" gifts in the ancient world. All "gifts"
implied obligations to the giver, including gifts from God.
From a cultural perspective, such gifts were made with
strings attached. This is what patronage is about. God's
"grace," that is his willingness to be patron, implies vertical
social standing since only the "haves" can give-in and

serve as patrons to the "have-nots." Being patron presupposes a want or need of a favor on the part of the client. Both the baptism of John and Jesus' proclamation of God's kingdom are premised on such a need of favor from God.

Charisma is the "favor" or gift-with-strings-attached that results from a patron in some upper social stratum giving to a client, one of a lower stratum. It is always a donation-with-strings-attached because all goods are limited. Thus, the God of Israel never simply "gives" in his interpersonal relationships with humans. He always "gives-in," because the God of Israel is patron in vertical dyadic relation (see **DYADISM**) with his arbitrarily chosen client. While God may have a need to give-in since he is honorable, he really has no need to give. And he really cannot "give" since "to give" necessarily presumes sheer equality, truly balanced reciprocity. If "to give freely" means to want nothing in return, then the God of Israel does not do this—and neither do people in peasant societies or in the contemporary Third World.

Theologically, to say God takes the initiative in giving grace means that he gives-in first. Minimally this image means God seeks the good-will, the openness of the one wanting or needing the "giving-in." The kingdom of heaven announced by Jesus indicates that the God of Israel is ready "to give-in again," as divine Patron. In the Pauline tradition, of course, the main difference between *charis* and *charisma* is that *charis*, God's readiness to be Patron, is shown to all human beings, while *charisma*, actual favor or patronage, comes to those "in Christ Jesus."

It is difficult to identify a parallel in Western culture to the Mediterranean concept of grace. The Western values of achievement and individualism direct members of this culture to feel self-sufficient and resist seeking special consideration. While gifts and favors are not ordinarily rejected, they are also not necessarily sought after. (Bruce J. Malina)

Cunningham, Robert B. 1993. *Wasta: The Hidden Force in Middle Eastern Society*. Westport, Conn.: Praeger.

Landé, Carl H. 1977. "Introduction: The Dyadic Basis of Clientelism." In *Friends, Followers, and Factions: A Reader in Political Clientelism.* Ed. Steffen W. Schmidt, et al. Pp. xiii–xxxvii. Berkeley: University of California Press.

Malina, Bruce J. 1988. "Patron and Client: The Analogy Behind Synoptic Theology." *Forum* 4/1:2–32.

GRATITUDE (DEBT OF)

This term describes the debt of interpersonal obligation for unrepayable favors received. The Hebrew word for this debt of gratitude is *ḥesed,* often translated "steadfast love" (see STEADFAST LOVE). Through such a debt of obligation, a person is bound to another in terms of ongoing generalized reciprocity, the idea that beneficiaries owe a debt of gratitude to their benefactors. Persons incur this sort of debt by birth (e.g., toward parents and grandparents, toward siblings), by choice (e.g., through marriage, through adoption) or by happenstance (e.g., help offered to a mortally wounded person; a favor given to a prospective client). On the other hand, those toward whom one has such a debt are equally obliged to maintain the relationship by further favors; this is ongoing reciprocity. The psalms endlessly hymn God's "steadfast love," his willingness to bestow further favors on those in covenant with him. This value is expressed throughout the Hebrew Scriptures.

The New Testament translates *ḥesed* with the Greek word for "mercy." For example, Hosea's "For I desire steadfast love and not sacrifice" (6:6) becomes: "Go and learn what this means, 'I desire mercy, and not sacrifice.' For I came not to call the righteous, but sinners" (Matt 9:13) and "And if you had known what this means, 'I desire mercy, and not sacrifice,' you would not have condemned the guiltless" (Matt 12:7). Pharisee opponents in Matthew are said to "have neglected the weightier matters of the law, justice, mercy and faith" (23:23, see Jas 2:13). And in Matthew 18:33: "should not you have had mercy on your fellow servant, as I had mercy on you?" the mercy involved is not simply feelings of compassion for one who suffers unjustly, but paying one's debt of interpersonal obligation by forgiving a trivial debt. In the conversation after the parable of the Samaritan in Luke 10, the good deed is described as "doing mercy," that is, doing an act of *ḥesed* (translated "showing mercy" Luke 10:37). God remembers his debts of interpersonal obligation (Luke 1:54) and "does mercy" (see Luke 1:50, 72, 78; Rom 12:8).

In a social system where debts of interpersonal obligation are prominent, "Lord, have mercy" means "Lord, pay up your debt of interpersonal obligation," or "I need your help right now, and you owe me!" Note that each time someone asks Jesus to heal them with a "have mercy" they use a title that underscores the basis for the debt owed, e.g., Lord (Matt 17:15; see Mark 5:19; Luke 17:13), Son of David (Matt 9:27; 20:30; Mark 10:47–48) or both Lord and Son of David (Matt 15:22; 20:31; Luke 18:38–39).

The writings of the Hebrew Bible frequently relate steadfast love and covenant (Deut 7:9–12; 1 Kgs 8:23; 2 Chron 6:14; Neh 1:5; 9:32; see also Ps 25:10; 89:28; 106:45; Isa 54:10; Dan 9:4). The reason is that the basis for this sort of debt of interpersonal obligation is a covenant or contract between unequals: between conqueror and conquered, between parents and their child(ren), between husband and wife or wives, between patron and client, between helper and accident victim. In each case, the superior party gives life to or sustains the life of the inferior one; persons thus are said "to receive mercy" (Rom 11:30–31; 1 Tim 1:13; Heb 4:16; 1 Pet 2:20). For such gifts the inferior owes, especially honor, e.g., "Honor your father and your mother" (Exod 20:12; Lev 19:3; Deut 5:16; Matt 15:4; Mark 7:10; Eph 6:2). Such honor entails practical support as well as full respect, such as not striking or cursing one's parents (Exod 21:15, 17). God is likewise to be glorified for his mercy (e.g., Rom 15:9).

And since such a covenant-rooted debt of obligation binds one in terms of ongoing generalized reciprocity, mention of God's "steadfast love" is often coupled with God's loyalty to his obligations, that is his "faithfulness" (Gen 24:27; Exod 34:6; 2 Sam 1:26; 15:20; 1 Kgs 3:6; 8:23; 2 Chron 6:14; Neh 9:17; Ps 25:10; 26:3; 36:5; 40:10–11; 57:3, 10 and frequently elsewhere in Psalms; Isa 16:5; Mic 7:20). On the other hand, for seeing to the honor and well-being of the superior, the superior likewise owes; God can be counted on to "grant mercy" to those in covenant with him (Heb 4:16; Jas 3:17; 1 Pet 1:3).

In the Western world, gratitude is not ordinarily on-going but rather episodic. One expresses gratitude for a gift or favor, but there is no expectation that this will continue in an ongoing process. The long-term, enduring relationships presumed, affirmed, and continued in the Middle Eastern world by this ongoing debt of gratitude simply are not highly valued in the West. (Bruce J. Malina)

Landé, Carl H. 1977. "Introduction: The Dyadic Basis of Clientelism." In *Friends, Followers, and Factions: A Reader in Political Clientelism.* Ed. Steffen W. Schmidt, et al. Pp. xiii–xxxvii. Berkeley: University of California Press.

Malina, Bruce J. 1988. "Patron and Client: The Analogy Behind Synoptic Theology." *Forum* 4/1:2–32.

Sakenfeld, Katharine Doob. 1977. *The Meaning of Hesed in the Hebrew Bible: A New Inquiry.* Harvard Semitic Museum 17. Missoula, Mont.: Scholars.

GROUP ORIENTATION

The people in the biblical world are dyadic (see **DYADISM**). This means that individuals basically depend on others for their sense of identity, for their understanding of their role and status in society, for clues to the duties and rights they have, and for indications of what is honorable and shameful behavior. Such people live in a world which is clearly and extensively ordered, a system which is well known to members of the group. Individuals quickly internalize this system and depend on it for needed clues to the way their world works. The group, whether it be clan, village, family, etc., communicates what is expected and proper, and individuals respond accordingly. Deference to the group is evident in the reverence given to "tradition" (see FAMILY-CENTEREDNESS). The tradition handed down by former members of the group is presumed valid and normative. Paul appeals to just this point when he prefaces his account both of the Eucharist (1 Cor 11:23) and the Resurrection (15:3) with an appeal to traditional authority, "I hand on . . . what I received." He expects the church to "maintain the traditions even as I have delivered them to you" (1 Cor 11:2); and he is critical of behavior which flaunts them (1 Cor 14:33–36). The Pharisees on occasion criticize Jesus precisely because he did not hew to the "tradition of the elders" (Mark 7:3–5). Hence, we find the exhortation to "stand firm and hold to the traditions which you were taught by us, either by word of mouth or by letter" (2 Thess 2:15; see 3:6). Likewise, the chief duty of Timothy is to "follow the pattern of the sound words which you have heard from me . . . guard the truth" (2 Tim 1:13–14; 3:14). Evidently the past is held in great esteem by the group.

Group orientation shows up in the constant injunction that disciples imitate their masters. Paul tells the Corinthians, "Be imitators of me as I am of Christ" (1 Cor 11:1). Paul himself imitates Christ by embodying the hymn in Philippians 2:6–12; like Jesus who gave up equality with God in obedience to the deity, he forgoes the former value found in the Law and seeks only to be conformed to the dying and risen Jesus (Phil 3:7–10, 17). The clouds of witnesses in Hebrews 11 illustrate the meaning of "faith" (see FAITH/FAITHFULNESS) for imitation; and Abraham is often held up as a model of faith in Galatians 3 and Romans 4. And of course, Jesus commands his disciples to be like him by denying themselves, taking up their cross and following him (Mark 8:34). The disciples must be like their master, either in acts of service (John 13:13–16) or in imitation of the master's fate (John 15:18–20).

Group orientation indicates that individuals should always "seek the good of the neighbor" (1 Cor 10:24) and not pursue individualistic objectives. Strong individualists at Corinth seem to have bucked the sense of accountability to the group, either by an unseemly marriage (5:1–2), or by eating proscribed foods (1 Cor 8:1–2, 7–11). Paul points out how the incestuous marriage harmed the group, as leaven pollutes flour (1 Cor 5:6–8); the unscrupulous eating of meats sacrificed to idols causes scandal to some, destroying the weak person for whom Christ died (1 Cor 8:11). Promoting one's interests, then, offends the group, and so comes under censure. Other people at Corinth luxuriated in their charismatic gifts, a behavior which Paul sought to moderate in terms of the good of the group. Prophecy is better than tongues for it "builds up" the group, whereas the speakers in tongues "edify" only themselves (1 Cor 14:3–4). Yet both prophecy and tongues should be regulated and subjected to controls for the sake of the group's "edification" (1 Cor 14:26–33). Evidently individualism is the nemesis of group orientation.

Nowhere is there greater criticism of what we would call individualism than in the Corinthian correspondence (see Introduction). In that faction-ridden community, certain people "puffed themselves up" by consciously disregarding the group's norms (1 Cor 4:6; 5:2; 8:1). Others boasted of their gifts and status, which put them above the considerations once shared with the group (1:31; 3:21). Boasting can also depreciate the role and status of legitimate authority in the group (2 Cor 11:12). Paul counters this with an appeal to what unifies the church and builds it up, and to what reaffirms the complex set of roles and statuses established by God.

Individuals are reminded that in regard to their own bodies, "you are not your own" (1 Cor 6:19). The sense of belonging to another is expressed in various ways. Paul insists that "you were bought with a price" (1 Cor 6:20;

7:23), that is, individuals are the property of Christ, his servants. In other places he stresses how individuals were freed from being slaves of Sin and Death and became slaves of God, slaves of righteousness (Rom 6:16–22). Although the language of freedom (see **FREEDOM**) is used, converts to Jesus become free in order to be bound in service to a faithful and noble Lord. Paul himself is always a "servant of God" or "steward of God's mysteries" (see **SERVICE**).

Group orientation is clearly expressed in the importance given to authority. God ascribes to certain people a role and status (see Introduction). In regard to the basic institution of the family, according to God's commandment parents are to be honored (Mark 7:10). The family considered in this cultural perspective also admits different roles to husbands and wives, roles which are constantly supported in the "codes of household duties" which are frequent in Christian preaching (Eph 5:21–33; Col 3:18–19; 1 Pet 3:1–7). In regard to civic life, "let every person be subject to the governing authorities" who hold authority from God (Rom 13:1–7). Within the church, Paul, precisely because he is authorized by Jesus (1 Cor 9:1) or by God (Gal 1:1, 15–16), exercises the role of apostle, prophet, and even father. Individuals, then, must respect the role and status of others in the group, whom God has so placed (1 Cor 12:28). John's Gospel illustrates this clearly by Jesus' insistence on his role as God's agent, the one whom God sent. The notion of faithfulness or loyalty further illustrates the importance of authority in group relations. Sons must honor and obey fathers; likewise slaves their masters. Even Jesus is praised for his faithfulness to God (Heb 3:1–3) and his obedience to him (Heb 5:8; Rom 5:14–21).

While group orientation is valued in the West, it is definitely a second-order value always subordinate to individualism. Individualism is cherished as the secret to success in a democracy. Even so, in times of crisis, individualism is subordinated to group orientation. In the corporation, the military, and other similar social contexts, individualism is readily sacrificed on the altar of group goals and objectives. Thus, while group orientation is a primary value in the Mediterranean world (the core value, honor, is basically a group value), it is a secondary value in the West. (Jerome H. Neyrey)

Malina, Bruce J. 1978. "Freedom: A Theological Inquiry into the Dimensions of a Symbol." *Biblical Theology Bulletin* 8:62–76.

———. 1993. "II. General Interpersonal Behavior." In *Windows on the World of Jesus: Time Travel to Ancient Judea.* Pp. 21–46. Louisville, Ky.: Westminster John Knox.

Malina, Bruce J., and Jerome H. Neyrey. 1991. "First-Century Personality: Dyadic, Not Individualistic." In *The Social World of Luke–Acts: Models for Interpretation.* Ed. Jerome H. Neyrey. Pp. 67–96. Peabody, Mass.: Hendrickson.

HANDS-FEET

These are correlative terms that refer to the human capabilities of doing, making, building, constructing, having physical effect on others and on one's environment. Briefly, the "hands-feet" area of human capability refers to purposeful activity. This is therefore a secondary value, a means for striving to acquire and preserve honor.

The "hands-feet" zone is one of the three interrelated zones that comprise distinctively human behavior. (The other zones are "eyes-heart" [see EYES-HEART] and "mouth-ears" which is treated in COMMUNICATIVENESS; DECEPTION; and EQUIVOCATION.) Just as society consists of a number of interpenetrating and yet distinct groups comprised of interpenetrating and yet distinct individuals, so too the individual is perceived to consist of interpenetrating yet distinct zones of activity. These zones of activity proceed from some inner, dynamic source, the individual's very life (often called "soul" in the Bible). Yet the existence and function of these zones is verified and validated on the basis of outward, external, concrete observations chunked in terms of three areas: eyes-heart, mouth-ears, and hands-feet. In more abstract terms, eyes-heart is the zone of emotion-fused thought; mouth-ears is the zone of self-expressive speech; and hands-feet is the zone of purposeful activity.

Any purposeful activity would be the outcome of a person's using the hands and/or feet. Thus, in the early account of creation in Genesis 2:4ff. we find God "forming" (v. 7) the first earthling (Hebrew: *adam*), "planting" (v. 8) a garden, "taking" and "putting" the earthling in the garden (v. 15), "forming" (v. 19) other creatures, and "taking" a rib from the earthling and "closing" (v. 21) it up with flesh. These are all "hands" activities, just as the "Lord God walking in the garden in the cool of the day" (3:8) is a "feet" activity.

Thus, the laying on of hands refers concretely to the activity of exerting force, including physical violence (e.g., Gen 22:12; Exod 7:4; Luke 20:19; 21:12; Acts 21:27). Because of this concrete usage, the laying on of hands becomes a natural symbol of the transfer of physical activity and force, i.e., a symbol of a person's past deeds and their effects, or of present power, or of both. (1) Thus, by laying hands on the head of an animal to be sacrificed, people transfer their past deeds and the effects of those deeds to the beast to have them annihilated and/or transformed with the destruction of the animal (e.g., Exod 29:10, 15, 19; Lev 3:2, 8, 13; Num 8:12). (2) Laying hands on the sick points to the transference of the power of the healer (Mark 5:23; 8:23; Acts 9:12, 17), just as laying hands on children wards off negative influence due to the imparted power of the one laying on hands (Gen 48:14; Mark 10:16). (3) Finally, people can hand over their power and have another exercise it on their behalf, effecting this by laying on their hands (Num 8:10; Acts 6:6; 8:17; 1 Tim 4:14), while some already wielding power over a group can hand it on to others by laying on their hands (Num 27:23; Deut 34:9; 1 Tim 5:22; 2 Tim 1:6).

People normally wore sandals (Exod 12:11; Deut 29:5; Josh 9:5; 1 Kgs 2:5; Acts 13:25) or shoes (Exod 3:5; Josh 5:15; Acts 7:33) as they performed their activities. To take off one's sandals or shoes indicated a halt to normal activity. This halt was further underscored by washing one's feet. For in the process of work, travel, or simply walking, the feet would get dirty. Hence, the common custom of washing the feet before or upon entering a dwelling (2 Sam 11:8) and the common courtesy of providing water to guests for this purpose upon their arrival (Gen 18:4; 19:2; 24:32; 43:24; Exod 30:19, 21; 40:31; Judg 19:21; Luke 7:44); slaves performed such an action for their owners (1 Sam 25:41).

Again as with the hands, because of the concrete behavior surrounding the feet, both the removal of footwear and the washing of feet became a natural symbol of removal of a person's normal social status (bare feet) or of a person's past deeds and their effects (symbolic foot washing). As for the first, Moses is directed: "Do not come near; put off your shoes from your feet, for the place on which you are standing is holy ground" (Exod 3:5; Josh 5:15; Acts 7:33). Similarly, during the mourning process, one was to remain unshod, removed from one's normal social status (Isa 20:2; Ezek 24:17–23). Then the well-known scenario of foot-washing in John's Gospel refers to the symbolic washing away of the disciples' past deeds and their effects, to Jesus' forgiveness of offenses against him before his "passing to the Father" (John 13:5–14).

"Feet" likewise refer to general behavior. God safeguards his people from public dishonor and contempt by keeping their feet from slipping (2 Sam 22:37; Job 12:5; Ps 17:5; 18:36; 66:9; 73:2) or stumbling (Ps 73:2; 116:8; see Jer 13:16). The wicked set "nets" or "snares" to trip up their neighbors, and thus shame them (Jer 18:22; Prov 29:5; see Ps 25:15; 56:13; Lam 1:13); but eventually they get tripped up in their own nets, i.e., their own misdeeds (Job 18:8). Since "hands-feet" refer to activity and power, to be set "under the feet of" someone means to be subject to that person, to be under that one's control (2 Sam 22:39; 1 Kgs 5:3; Ps 8:6; 18:38; 47:3; Mal 4:3; Mark 12:36; Matt

22:44; Rom 16:20; 1 Cor 15:25, 27; Eph 1:22; Heb 2:8; Rev 12:1). Similarly, to put one's foot on the neck of a person is to indicate total defeat and control (Josh 10:24). The neck both holds up a person's honor which is associated with the head-face (Isa 3:16), and is the channel of life because the breath-soul passes through it. Finally, "the feet" is a frequent euphemism for the male genitals, undoubtedly a symbol of potency, the power to generate offspring (Gen 49:10; Exod 4:25; Ruth 3:4, 7, 8; Isa 6:2; Ezek 34:18–19).

There is much more to note about this hands-feet zone in biblical writings. Suffice it here to note that the zone of purposeful action is referred to with the following words: hands, feet, arms, fingers, legs, and the activities of these organs: to do, act, accomplish, execute, intervene, touch, come, go, march, walk, stand, sit, along with specific activities such as to steal, kidnap, commit adultery, build, and the like. The following representative nouns and adjectives pertain to this zone: action, gesture, work, activity, behavior, step, walking, way, course, and any specific activity; active, capable, quick, slow, and so forth.

In the prevailing culture of the United States, the reality that corresponds to the hands-feet zone in biblical literature is outward human behavior, all external activity, human actions upon the world of persons and things. While the operations are similar, the ways of explaining and describing the operations are quite different. By and large, people in the Unites States fall back upon interior motivations and psychological explanations for external activities, particularly when these activities have more than utilitarian or functional purpose. We wonder how a person's activities fit into a life-plan or purpose in life. We ask "what's in it for them?" because we always assume that people act out of enlightened self-interest. While healing in the ancient world is a "hands" activity involving power and restoration of meaning to a person's life, this same external activity in Western culture is viewed predominantly from a technological perspective and serves to restore people's productivity or gainful employment. (Bruce J. Malina)

Bremmer, Jan, and Herman Roodenburg, eds. 1991. *A Cultural History of Gesture*. Ithaca, N.Y.: Cornell University Press.

Géradon, Bernard de. 1958. "L'homme à l'image de Dieu." *La nouvelle revue théologique* 80:683–95.

Malina, Bruce J. 1993. *The New Testament World: Insights from Cultural Anthropology*. 2d rev. ed. Louisville, Ky.: Westminster John Knox, 73–81.

HEALING

Healing is a cultural technique or strategy for restoring a person to well-being. Lack of human well-being is a shameful situation, hence restoration to proper human well-being, or healing, is a restoration to honor, a restoration of meaning to life. Proper human well-being, sometimes narrowly described as health, is therefore a means value, a condition that allows a person to fully participate in cultural activities the main purpose of which, in the Mediterranean world, is to maintain or augment honor.

Medical anthropology and the definitions it proposes help an investigator to better understand the reality of human well-being or lack of it as this is experienced and interpreted in different cultures. Consider the modern experience called cancer. In today's Western medical perspective, cancer is an umbrella word that describes over one hundred different diseases. Cancer specialists attack the problem with a battery of strategies, chief among which are surgery, radiation, and chemotheraphy. If medical tests subsequent to these therapies find no sign of the disease in a person, that person is considered to be in remission. Only after a person remains in remission for five years does medical science declare the person "cured." Medical anthropologists define a cure as the elimination of a disease and point out that a cure is a very rare occurrence.

On the other hand, medical anthropologists define healing as the restoration of meaning in life whether or not the disease is affected, that is, whether or not the physical condition is improved. In this perspective, healing takes place always and unfailingly. All people eventually make some sense of life after the experience of misfortune, including those in the realm of human well-being.

Like all anthropological disciplines, medical anthropology is a helpful tool for grasping and understanding differences and similarities between cultures. The reality of human well-being, sometimes narrowly viewed as health, is culturally constructed and interpreted, and therefore differs from culture to culture. Real misfortune in the realm of human health is called sickness. This reality can be viewed and interpreted with the aid of two explanatory concepts: disease and illness. Medical anthropologists insist that these are not realities but rather hermeneutic concepts that represent two contrasting viewpoints.

The term "disease" reflects the Western, scientific perspective and describes abnormalities in the structure or function of organ systems. These pathological states do exist, whether or not cultures recognize them. The germs and viruses that cause some of these abnormalities can be seen with a microscope. To cure the disease one employs scientific interventions (surgery, radiation, chemothrapy, pharmaceuticals, etc.) by specialists. As noted above, a cure is a rare occurrence.

The concept of illness is another way to describe a pathological state, even if it is not recognized as such. Labeling something as an illness interprets misfortunes in human well-being beyond pathological states. Illness thus reflects a social and cultural view of socially disvalued states and includes more than what science identifies as disease. Since the illness state is socially disvalued, it is possible for society or segments of it to reinterpret the state and provide it with new social value or meaning.

This strategy is called healing, or restoring meaning to life, and as noted above, it occurs unfailingly in every instance.

Did Jesus cure people such as lepers? Possibly, but without confirming evidence from lab tests, x-rays, cat scans, and other such modern inventions, no one can say for certain. We did not examine the patient before and after treatment. In fact, it is very likely that Jesus did not cure leprosy, because there is no scientific evidence that it existed in first-century Palestine. Of all the human bones excavated and examined in modern Israel, to this date none have been discovered with traces of Hansen's disease. Then did Jesus heal people such as these so-called lepers, that is, did he restore meaning to their lives? Yes, most of the time, but not always (Mark 6:5).

Though the Bible speaks of "leprosy" and identifies people afflicted with it, the symptoms described are not those of Hansen's disease or perhaps any disease. The real problem seems to be a repulsive, scaly or flaky condition that affects clothing and houses as well as people. The dominant concern in the texts that discuss this problem is whether or not the scales or flakes indicate that the skin/cloth/wall has been "broken" or "penetrated" (Lev 13–14). The concern is about boundaries: are they firm and impenetrable or have they been breached? Thus, from a biomedical perspective the "leprosy" described is not a disease, perhaps not even a pathological situation. Rather, the concern is an illness, a socially dis-valued condition with unwelcome social consequences. The problem is that some people are viewed as being un-clean, impure, not-holy, rather than clean, pure, and holy. This condition is serious because it violates God's will: "You shall be holy because I the Lord am holy" (see Lev 11:44–45). The texts clearly indicate that what the community fears is pollution not contagion (Hansen's disease is minimally contagious anyway—a spouse does not normally contract it from an infected partner), and their polluting capability is the reason why afflicted per-

sons must depart from the holy community and live outside the camp, beyond the boundaries of society (Lev
13:45–46).

The so-called lepers who seek Jesus' intervention all
have the same request: to be made clean (Matt 8:2–3;
Mark 1:40–42; Luke 5:12–13). Jesus' response in the
["theological"] passive voice emphasizes that God does
the cleansing. Jesus is only God's broker, an inter-
mediary (see **PATRONAGE**). In Luke's account of the ten
so-called lepers, the afflicted persons ask Jesus to have
mercy. Translated in line with Mediterranean cultural
values, their request is: "I need your help right now, and
you owe me!" or "Lord, pay up your debt of interpersonal
obligation!" (see **GRATITUDE, DEBT OF**). Jesus is recognized
here and throughout the gospels as one who has ability
(see **POWER**) to restore meaning to life, and he owes it to
people to do so. The end result is that these people are indeed healed, that is, meaning has been restored to their
lives, when Jesus proclaims them "clear, pure, holy" and
fit to return to life in the holy community.

The temple priests might have refused to confirm Jesus' judgment, and a lengthy debate might have followed. The scenario is very plausible and highly likely.
Jesus' opponents did not deny Jesus' healing ability. They
were concerned about its source (Matt 12:22–45) because
they knew that they, the authorities, did not grant it to
him or authorize him to use it (Matt 21:23). By healing
people's ills, Jesus provided fresh meaning to their lives
and subverted the meaning dictated and supported by his
opponents, the authorities. Using power without authorization is a treasonous political action deserving death.
The authorities had no choice but to condemn him (Matt
26:3–5).

Thanks to television and other modern media, even
the least formally educated Western Bible reader possesses an astonishing amount of scientific knowledge
about human health and disease. Very few recognize
how heavily overlaid medical science is with Western

cultural presuppositions and assumptions. Those who practice medicine internationally become painfully aware of this in their daily experience and recognize that so-called cosmopolitan scientific medicine cannot become truly "cosmopolitan" until it sheds these cultural peculiarities. This cross-cultural challenge for delivering Western health care on an international and culturally diverse level is the same challenge facing the average medically sophisticated Bible reader. Asking scientific questions of the Bible guarantees it will be misunderstood and misinterpreted. Taking the natives at their word is always reliable. Healing, or the restoration of meaning in life, is the common human experience in modernity as in antiquity. Cures that are so rare in the modern world were probably equally rare in the ancient world. (John J. Pilch)

Pilch, John J. 1981. "Biblical Leprosy and Body Symbolism." *Biblical Theology Bulletin* 11:108–13.

———. 1988. "Understanding Biblical Healing: Selecting the Appropriate Model." *Biblical Theology Bulletin* 18:60–66.

———. 1991. "Sickness and Healing in Luke–Acts." In *The Social World of Luke–Acts: Models for Interpretation.* Ed. Jerome H. Neyrey. Pp. 181–209. Peabody, Mass.: Hendrickson.

———. 1992. "BTB Readers Guide: Understanding Healing in the Social World of Early Christianity." *Biblical Theology Bulletin* 22:26–33.

———. 1995. "Insights and models from medical anthropology for understanding the healing activity of the Historical Jesus." *Hervormde teologiese studies* 21:314–37.

HEART-EYES—SEE EYES-HEART

HOLY/HOLINESS—SEE WHOLENESS

HONOR/SHAME

These are the core values in the Mediterranean world in general and in the Bible as well. Honor is a claim to worth that is publicly acknowledged. To "have honor" is to have publicly acknowledged worth. To "be honored" is to be ascribed such worth or be acclaimed for it. Shame, as the opposite of honor, is a claim to worth that is publicly denied and repudiated. To "be shamed" is always negative; it means to be denied or to be diminished in honor. On the other hand, to "have shame" is always positive; it means to be concerned about one's honor. All human beings seek to have shame, no human being cares to be shamed.

Honor is primarily a group value. Individual members of a group share in its honor. Kinship groups are said to inherit honor from their honorable ancestors. This inherited honor must be maintained and defended by the current generation, male and female. However, within the framework of the kinship group and gender-based society (see Introduction), honor is a value embodied by adult males, while (positive) shame is a value embodied by adult females. Individual males must achieve honor in public contests. It must be claimed, gained, and defended before one's peers. Honor is associated with a value cluster that includes: strength, courage, daring, valor, generosity, and wisdom. Weakness, cowardice, and lack of generosity indicate lack of honor, and hence, are despised. This value cluster and the honor underpinning it are most intensely lived in a small group, where everybody knows everybody else, where all are "equal" in honor, where the individual exists only through the group, and where kinship rules prevail.

The female domain is that of shame in the sense of focal concern for honor; such shame is neither won nor claimed. It is, rather, presupposed and then maintained as a veil of privacy and of personal and sexual integrity. Shame is therefore not associated with strength or wisdom or courage, but rather with privacy, reserve, and purity.

For a male, "to lose honor" is "to be shamed." Being shamed involves a loss of repute and worth in the eyes of others, especially of one's peers. It results from a public exposure of a man's weakness or cowardice or pretension or foolishness. But what exactly counts as weakness, what concrete behavior is really cowardly, what specifically can be rated as folly? The terms "honor" and "shame" are vacant in this respect. They are really high context words whose content must be deduced from actual social behavior. In other words, while one can readily say that where honor is the highest value, public humiliation is a fate worse than death, one must still describe what in a given social group or society counts as honorable behavior.

Thus, Israel's claim to honor is its special relationship to the Lord (Isa 43:1–7), the evidence that God is on the side of Israel (Ps 44:1–8). This claim depends on evidence for God's continued interest in his chosen people. National defeat proves God's abandonment with resultant shame for Israel (Ps 44:13–16). The victors may also mock the God of Israel, who seems to them to be powerless to save Israel. In the face of misfortune, Israel becomes confused and questions either its own integrity before the Lord (Ps 44:17–22) or the Lord's continuing support and election of Israel (Ps 44:9–16) or both (Isa 59:1–19). The prophets have often pointed out Israel's sins as the cause of the Lord's displeasure (Isa 2:6–3:26), hence, the cause of their being shamed.

Children are expected to honor their parents (Exod 20:12; Deut 5:16) specifically by supporting them, not beating or cursing them (Exod 21:15, 17; Prov 19:26; 20:20; 28:24). Jesus questions the "Qorban" custom of devoting money to the temple by children whose primary obligation is to "honor" parents by physical support (Mark 7:9–13; Matt 15:4–6). A dishonoring son is one who is "stubborn and rebellious . . . , who will not obey the voice of his father or the voice of his mother"; he is best put to death (Deut 21:18–21) since he is cursed (Deut 27:16).

The righteous person's claim to honor is evidence of special relationship with God because of reliance on God's help (Ps 54; 55). A calamity points in the opposite

direction and allows one's enemies full rationale for deri-
sion, hatred, and denial of God's concern. The sufferer
must then demonstrate the opposite: insist on his own
righteousness, confess his guilt before the Lord, and appeal for help to the Lord's steadfast love (see STEADFAST
LOVE; GRACE/FAVOR; AUTHORITARIANISM). God's punishment of one's enemies is likewise evidence of honor due
to special relationship with God (cf. Ps 35:4; 69; 70:2;
71:13; 83:16–17).

Disobedience to God is often mentioned in the Psalms
and Prophets as reason for God's rejection (Ps 44; 69;
109:28–29) with resulting shame and confusion before
others. These others are one's local peers (Ps 44:16) or
other nations or cities (Ezek 16:37). Another reason is reliance on the wrong allies; Isaiah (20:3–5) warns Judea
that those who seek the protection of the power of Egypt
and Ethiopia will see the shame of these nations; their
own shame will be like the shame of their protectors.
Likewise he warns, "Therefore shall the protection of
Pharaoh turn to your shame, and the shelter in the
shadow of Egypt to your humiliation . . . every one
comes to shame through a people that cannot profit
them" (Isa 30:3–5).

For its behavior, Jeremiah threatens Jerusalem with
shame in the form of public exposure or "nakedness" (see
NUDITY), as the Lord says, "I myself will lift up your skirts
over your face, and your shame will be seen. . . . Woe to
you, Jerusalem" (13:26–27; cf. 51:51). Those who complain
of "the burden of the Lord," hear the Lord's response: "I
will bring upon you everlasting reproach and perpetual
shame, which shall not be forgotten" (23:40). Threats of
identical public exposure against Jerusalem for its iniquity
and disloyalty occur also in Ezekiel 16:36–54 (cf. Hos 2:10;
Nah 3:5). Public exposure is a typically female punishment, used here because in the ancient Mediterranean,
cities were considered female entities.

Second Isaiah (a term that identified the author of
Isaiah 40–55) announces a reversal of the situation of

exile, resulting in the opposite of being shamed. Thus, in
54:4 the Lord comforts the exiles, saying, "Fear not, for
you will not be ashamed; be not confounded, for you will
not be put to shame; for you will forget the shame of
your youth." And in Isa 61:7 the Lord reassures the Israelites, saying, "Instead of your shame you shall have a
double portion, instead of dishonor you shall rejoice in
your lot."

In the writings of Paul, one can see what Paul holds
as honorable by considering what he boasts about: his
ethnic, kinship origins and group affiliation in Israel
(Phil 3:5–6), as well as his own status among his people
(2 Cor 11:22) and his manly endurance of sufferings
(2 Cor 11:23–28). Yet in another context, he dismisses
this kinship basis for honor in favor of a new standard.
"But whatever gain I had, I counted as loss for the sake
of Christ. Indeed I count everything as loss because of the
surpassing worth of knowing Christ Jesus my Lord. For
his sake I have suffered the loss of all things, and count
them as refuse, in order that I may gain Christ" (Phil
3:7–8; see also 3:10–11).

Thus, status in Israelite and local Tarsus society is
no longer the apostle's supreme value; now it is status in
the Christian group: Christ is now his supreme worth. Instead of boasting of his own power and courage, the
apostle now accepts weakness, lowliness, suffering, and
fear (1 Cor 2:1–5) for the sake of the gospel. Instead of
seeking recognition in the eyes of others, he wants to be
found in Christ, his Lord and his judge (1 Cor 4:1–5;
2:1–5). He does not seek human approval (1 Thess 2:4)
but only God's approval (cf. Gal 1:10). He insists on his
status and role as legitimate apostle (Gal 1 and 2).

For this reason, Paul was often in conflict with com-
peting Judean apostles who insisted that Greeks and Romans had to first be "in Israel" before they could be
accepted "in Christ" (2 Cor 11:5–6; 12:10). In Paul's view,
those "in Christ" need to reassess what they once considered honorable in favor of a new set of standards. For ex-

ample, when the Corinthians began to boast about their spiritual accomplishments, he reminded them that God called them when they were lowly, weak, and foolish in order to shame the strong, the wise, and the noble. God did this so that no human being should boast before him. God himself, then, is the source of their "life in Christ" (1 Cor 1:26–31; 4:6–10). While those who believe in Christ will not be put to shame before anyone (Rom 9:33), Paul's only fear is that he himself or the community may be put to shame before Christ on the last day (1 Thess 3:13; cf. 5:23; 2 Cor 5:10). Shameful behavior, for Paul, includes homosexual relations and all kinds of other sins among Greeks and Romans, allowed by God for their perverting the truth (Rom 1:24, 26, 28). Similarly, and in agreement with the traditions of the churches in Palestine, he states that if a man prophesies with his head covered he "dishonors (*kataischynei*) his head." On the other hand, if a woman prophesies with her head uncovered, she dishonors her head. In that case it is as if she had shaved her head (1 Cor 11:6) and disgraced herself (vv. 3–16).

While the Gospel tradition reports Jesus speaking only rarely about honor and shame, the narrative is replete with honor concerns. This feature is clearly underscored in the many scenarios in which Jesus demonstrates considerable skill at challenge and riposte and thereby reveals himself to be an honorable man, capable of defending God's honor, his group's honor, and his own honor.

The contest begins with a challenge (almost any word, gesture, action) that seeks to undermine the honor of another person and a response that answers in equal measure or ups the ante (and thereby challenges in return). Both positive (gifts, compliments) and negative challenges (insults, dares) must be answered to avoid a serious loss of face. His challengers include scribes (from Jerusalem), the Pharisees, the elders, the Sadducees, and the High Priests. These social categories attempt to show Jesus up, thus in effect to keep Jesus out of their status ranks.

For example, in Mark (and parallels) we find these challenge-riposte scenarios presented, first of all, in an initial set of five: 2:1–12; 2:15–17; 2:18–22; 2:23–28; 3:1–6; and then interspersed throughout the work: 3:20–35; 7:1–8; 10:1–12; 11:27–33; 12:13–17; 12:18–27.

Jesus demanded loyalty from his disciples both toward himself and toward his message. His experience indicated that opponents would attempt to discredit, and therefore dishonor, both. Hence, disciples are warned: "Whoever is ashamed of me and of my words in this adulterous and sinful generation, of him will the Son of man also be ashamed, when he comes in the glory of his Father with the holy angels" (Mark 8:38).

Family ties, the strongest of Mediterranean social bonds, must have proved a significant hurdle to loyalty to Jesus and his task (Matt 10:37; Luke 14:26). Luke presents a comparison emphasizing the dishonor involved in taking up after Jesus and then backing out. "For which of you, desiring to build a tower, does not first sit down and count the cost, whether he has enough to complete it? Otherwise, when he has laid a foundation, and is not able to finish, all who see it begin to mock him, saying, 'This man began to build, and was not able to finish' " (Luke 14:28–30). In the same vein, Jesus prepares his disciples for the dishonor opponents will attempt to heap on them: "Blessed are you when men revile you (*oneizō*) . . . and utter all kinds of evil against you falsely on my account" (Matt 5:11; Luke 6:22). He predicts: "A disciple is not above his teacher. . . . If they have called the master Beelzebul, how much more will they malign those of his household" (Matt 10:24–25).

In typical Mediterranean fashion, Jesus' disciples are reported to have once discussed "with one another who was the greatest" (Mark 9:34; Matt 18:1; Luke 9:46). On this occasion, Jesus rejects contemporary standards for assessing what might be honorable and shameful. As Luke articulates it here: "for he who is least among you all is the one who is great" (9:48). And in another context where control of other people, authority, is labelled the hallmark of "the Gentiles," i.e., Greeks and Romans, Jesus urges: "whoever would be first among you must be slave of all" (Mark 10:44; Matt 20:27); or in Luke's tradition: "let the greatest among you become as the youngest, and the leader as one who serves" (Luke 22:26). Finally, in Matthew's Gospel, Jesus warned the disciples to forgo titles of honor such as rabbi, father, master (Matt 23:8–10); instead: "He who is greatest among you shall be your servant; whoever exalts himself will be humbled, and whoever humbles himself will be exalted" (23:11–12; cf. Luke 14:7–11).

Honor and shame as they touch Jesus are best evidenced in the Passion account, and this in a culture where crucifixion was the most humiliating of all possible forms of death. First of all, the political implications of Jesus' humiliating death are foreshadowed in the parable of the Wicked Husbandmen (Mark 12:1–12; Matt 21:33–46; Luke 20:9–19), where the tenants shame the second servant sent by the master, who finally sends his own son. Instead of honoring the son, the tenants kill him. Everyone knows that the owner, to get satisfaction for his honor, will have to destroy the tenants and lease the vineyard to others.

Then the implications for Jesus are laid out as he is publicly shamed, and this in terms of three social roles: prophet, king, and Son of God. Thus, after Jesus is interrogated by the high priest, some of those present insult him by spitting on him, then cover his head and strike him, challenging him to "Prophesy!" (Mark 14:65; Matt 26:67–68; Luke 22:63–65). Jesus' silence indicates to his challengers that he cannot defend his claim; God is not with him.

In the next scene, it is the turn of some Roman soldiers to shame Jesus (Mark 15:16–20). They clothe him with a purple cloak, press a crown of thorns on his head, and salute him: "Hail, King of the Judeans!" They too spit on him, strike his head with a reed, and make mock obeisance. Jesus' powerlessness indicates to his challengers that he cannot sustain this claim (cf. Matt 27:27–31; John 19:1–3).

The third mocking scene presents Jesus hanging on the cross, utterly humiliated, publicly shamed (Mark 15:29–32). Passers-by shake their heads in contempt, adding words of insult. The chief priests and scribes add to his injury by their contemptuous and vengeful observations: "He saved others; he cannot save himself. Let the Christ, the King of Israel, come down now from the cross, that we may see and believe" (15:29–31). In Luke's Gospel, Jesus is mocked as "the Christ of God, his Chosen One" (Luke 23:35). In Matthew's Gospel, the revilers also say, "He trusts in God; let God deliver him now, if he desires him; for he said, 'I am the Son of God' " (Matt 27:43).

God's raising Jesus from the dead demonstrates God's vindication of Jesus and the ascription of paramount honor to him. It equally underscores God's approval of Jesus' standards for what is honorable and what is shameful. The tradition that puts Jesus now standing (Acts 7:55–56; Rom 8:34) or seated (Eph 1:20; Col 3:1; Heb 1:3; 8:1; 10:12; 12:2) at the right hand of God likewise underscores his honorable status. And early Christian hymns, such as the one in Philippians 2:5–11, expect universal acknowledgement of Jesus' status of ultimate honor as Lord.

In Western culture, it is not honor and shame so much as guilt that drives human behavior. Honor and shame are public and therefore reflect external social pressure to conform to social norms. Guilt is rather internal. Cultures such as the U.S., where behavior is driven by guilt concerns, require that human beings internalize a sense of obligation and feel appropriate internal sentiments about observing social norms or failing to observe them. (Joseph Plevnik)

Peristiany, John G., ed. 1966. *Honor and Shame: The Values of Mediterranean Society.* Chicago: University of Chicago Press.

Peristiany, John G. 1992. *Honor and Grace in Anthropology.* Cambridge: Cambridge University Press.

Pitt-Rivers, Julian. 1961. "Honor." In *International Encyclopedia of the Social Sciences.* Ed. D. L. Sills. 6:503–11. New York: Macmillan.

Gilmore, David D. 1982. "Anthropology of the Mediterranean Area." *Annual Review of Anthropology* 11:175–205.

_____. 1987. *Honor and Shame and the Unity of the Mediterranean.* American Anthropological Association Special Publication 22. Washington: American Anthropological Association.

Klopfenstein, Martin A. 1972. *Scham und Schande nach dem Alten Testament: Eine begriffsgeschichtliche Untersuchung zu den hebräischen Wurzeln bos, klm und hpr.* Zurich: Theologischer.

Malina, Bruce J. 1986. *Christian Origins and Cultural Anthropology: Practical Models for Biblical Interpretation.* Atlanta: John Knox.

_____. 1993. *The New Testament World: Insights from Cultural Anthropology.* Rev. Ed. Louisville, Ky.: Westminster John Knox.

Schneider, Carl D. 1992. *Shame, Exposure and Privacy.* New York: Norton.

Neyrey, Jerome H. 1990. *Paul, In Other Words: A Cultural Reading of His Letters.* Louisville, Ky.: Westminster John Knox.

_____., ed. 1991. *The Social World of Luke–Acts: Models for Interpretation.* Peabody, Mass.: Hendrickson.

HOPE—SEE TRUST

HOSPITALITY

This is the process of "receiving" outsiders and changing them from strangers to guests. This value clearly serves as a means for attaining and preserving honor, the core cultural value. In the world of the Bible, hospitality is never about entertaining family and friends. Hospitality always is about dealing with strangers. To show hospitality to strangers is "to receive" them. If strangers are not to be done away with, either physically or socially (see Matt 10:14–23), their reception occurs in three stages:

(1) Strangers have to be tested. Strangers pose a threat to any community since they are potentially anything one cares to imagine. Hence, they must be checked over both as to how they might fit in and as to whether they will subscribe to the community's norms. Officials

(Josh 2:2–3) or concerned citizenry (Gen 19:4–5) might conduct such tests; the invasion of the outsider must be repelled (Mark 5:17: the Gerasenes ask the stranger Jesus to leave). An invitation to speak can be a test (Acts 13:14–15), while letters of recommendation can excuse from a test, although sometimes not (e.g., 2 and 3 John; Rom 16:3–16; 1 Thess 5:12–13). The ritual of foot washing marks the movement from stranger to guest (see Gen 18:4; 19:2; 24:32; lacking in Luke 7:36–50; see **HANDS-FEET**).

(2) The stranger takes on the role of guest. Since transient strangers lacked customary or legal standing within the visited community, it was imperative that they find a patron, a host (see **PATRONAGE**). Hosts would be established community members, and through a personal bond with them (something inns cannot offer), the stranger was incorporated as guest or client. The traditional name for a protected client is "protégé." To offend the guest is to offend the host, who is protector and patron of the guest (poignantly underscored in the case of Lot, Gen 19:1–10). Yet such patronage can yield more trouble than honor (e.g., Prov 6:1–3).

The rules of hospitality require the guest: (a) To refrain from insulting the host and from any show of hostility or rivalry; a guest must honor the host (Jesus eating with sinners neither accuses them of being sinners nor asks them to change: Matt 9:10; Luke 5:29). (b) To refrain from usurping the role of the host, e.g., making oneself at home when not yet invited to (in the home of another, Jesus heals when asked: Mark 1:30–31); taking precedence (see Luke 14:8); giving orders to the dependents of the host (Jesus refuses to command Mary: Luke 10:40–42); making claims or demands on the host or demanding or taking what is not offered (see Luke 7:36–50, where Jesus is the perfect guest; and the rules for travelling disciples: Mark 6:10 and parallels). (c) To refrain from refusing what is offered; to refuse is to infringe on the role of guest. The guest is above all bound to accept food (see Luke 10:8; the directives to disciples for their travels would force them to accept patronage: Mark 6:8 and parallels; see 1 Cor 9:4). On the other hand, the rules of hospitality require that a host: (a) Refrain from insulting one's guests or from any show of hostility or rivalry. (b) Protect one's guests and their honor. For guests individually are embedded in the host. Thus, while fellow guests have no explicit relationship, they are bound to forgo hostilities, since they offend their host in the act of offending one another. The host must defend each against the other since both are his guests (thus Paul's problem at the "Lord's Supper" in 1 Cor 11:17–34). (c) Attend to one's guests, to grant them the precedence which is their due, to show concern for their needs and wishes or in general to earn the good will which guests should show. Note how in Luke 7:36–50 Simon the Pharisee fails on all counts with his guest, Jesus: no foot washing; no kiss; no anointing; no keeping away the sinful woman; the parable in Luke 7:40–42 represents Jesus' defense of his honor as guest. Finally, failure to offer the best one has is to denigrate the guest (John 2:10).

While element (a) is the same for both guest and host, elements (b) and (c) are complementaries. This assures that a stranger will rarely, if ever, reciprocate hospitality. Hence, its necessity and value (see Matt 25:38, 43) among the traditional Judaic works of mercy. Yet while hospitality does not entail mutual reciprocity between individuals, it can nevertheless be viewed as a reciprocal relationship between communities. Such hospitality to travelling Christians is both urged (see Rom 12:13; 1 Pet 4:9) and much practiced (e.g., Acts 17:7; 21:17; 28:7; Rom 16:23).

(3) The guest never leaves the host with the same status as upon arrival, for the stranger-guest will leave the host as either friend or enemy. If as friend, the guest will spread the praises of the host (e.g., 1 Thess 1:9; Phil 4:15), notably to those who sent the stranger to the host (e.g., Mark 9:37). If as enemy, the one aggrieved will have to get satisfaction (e.g., 3 John).

In the context of the practice of hospitality, John 1:11, "his own . . . received him not," means that the "Word made flesh" was given no welcome, shown no hospitality. In turn, Jesus gives this word of honor: "Truly, truly, I say to you, he who receives any one whom I send receives me; and he who receives me receives him who sent me" (John 13:20; in the Synoptics, the saying is referred to a "child," the least among the Christians: Luke 9:48; Matt 18:5; Mark 9:37). Of course such sayings were significant in a world unaccustomed to travel and social services.

In the United States, hospitality is reserved almost exclusively for friends. Strangers are directed to motels or hotels, and those in need are sent to social service agencies that regularly provide food and lodging to needy people who will remain anonymous throughout. (Bruce J. Malina)

Hobbs, T. Raymond. 1993. "Man, Woman and Hospitality (2 Kings 4:8–36)." *Biblical Theology Bulletin* 23:91–100.

Malina, Bruce J. 1986. "The Received View and What It Cannot Do: III John and Hospitality." In *Social-Scientific Criticism of the New Testament and Its Social World.* Ed. John H. Elliott. *Semeia* 35:171–94.

Pitt-Rivers, Julian. 1969–70. "The Pattern of Guest Welcome in the Odyssey." *Classical Journal* 65:124.

_____. 1977. *The Fate of Shechem or the Politics of Sex: Essays in the Anthropology of the Mediterranean.* Cambridge: Cambridge University Press.

HUMILITY

This value directs persons to stay within their inherited social status. The strategies for being humble include not presuming on others and avoiding even the appearance of lording it over another. Humble persons do not threaten or challenge another's rights, nor do they claim more for themselves than has been duly allotted them in life. They even stay a step below or behind their rightful status (e.g., the "unworthy" John the Baptist, Mark 1:7). Thus, humility is a socially acknowledged claim to neutrality in the competition of life.

Conversely, to attempt to better oneself at the expense of others, to acquire more than others, to strive for honors others now enjoy, are all instances of proud and arrogant behavior. God humbles such proud people (Matt 23:12; Luke 18:14; see Deut 8:2, 16; Ps 55:19), while he exalts the humble (2 Sam 22:28; Ps 18:27; Luke 1:52; 14:7–11). Hence, humility has precedence over honor (Prov 15:33; 18:12). To humble or humiliate others is to shame them (e.g., Dinah in Gen 34:2; "women" in Ezek 22:10; Isa 2:9, 11, 17). To humble or humiliate oneself is to declare oneself powerless to defend one's status (e.g., 2 Chron 33:23; 36:12; Phil 2:8), and then to act accordingly either factually (becoming powerless, like the low-born; see "humble in spirit" in Isa 57:15; 66:2; or "the humble of the land" in Zeph 3:12), or ritually (by a rite in which the use of power is set aside, symboled by behavior typical of the low-born: fasting, rending garments, weeping, lamenting, confessing—e.g., Lev 26:41; 1 Kgs 21:29; 2 Kgs 22:8–20; Ps 69:10). Such self-humiliation before God is praiseworthy and obtains God's favor (see **GRACE/ FAVOR**; **PATRONAGE**; Prov 3:34; Jas 4:10; 1 Pet 5:5–6; also 2 Cor 12:21). Matthew's tradition insists that Jesus was no arrogant teacher, but "meek and humble of heart" (Matt 11:29). And Matthew alone notes how Jesus' entry into Jerusalem is an unpretentious one: "Tell the daughter of Zion, Behold, your king is coming to you, humble, and mounted on an ass, and on a colt, the foal of an ass" (Matt 21:5, quoting Zech 9:9); the horse was the traditional war animal of power and status, the ass was simple transportation.

Yet the Gospel tradition notes that Jesus did not exhort followers to practice traditional forms of self-humiliation. An indication of this is the tradition about Jesus and fasting. The traditional Hebrew name for fasting is (self) humiliation (*taanith*; see Isa 58:5; Ezra 8:21). The tradition had it that Jesus did not fast (Mark 2:18–20; Matt 9:14–17; Luke 5:33–39), nor did he expect his disciples to fast in public (Matt 6:16–18). Rather, Jesus urged simply that one not challenge the honor of others (Matt 23:12; Luke 14:11; 18:14), as though one were as powerless to do so as a child (Matt 18:4). Such humility is a valued quality (Eph 4:2; Col 3:12). Humility is thus a means value, that is, a course of action or behavior which facilitates the realization of honor, the core value of Mediterranean culture.

In the Western world, humility is not widely practiced. Because of Western culture's emphasis on achievement, it is imperative to record such achievements in résumés and record books and to publicize them in press releases and newspaper reports. Humility does not accord well with the popular wisdom that "winning isn't everything, it's the only thing!" (Bruce J. Malina)

Wengst, Klaus. 1988. *Humility: Solidarity of the Humiliated: The Transformation of an Attitude and Its Social Relevance in Graeco-Roman, Old Testament-Jewish, and Early Christian Tradition.* Philadelphia: Fortress.

HYPOCRISY—SEE EQUIVOCATION

IDEALISM (THE PRACTICE OF SAYING "YES" BUT NEGLECTING TO ACT ACCORDINGLY)—SEE EQUIVOCATION

INDIVIDUALISM—SEE DYADISM; GROUP ORIENTATION

INTROSPECTION/LACK OF INTROSPECTION—SEE AUTHORITARIANISM

JEALOUSY—SEE ZEAL/JEALOUSY

JUSTICE—SEE PATRONAGE

LAW-MINDEDNESS—SEE TORAH ORIENTATION

Likability

The God of the Bible likes his creatures when they live up to his expectations that they all be saved (1 Tim 2:4). He especially likes the Son who proclaims that he came to do God's will (Heb 10:7, 9) and who affirms that he always does what the Father likes (John 8:29). Jesus did not seek to please himself (Rom 15:3). Among those whom God likes are: the just when they act according to his inspirations by doing what is within their power for their fellow believers (Heb 10:38; 2 Cor 8:12) and those who fear him and obey his commandments (Acts 10:35; 1 John 3:22). But God does not like those who live in the flesh (Rom 8:8) and those who do not love truth (2 Thess 2:12).

This picture of the God with strong likes and dislikes becomes the criterion for what believers should like and dislike, rather than allowing one's personal bent to determine the standard. It flows from their sense of being part of God's army (2 Tim 2:4), members of a group that walks by faith (2 Cor 5:7), chosen by God to enjoy the blessings of salvation (2 Cor 6:2). The strong should refrain from doing what they like when it hinders the salvation of weak members of the community (Rom 15:1–2). Being likable is an attitude controlled by a dualistic view of reality. Each person is under the eye of God who judges the heart to reward the good and punish sinners. This belief prevents members from acting merely to satisfy human desires.

Thus, Paul likes even his weaknesses and sufferings because they are for the cause of Christ and gain him God's strength (2 Cor 12:10). His only ambition is to be liked by God (2 Cor 5:9). From this perspective he warns community members about the responsibilities of the married state. They can prove an obstacle to being liked by God because the married are pressured to do what their partners like (1 Cor 7:32–34). That kind of conduct is characteristic of slaves (Col 3:22).

This context accounts for paradoxical statements in Paul. At one time he says that he does not do what people like (Gal 1:10; 1 Thess 2:4), and yet he boasts that he does what others like (1 Cor 10:33) where he refers to doing everything he thinks will advance their salvation. It is in this spirit that the faithful of Macedonia and Achaia contribute to Paul's collection for the poor Christians of Jerusalem (Rom 15:26–27). By contrast, Jesus experiences the fate of a prophet in not being likable to the people of his home town (Luke 4:24). They are typical examples of sinners who like themselves, that is, who yield to their fleshy desires.

Americans typically find these biblical norms of likability foreign to their taste and prefer a developmental stance of experimentation. They try to expand the arena of their likes by pursuing new experiences. Personal preferences provide norms for using one's resources and time to cultivate persons and things that provide personal satisfaction. The cultural preference of "taking care of Number One" has greater weight in United States culture than the traditional expression of "the will of God," to love God above all else. (†James M. Reese)

Antoun, Richard T. 1972. *Arab Village: A Social Structural Study of a Transjordanian Peasant Community*. Bloomington: Indiana University Press.

Eickleman, Dale F. 1981. "Personal and Family Relationships." In *The Middle East: An Anthropological Approach*. Pp. 105–34. Englewood Cliffs, N.J.: Prentice Hall.

LIMITED GOOD

"Limited good" is a social construct, that is, a product of human imagination and reasoning, which views the world as a zero-sum game. Residents of modern industrial countries tend to think of an "expanding" economy that has access to unlimited reserves of minerals and power; this modern economy preaches that all workers can expect an ever-rising standard of living. Nothing could be more foreign to the thinking of the peasants of the ancient world. As the value map on page xxv of the Introduction to this book indicates, ancient peasants perceived themselves as subject to "nature," not its master. Their economy was that of a heavily taxed agricultural peasantry who could not gain a better lifestyle since they lived in a patron-client relationship with those who controlled access to limited resources and power. Moreover, one of the distinctive elements of the peasant's outlook on life was the perception that all the good things of this world—beauty, health, wealth, land, and even reputation—existed in very limited supply. This limited supply must be divided among all the inhabitants of the village, region or city, since the total supply will not increase.

Anthropologist George Foster, who articulated this perspective, succinctly defines "limited good" as follows:

> By "Image of Limited Good" I mean that broad areas of peasant behavior are patterned in such a fashion as to suggest that peasants view their social, economic, and natural universes—their total environment—as one in which all of the desired things in life such as land, wealth, health, friendship and love, manliness and honor, respect and status, power and influence, security and safety, exist in finite quantity and are always in short supply, as far as the peasant is concerned. Not only do these and all other "good things" exist in finite and limited quantities, but in addition there is no way directly within peasant power to increase the available quantities (1965, 296).

What are the likely outcomes if one perceives the world in this fashion? Drawing on extensive cross-cultural data, Foster links the "image of limited good" with the pervasive envy he finds in peasant societies (see ENVY and ZEAL/JEALOUSY). He spells out the behavioral implications of this perception, noting that "any advantage achieved by one individual or family is seen as a loss to others, and the person who makes what the Western world lauds as 'progress' is viewed as a threat to the stability of the entire community" (1972, 169). Why? If the supply of good things is radically limited, the gain by one person must come through loss by another.

Several things tend to occur when people perceive the world from this point of view: first, they will be reluctant to advance beyond their peers because of the sanctions they know will be leveled against them; and second, the one who is seen or known to acquire more becomes much more vulnerable to the envy of his neighbors (Foster 1972, 169). Thus, any increase of goods which are perceived to exist only in a limited supply means that someone in the village or neighborhood is losing out. Hence one would expect some process of social control to be operative, both to prevent gain at the expense of others and to level the situation back to the status quo if gain has occurred.

What does this look like in the ancient world and the world of the Bible? The bulk of the examples we will examine all have to do with that most precious of goods in antiquity, honor (see **HONOR/SHAME**). But if the principle is valid in this regard, it will be true of other goods in society. The clearest example of this perspective is found in a fragment of the pre-Socratic philosophers: "People do not find it pleasant to give honor to someone else, for they suppose that they themselves are being deprived of something" (Anonymous Iamblici in H. Diels, ed., 1957. *Die Fragmente der Vorsokratiker.* 2.400. Hamburg: Rowohlt.). Centuries later Plutarch describes the discomfort of a person hearing a lecture, who perceives the success of the speaker as his own loss of reputation: "As though commendation were money, he feels that he is robbing himself of every bit that he bestows on another" (*On Listening to Lectures* 44B). Plutarch's contemporary, Josephus, tells of his rival's envy at Josephus's success. The rival seeks to persuade Galilee "to abandon their allegiance to [Josephus] and go over to him, asserting that they would find him a better general than [Josephus] was" (Josephus, *Life* 122–123). Josephus explains the reason for the rival's animosity: the rival believed "that [Josephus's] success involved his own ruin." In another place, Plutarch seems to be describing the hostile reaction that sets in when people see others gaining: ". . . men attack other kinds of eminence and themselves lay claim to good character, good birth, and honor, as though they were depriving themselves of so much of these as they grant to others" (*Old Men in Public Affairs* 787D). Finally, Philo of Alexandria caricatured the Egyptians as chronically envious, which is grounded in their perception of limited good: "But jealousy is part of the Egyptian nature, and the citizens were bursting with envy and considered that any good luck to others was misfortune to themselves" (*Flaccus* 29).

Hence, it is perfectly obvious why the disciples of the Baptizer are so distressed to learn of Jesus' success and growing fame; they perceive that they and their master are losing as a result (John 3:26). The response of the Baptizer acknowledges that their analysis of the situation is correct, but he himself does not react in envy. The Baptizer accepts the fact that Jesus' gain is his loss: "He must increase, but I must decrease" (John 3:30); since he is only the friend of the bridegroom, it is his role to see to the honor and happiness of Jesus. Similarly, the Pharisees and the Jewish council interpreted Jesus' success as their own loss: "This man performs many signs. If we let him go on thus, every one will believe in him, and the Romans will come and destroy . . . our holy place" (John 11:47–48). Unlike the Baptizer, they resent their loss. They plot to restore equilibrium to the social situation by killing Jesus.

Thus far we have viewed the image of limited good as it applies to the realm of mortals. There is a very interesting body of data which views the affairs and fortunes of God and the gods from the same perspective of limited good. Philo, the apostle of monotheism, explains that when polytheism expanded, the honor due the only God was diminished as other gods gained in reputation: "God's honor is set at naught by those who deify the mortal" (*Drunkenness* 110). In another place, Philo argues that the Roman emperor Gaius was increasingly demanding honor and respect on earth, which constituted a threat to the sovereignty of the Jewish deity: "You deem God worthy of nothing in our world here below, no country, no city, but even this tiny area hallowed for Him and sanctified by oracles and divine messages you propose to take away, so that in the circumference of this great earth no trace or reminder should be left of the reverence and honor due to the truly existing veritable God" (*Embassy* 347). Thus Gaius' increase in worldly power comes at the expense of the Deity. The clearest evidence of this limited good perspective is found in the words of God to Gideon when he summons him to battle. The Deity will allow Gideon but a few hundred soldiers to fight and defeat the enemy. If a greater army were used it would claim victory was the result of its own strength and size and not of the power of God: "The Lord said to Gideon, The people with you are too many for me to give the Midianites into their hand, lest Israel vaunt themselves against me, saying, 'My own hand has delivered me' " (Judg 7:2). If Gideon increases in honor, it will be at God's expense.

In contrast, the modern Western world believes in limitless good. While the ancients believed "there is no more where this came from," the modern Western world believes "there is always more where this came from." Thus, to surpass the honor or reputation of a renowed person, all one needs is a better publicity agent and increased exposure. This takes nothing away from the reputation of the other. That reputation is not diminished when it is surpassed by the fame or honor of another. (Jerome H. Neyrey)

Cohen, David. 1991. *Law, Sexuality, and Society: The Enforcement of Morals in Classical Athens.* Cambridge: Cambridge University Press. Pp. 183–98.

_____. 1995. *Law, Violence and Community in Classical Athens.* Cambridge: Cambridge University Press. Pp. 63–70.

Foster, George M. 1965. "Peasant Society and the Image of Limited Good." *American Anthropologist* 67:293–315.

_____. 1972. "The Anatomy of Envy: A Study in Symbolic Behavior." *Current Anthropology* 13:165–86.

Kennedy, John G. 1966. "Peasant Society and the Image of 'Limited Good': A Critique." *American Anthropologist* 68:1212–25.

Malina, Bruce J. 1993. *The New Testament World: Insights from Cultural Anthropology.* Rev. ed. Louisville, Ky.: Westminster John Knox.

Neyrey, Jerome H. 1993. *2 Peter, Jude.* Anchor Bible 37C. New York: Doubleday.

Piker, Steven. 1966. "The Image of 'Limited Good': Comments on an Exercise in Description and Interpretation." *American Anthropologist* 68:1202–11.

LOVE

This is the value of group attachment and group bonding (see **GROUP ORIENTATION**). It may or may not be coupled with feelings of affection. Such group attachment and group bonding are one type of social glue that keeps groups together (see **FAITH/FAITHFULNESS**; the value Love is not to be confused with Steadfast Love, for which see **GRACE/FAVOR**). Thus, to love someone is to be attached and bonded to the person: "to love the LORD your God . . . and to cleave to him" (Josh 22:5); "If I am still alive, show me the loyal love of the LORD . . ." (1 Sam 20:14); "Solomon clung to these (his foreign wives) in love" (1 Kgs 11:2); "Because he cleaves to me in love, I will deliver him" (Ps 91:14). To love wisdom, for example, is to adhere to and not forsake it (Prov 1:20–23; 4:6). Attachment to a female is often simply abiding sexual attraction (2 Sam 13:4; Ezek 16:8; 23:17; Hos 3:1); yet to truly love one's wife is to be detached from ("to leave") father and mother and "to cleave" or "to be joined" to her (Gen 2:24; Mark 10:7; Matt 19:5), even while continuing to live with father and mother as is customary for men in Mediterranean culture. Women normally marry out of their families (see Ezek 44:25; Mic 7:6; Matt 10:35; Luke 12:53).

One can be attached to food (Gen 27:4), or to behavior such as lying (Ps 52:3–4), or to abstract values such as righteousness and justice (Ps 33:5), truth and peace (Zech 8:19), or God's rescue (Ps 40:16), or even to God's revelation, the Torah (Ps 119 passim) and wisdom (Prov 5:19; 8:17, 21). Jesus' opponents are attached to praying in public view (Matt 6:5), to the best seats and places of honor (Matt 23:6), to being saluted (Luke 11:43) as they dress in long robes (Luke 20:46).

Yet normally attachment is to persons, e.g., a son (Gen 22:2); a future wife (Gen 29:20); a wife (Gen 29:32); a neighbor, defined as "sons of your own people" (Lev 19:18) and resident aliens (Lev 19:34); "the house in which [God] dwells" (Ps 26:8, NAB); the future king (1 Sam 18:22); the Lord your God (Deut 6:5; 11:1); the name (person) of God (Ps 5:11). Jesus likewise insists on loving God above all as in Deut 6:5 (Mark 12:30–31; Matt 22:37; Luke 10:27; see also Jas 1:12; 2:5; 1 Pet 1:8); and one must love one's neighbor as well (Matt 19:19; 22:39).

In the Johannine literature, this value of attachment becomes a constant theme: God was so attached to human society, i.e., the world, that he sent his only Son (John 3:16) whom he likewise loves (John 17:24–26). Israel is to be attached to God (John 5:42), an attachment that would be apparent if only it were attached to Jesus: "If God were your Father you would love me" (John 8:42). Jesus' disciples are to love, i.e., be attached to, him (John 14:15, 21, 23, 24 and 21:15–17).

Paul too underscores "God's love" (Rom 5:5, 8; 8:39). Yet he has little about love of "neighbor" as Matthew and Luke. Rather Paul's concern, like that of John, was the larger problem of getting those who joined their Christian groups to become attached to each other, their new "neighbors." Both John (13:34–35; 15:12–13, 17) and Paul (Rom 12:10; 13:8–10; 14:15; 1 Cor 13; Eph 4:15; Col 1:4; 1 Thess 4:9–10; 2 Thess 1:3) repeatedly insist on mutual love.

Often such a contrast is made between what one loves and what one hates that not to love is to hate and vice-versa, with no middle ground (see **EMOTION/ DEMONSTRATION OF FEELINGS**). "You only hate me, you do not love me" (Judg 14:16). "Then Amnon hated her with very great hatred; so that the hatred with which he hated her was greater than the love with which he had loved her" (2 Sam 13:15). "You love those who hate you

and hate those who love you" (2 Sam 19:6). To "love
those who hate the LORD" is to help the wicked (2 Chron
19:2). "I the LORD love justice, I hate robbery and wrong"
(Isa 61:8). "There I began to hate them. . . . I will love
them no more" (Hos 9:15). "Hate evil, and love good"
(Amos 5:15); "You who hate the good and love the evil"
(Mic 3:2). If love is attachment, hate is dis-attachment or
detachment, a withdrawal of the sense of being bonded.
To love and to hate mark the either/or, on/off switches
of social connectedness.

Thus, one cannot serve two masters; it is either God
or greed one must serve (Matt 6:24//Luke 16:13). While
Matthew defines enemy as "those who persecute you"
(Matt 5:44), Luke defines enemy as "those who hate you"
(Luke 6:27). "To love one's enemy," then is to act with
social attachment toward those with whom one is disat-
tached. Even "neighbor" includes the enemy, not just
one's fellow ethnics. This is illustrated in the parable of
the Good Samaritan (Luke 10:29–37).

Since Mediterranean societies, in their value preferences, stress being over doing (see Introduction), the normal difficulty with "loving" God or other persons is that
no activity or doing is involved. Hence, the constant
need to motivate Mediterranean persons to action. And
hence, the theme of "loving and doing": God shows his
steadfast love to those "who love me and keep my commandments" (Exod 20:6; Deut 5:10; 7:9; Josh 22:5; 1 Kgs
8:23, etc.). "You shall therefore love the LORD your God,
and keep his charge, his statutes, his ordinances, and his
commandments always" (Deut 11:1). The same theme is
found in the story of Jesus. After teaching the new righteousness in Matthew's Sermon on the Mount, Jesus con-
cludes with a whole section on doing it (Matt 7:13–27).
John in turn has the theme: "If you love me, you will
keep my commandments" (John 14:15; 15:10). And after
describing love in 1 Corinthians 13 and concluding that
"group attachment" is the greatest of these, Paul con-
cludes: "Make love your aim!" (1 Cor 14:1).

In Western culture generally speaking, love is an affect of the heart which is usually experienced individualistically toward another or other individuals. It does not necessarily involve attachment. In fact, given the strong sense of individualism that permeates this culture, attachment and especially group attachment is not a high priority. In this culture, individuals join groups but only on the basis of an implied contract. One remains with the group only as long as it meets personal interests. When that fails, it is time to leave the group. No stronger attachment than this is established between the individual and the group. (Bruce J. Malina)

Eisenstadt, Shlomo N., and Louis Roniger. 1984. *Patrons, Clients and Friends: Interpersonal Relations and the Structure of Trust in Society.* Cambridge: Cambridge University Press.

Hatfield, Elaine, and Richard Rapson. 1993. "Love and Attachment Processes." In *Handbook of Emotions.* Ed. Michael Lewis and Jeannette M. Haviland. Pp. 605–16. New York: Guilford.

LOYALTY—SEE FAITH/FAITHFULNESS

MANLINESS—SEE DRAMATIC ORIENTATION; PARENTING; AUTHORITARIANISM

MEDIATOR—SEE POWER

MEEKNESS

This is the value of humility when coupled with gentleness or non-violence (see HUMILITY). This gentleness or non-violence presupposes that one can readily obtain and use force. It differs from pacifism in that non-violence renounces force in order to communicate something to others (e.g., that the opponent is unworthy, cowardly, too weak; that non-retaliation reflects obedience to or trust in God, etc.), while pacifism renounces force because it will only harm the person using it (e.g., bad karma, fear of punishment now or in the hereafter, etc.). The meek person not only does not threaten or challenge others but accepts others openly and confidently. For example, Moses is considered the meek person, par excellence (Num 12:3). Since for Matthew, Jesus is a prophet, a new Moses, we find him as teacher to be meek and humble of heart (Matt 11:29). This aspect of Jesus' behavior is underscored again in the scene of Jesus' arrest; Matthew is the only evangelist to have Jesus renounce power to "fulfill the scriptures," although such power was available to him: "Then Jesus said to him, 'Put your sword back into its place; for all who take the sword will perish by the sword. Do you think that I cannot appeal to my Father, and he will at once send me more than twelve legions of angels? But how then should the scriptures be fulfilled, that it must be so?' " (Matt 26:52–54). Paul, too, knows of "the meekness and gentleness of Christ" (2 Cor 10:1).

In Psalm 37 the meek are persons whose lands have been taken away by greedy and vicious fellow Israelites; the meek protest this loss yet do not take up arms but look to God to right the wrong. After all, the land in question is God's land, the Holy Land. The expected outcome: "But the meek shall possess the land, and delight themselves in abundant prosperity" (Ps 37:11; cf. Ps 10:17; for the same idea see also Isa 11:4; 29:19). Again in Matthew we find Jesus taking up this promise of the Psalmist: "Blessed are the meek, for they shall inherit the (holy) land" (Matt 5:5, NAB). Early Christians were urged to espouse such meekness in the face of injustice (Eph 4:2; Col 3:12; Jas 1:21; 3:13).

Meekness is not highly prized in Western culture. Popular wisdom teaches: "If you don't blow your own horn, nobody else will!" In other words, in the West, the meek will be left in the dust. This is a natural consequence of the West's primary value orientation toward individualism and achievement. (Bruce J. Malina)

Hauck, F., and S. Schulz. 1968. "praüs, praütes." *Theological Dictionary of the New Testament* 6:645–51.

Romilly, Jacqueline de. 1979. *La douceur dans la pensée grecque.* Paris: Belles Lettres.
Winkler, Klaus. 1955. "clementia." *Realencyklopedie für Antike und Christentum* 3:206–31.

MERCY—SEE GRACE/FAVOR; GRATITUDE; STEADFAST LOVE

MIRTH

This cognitive experience produces exuberance of spirit which manifests itself externally in physical expressions, such as smiling or laughter. Mirth can be subdivided into such categories as laughter, humor, puns, hyperbole, irony, ridicule and satire. As such, mirth is a secondary or means value. Persons skilled in the use of puns, hyperbole, humor and the like can easily enhance their honor rating among peers and outsiders, for such mastery of language is certainly an acquired or achieved competence or skill.

Mirth is essentially social in character. It shows that one is involved emotionally in a social situation. A joke combines pleasure and cognitive experience, and its effect depends in large measure upon the intellectual abilities of the reader or hearer.

Plato (c. 429–327 BCE) took a negative view of mirth and thought that it was destructive of wisdom, religion, art, and morals:

> Philebos says that to all living beings enjoyment (*to chairein*) and pleasure (*hedonen*) and gaiety (*terpsin*) and whatever accords with that sort of thing are a good; whereas our contention is that not these but wisdom and thought and memory and their kindred, right opinion and true reasoning, are better and more excellent than pleasure . . . (*Philebos* 1).

This was neither a semitic approach nor a modern one. Nowadays most psychologists and social scientists would see the positive side of mirth.

Very often mirth is closely associated with incongruity, e.g., when Jesus speaks of placing a lamp under a bushel (Matt 5:15) or someone having a plank (*dokos*) in his eye (Matt 7:3). It is the incongruity, often absurdity, or other rhetorical techniques, which initiate the mirth.

The occasions for the manifestation of mirth include community celebrations, such as weddings, circumcision ceremonies, celebration of victory, and feasting in general. The outward manifestations of mirth on these occasions are: the cleansing of the body, often with anointing; donning of clean or new clothes; singing and dancing; and clapping of hands with an important stress on rhythm. These assist in creating bonding or solidarity within a community and can also result in psychic liberation, creativity, and reconciliation.

However, mirth may also arise in stressful, ambiguous, or threatening circumstances, and on these occasions it serves to relieve tension. A critic of social or religious conditions (often identified with the role of prophet in the NT) may also use mirth to convey his/her message, and in doing so s/he has recourse to various rhetorical devices, such as hyperbole, irony, etc. Thus, John the Baptist used the image of snakes fleeing from a forest or field fire in his trenchant criticism of certain groups of scribes and Pharisees. He calls them a generation of vipers (Matt 3:7): the metaphor is all the more pungent because reptiles were unclean animals and Pharisees were known for their strict observance of the purity laws. Jesus ridicules the lawyers and Pharisees for traversing land and sea to make one convert (Matt 23:15) and "straining out a gnat and swallowing a camel" (Matt 23:24). Here mirth attempts to reduce the pomposities of authoritative figures.

Mirth is an expression of communal joy, and thus one often finds the Greek prefix *syn* with verbs of rejoicing (Luke 5:15; Luke 1:58). Mirth is expressed in a joke or pun which may contain an important truth. For example in Matthew 3:9 and 21:42 we find a play on the words "stones" and "sons" because the Hebrew consonants of both words are identical (*'bn*): the figure of speech used here is called *parechesis* (the sounding of one word beside another).

Mirth results in the solidarity of the community, but it can also polarize the community; e.g., in Acts 17:32 some of the crowd reacted to Paul's speech by mockery (*chleuazō*) but others were ready to hear the apostle again. Mirth can release surplus energy in various ways. It can manifest itself as "glee" in malicious mirth, e.g., over the defeat of an enemy. It can also serve a cathartic effect for aggressive feelings and is a mode of expressing conflict which enables participants to suspend temporarily the ordinary rules of conduct. It is a safe violation of social and religious taboos and a cover for forbidden conduct, wishes, and criticism. This is especially exemplified in status reversal, a ceremony implemented in many cultures. It may be seen in the mockery of Jesus (Matt 27:27–31; Mark 15:16–20; John 19:2–3). V. W. Turner has described this mirth as "white laughter."

Mirth and foolery are important phenomena in society because they cross the boundaries of the sacred and profane. Sexuality and sacredness are potentially destructive but also creative in society and thus both form a basis of mirth and satire.

The Bible, especially the OT, predicates mirth of God (e.g., Ps 2:4; 37:13; 52:6; 59:8). However, the study of mirth in English or other translations of the Bible is difficult for the following reasons. A translation (even from oral to written tradition) cannot adequately express a play on words and other rhetorical devices designed to produce mirth in the audience. Mirth varies according to the culture. But, most importantly, in the Bible the lack of nonverbal communication makes the presence of mirth in a text difficult to discern for modern readers. For example, Jesus' use of non-verbal communication in his teaching now collected in the Sermon on the Mount (Matt 5–7) may have added considerably to the effect of his teaching. It is sometimes difficult to know whether Jesus is joking, although his use of hyperbole is a useful hint that he is.

Jesus' parables are a prime example of a teaching method which contains an important element of incongruity which must have caused hilarity in his audience and increased the persuasiveness of his teaching, e.g., a business person selling all that he has for one pearl (Matt 13:45–46) or a harvest which yields one hundred percent (Matt 13:1–9; see also **DRAMATIC ORIENTATION**).

Unbelievers in Jesus' *charismata* also indulged in mirth (*katangelein*) e.g., when he stated that the young girl was sleeping, not dead (Matt 9:24). In Luke 16:14 the Pharisees sneer at Jesus: the Greek word *ekmyktērizō* means "turning up one's nose."

The belief in the afterlife, especially when this includes an anticipation of the transformation of the body, is often expressed in the terms of feasting and merriment as well as more spiritual behavior, such as praising God (cf. Matt 8:11). An anticipatory eschatological mirth is experienced in the rites of initiation, particularly in the outpouring of the Spirit and in community prayer and meals, especially Eucharist: all of these events are characterized by joy (Acts 8:8; 13:52; 15:3). In these cases mirth presupposes a certain understanding of symbolic language. It may produce retrogression of the ego manifested by childlike innocence and play (e.g., in the practice of glossolalia). Innocent mirth is closely associated with the Holy Spirit. It is rare to find true mirth associated with the demonic.

Mirth in Western culture bears many similarities to mirth as manifest in these ancient Mediterranean texts. In the West, however, some people specialize in mirth mainly for purposes of entertainment. Comedians appear in films, on TV, in nightclubs, and in many other places in an effort to earn a living by making people laugh. While success in this regard is richly remunerative for the comedian, such success is never associated with honor as in the Mediterranean world. Here is a major contrast between the cultures of the United States and the ancient Mediterranean world, the contrast of key social institutions: economics for the U.S., but kinship for the Mediterranean people (see Introduction). (Josephine Massyngbaerde Ford)

Ruch, Willibald. 1993. "Exhilaration and Humor." In *Handbook of Emotions.* Ed. Michael Lewis and Jeannette M. Haviland. Pp. 605–616. New York: Guilford.

MOUTH-EARS—SEE COMMUNICATIVENESS; DECEPTION; EQUIVOCATION

NUDITY

The Hebrew Scriptures relentlessly censure nudity (but this was hardly the case in Greece [Thucydides I.vi.4–6]). Although God presumably made Adam and Eve naked, they became aware of it with the shame of being discovered as sinners (Gen 2:25). God's first act of mercy to them was to cover them with garments of skin (Gen 3:21). Thus, nudity became inextricably linked with sin and "shame"; it was unacceptable in God's presence. Analogously, great concern was shown for the dress of the priest who offered sacrifice, first that he not have to ascend stairs lest his nude loins be revealed in sacred space (Exod 20:26), and then that he wear breeches to prevent accidental exposure (Exod 28:42). Thus, nudity was linked with issues of purity and pollution in myth and practice. As Genesis and Exodus indicate, if we would understand the cultural perspective of the ancient Jews toward nudity, we must see the issue through the eyes of two complementary models, namely, honor/shame and purity/pollution.

Nudity and Shame: Cultural attitudes toward women in ancient Judaism directed that they be defensive of their chastity. This concern was expressed by the expectation that women would be oriented toward the private space of the house, which would keep them from public areas where their virtue might be compromised. Such concern for female virtue was also realized in the expectation that women's bodies be clothed as fully as possible, with the result that loss of clothing was synonymous with loss of virtue. Public nudity inevitably meant "shame" for them, for their chastity was compromised: their physical body was no longer exclusively the property of their husbands (see Plutarch, *In Praise of Women*, 258E). Hence, we read of "shame" in conjunction with a woman's "nakedness." "Your *nakedness* shall be uncovered, and your *shame* shall be seen" (Isa 47:3; see Lev 20:17; 1 Sam 20:30; Ezek 16:36; Lam 1:8; Mic 1:11; Rev 3:18).

Even in regard to men we find a comparable pattern. Just as the woman's sexual organs are occasionally called her "shame" (*Jub* 3:21), so also the penis is Adam's "shame," in phrases such as "he covered his shame . . . to cover his shame" (*Jub* 3:27, 30). Paul too spoke of the "shameful" parts of the body, meaning the sexual organs (1 Cor 12:23). Although in Jewish propaganda a man's circumcised penis was called his "glory" (Gal 6:13; Phil 3:19), he may be shamed if he is stripped of his clothes by an aggressor and thus his male member is displayed, as we find on the stele of Sargon, the Megiddo ivory, and certain Egyptian drawings from Karnak (see Acts 19:16).

This kind of shame occurs as well by the involuntary exposing of the naked buttocks of exiles and captives. Isaiah describes just such a shameful parade of naked captives: ". . . so shall the king of Assyria lead away the Egyptians captives and the Ethiopians exiles, . . . naked and barefoot, with buttocks uncovered" (Isa 20:4; see Deut 28:48). On one occasion David's servants were shamefully treated by Hanun, king of the Ammonites, who "shaved off half the beard of each, and cut off their garments in the middle, at their hips" (2 Sam 10:4; 1 Chron 19:4). The higher the social ranking of the naked captive, the greater the shame (Job 12:17, 19).

Comparable shame might occur during judicial punishment when prisoners were stripped naked (see *Esther Rabbah* 3.14). An adulterous woman, even Israel, was punished in this manner (Isa 32:11; Ezek 23:10, 26–30;

Hos 2:3, 10). In Nahum 3:5 we read the classic example of this: I "will lift up your skirts over your face; and I will let nations look on your nakedness and kingdoms on your shame." Prisoners who were stripped naked before scourging and death suffered as much from the shame of involuntary nakedness as from the lash (4 *Macc* 6:2; Matt 27:28, 31).

One is shamed, then, when involuntarily stripped naked by another. Yet a person may also be shamed if someone aggressively exposes either his penis or buttocks to him. Such a display is a claim of power and superiority, for masculine strength is symbolized by the penis. For example, Josephus reports that a Roman soldier on the wall above the Jerusalem temple lifted his tunic and exposed his backside to those below in the temple, accompanying this with an appropriate noise; this shamed the Jews and provoked a riot (Josephus, *War* 2.224). Similarly, at Qumran a censure was placed on a man who allowed "'the hand' (i.e., the penis) to protrude from beneath the garment . . . and reveal his nakedness" (1QS 7:13–14). This parallels the concern of the priests not to expose their loins in the presence of the Holy One (for God would be shamed by being exposed to nakedness of this sort); priests would be thereby challenging God's power and supremacy. In this light we evaluate the concern of Paul to put on a "heavenly tent" or garment at death, so that he may "not be found naked" in the presence of the honorable God (2 Cor 5:1–4, author's trans.).

Nudity and Purity/Pollution: Purity refers to the perception of things, persons, etc. being "in place" according to the value system of a given culture. And pollution refers to what is "out of place." Nudity was always "out of place" in the presence of the holy God: "One must not stand nude in the presence of the Divine Name" (*b. Shab.*, 120b; yet 1 Sam 19:24; 2 Sam 6:20). Even the accidental exposure of a priest's groin or buttocks was judged to be "out of place" in the worship of God (Exod 20:26), so nudity was not just shameful but unclean (see Aulus Gellius, *Attic Nights* X.15.19–20; Plutarch, *Roman Questions* 274A–B). As Torah extended purity concerns to daily life, Jews entering a privy were told not to face east or west when stripping for the toilet, for this is the axis of the Holy of Holies in the temple and it would be shaming God to expose one's buttocks or penis in that direction: "Let no man stand naked facing the chamber of the Holy of Holies. If one enters a privy, let him turn his face neither to the east nor to the west, but sideways. Nor should he uncover himself standing up, but sitting down" (*'Abot de Rabbi Nathan* 40; see *b. Ber.* 62a). We find rules for the Essenes at Qumran that they must not expose their male members when they defecate in the fields; after digging a hole, they "wrap their mantle about them, that they may not offend the rays of the deity, [and] sit above it" (Josephus, *War* 2.148–149). Given the fact that nudity is shameful, it is "out of place" especially in the sight of God. Comparably, on the great day of the Lord, they are "blessed" who "have kept their garments that they may not be naked and be seen exposed" (Rev 16:15).

For second-temple Jews, the physical body was regulated with the same systematic concern for order as the temple and the body politic. This meant concern for precise classification: (a) concern over exact role and status and (b) regulation of who's "in" or "out." Whenever role and status become blurred or ambiguous, the orderly system is threatened; whatever enters and leaves is the object of great scrutiny, for such things belong to the realm of the unclean. On the level of the physical body, these social controls are expressed in concern over nudity, either the absence of clear boundaries, the loss of distinguishing marks of status, or the "uncovering of nakedness" in prohibited sexual unions and marriages.

Purity has to do with the making and maintenance of boundaries. As a people "set apart," Jews defined themselves by territorial, psychological, and physiological boundaries; certain marriages were forbidden and certain foods proscribed. Moreover, to protect the core of their political-religious identity, they "built a fence around Torah." (This term describes the rabbinic practice of urging believers to observe a little more than was required in order to make certain that the commandment would be in no danger of being violated by even an unintentional omission.)

Clothing is also such a boundary for the physical body, which is a microcosm of the social system. Nudity means the complete absence of boundaries; the body is accessible to any and every one, thus destroying its exclusivity as something "set apart." Boundaries must be maintained, and so nudity is unclean.

One's place in society was signaled by one's clothing; observant Jews wore long tassels and broad phylacteries to signal their devotion to Torah (Matt 23:5). Priests wore specific articles of clothing for liturgical actions: "The High Priest ministers in eight pieces of raiment, and common priest in four—in tunic, drawers, turban and girdle. To these the High Priest adds the breastplate, the apron, the upper garment and the frontlet" (m. Yoma 7:5). Hellenized Jews wore the "Greek hat" (2 Macc 4:12) or wreathes of ivy (6:7). And so clothing begets clarity, and clarity denotes purity. But when people are naked, all such defining marks vanish, and one's identity, role, and status become ambiguous. Thus, disorder occurs because the physical body is no longer appropriately marked to indicate its classification according to the social system. Nudity erases social clues and so is unclean (see Luke 10:30).

Symbolic of its exclusivity, Jewish life strictly governed the bodily orifices such as the mouth against the entrance of unclean foods (see Mark 7:15; Acts 10:14). Comparably, we find rules concerning the sexual orifice which proscribe certain sexual relationships and marriages as "unclean." These prohibited crossings of the sexual orifice are called the "uncovering the nakedness of . . ." (Lev 18:6–18; 20:11, 17–21; see 1 Cor 5:1–2; 1 Thess

4:3–7). Maintenance of identity was symbolized by kosher marriages as well as kosher foods.

Jewish purity concerns were severely tested by the advent of Hellenistic customs into Israel. As part of his Hellenization of Jerusalem, Antiochus erected a gymnasium there (1 Macc 1:14; 2 Macc 4:9–15; Josephus, *Antiquities* 12.240–241), a form of school for the training of youths. It was also the place where men engaged in athletic exercises in the nude. Protesting against places such as gymnasia and baths, the book of *Jubilees* maintained that it is prescribed on heavenly tablets that "they should cover their shame, and should not uncover themselves as the Gentiles uncover themselves" (3:31). Given the cultural perceptions noted above, nudity would be shameful enough, but it led to attempts to remove the marks of circumcision, so evidently visible when naked (1 Macc 1:15). Thus, nudity at gymnasia and baths led to a further rejection of formal Jewish customs such as circumcision, and so became doubly polluting. Yet we read of games celebrated at Jerusalem, first by Antiochus (2 Macc 6:7) and then by Herod (Josephus, *Antiquities* 15.268–270), as well as games at Tyre and Caesarea.

Nudity in the Western world carries different meanings which have also changed over the course of time. Earlier in U.S. history under Puritan influence, attitudes toward nudity reflected biblical attitudes in general, though obviously without the context of the core values of honor and shame. Gradually these views were relaxed and even changed to the point that at the present time, (public) nudity is often viewed as a legitimate and protected constitutional right within the category of free speech (see Introduction). (Jerome H. Neyrey)

Beidelman, T. O. 1968. "Some Nuer Notions of Nakedness, Nudity, and Sexuality." *Africa* 38:113–31.

Bonfante, Larissa. 1989. "Nudity as a Costume in Classical Art." *American Journal of Archeology* 93:543–70.

Smith, Jonathan Z. 1978. "Garments of Shame." In *Map Is Not Territory: Studies in the History of Religions.* Pp. 1–23. Leiden: Brill.

Warren, H. C. 1933. "Social Nudity and the Body Taboo." *Psychological Review* 40:160–83.

OBEDIENCE (SUBMISSION)

This quality pervades the hierarchical universe created by God, who makes his will known by his law (Ps 119). In Mediterranean culture of past and present, those in subordinate positions should subject themselves or be subjected to authority above them. Even inanimate objects obey God's agents (Mark 4:41; Luke 17:6). It is the mark of a sinner not to obey (Rom 8:7). All those living under a government should obey the prevailing political authority (Titus 3:1), which is ordained by God, the author of all order (Rom 13:1).

Families mirror nature's hierarchical subjection: wives to husbands (Eph 5:22; Col 3:18; Titus 2:5; 1 Pet 3:1, 5); slaves to masters (Eph 6:5; Col 3:22; Titus 2:9; 1 Pet 2:18); children—including Jesus (Luke 2:51)—to parents (Eph 6:1; Col 3:20). Even in his adulthood, Jesus—like every other adult male in his culture—valued obedience to his Father's will enough to die for it (Phil 2:8; Heb 5:8; see also **PARENTING**). That obedience brought to humanity reconciliation with the Father who rules all (Rom 5:19; Heb 5:9).

The rule of obedience prevails in the community of believers (1 Cor 16:16). As apostle, Paul does not hesitate to require obedience from all members (2 Cor 2:9). Within special charismatic groups some form of obedience exists, as prophesying is subject to the prophetic group (1 Cor 14:32–33). At the same time this value of obedience is tempered by the new law of love so that members subject themselves to one another out of love for Christ (Eph 5:21). To him are subject not only elements of the church (Eph 5:24) but all things (Phil 3:21; Heb 2:8; 1 Cor 15:27–28).

Paul clearly believes that this multilevel obedience is a reflection of the wisdom and power of God who gives all persons their clearly defined role in his plan (Rom 13:5). God punishes those who do not remain in their status, which is also a basic Mediterranean cultural imperative (see HUMILITY; HONOR/SHAME). He rewards the humble because their obedient subjection to God is at the same time a rejection of the devil (Jas 4:5–7).

Modern Americans do not envision humans as fixed in a closed, static universe controlled by God and his agents. They have utmost confidence in the effectiveness of human initiative. Wives and husbands dialogue as equal partners to build community. Slavery has been eliminated. Children are encouraged to experiment and to exercise initiative in forging new lifestyles. The American dream believes in self-expression, education, and scientific research as keys that unlock human progress, not in submission to any form of authority. The kind of obedience that pervades all of life in the Bible occurs in the United States only in the military, health care, the corporate world, and some religious organizations. It is therefore a secondary value in the U.S., but a primary value in ancient Mediterranean culture. (†James M. Reese)

Malina, Bruce J. 1993. "Honor and Shame." In *Windows on the World of Jesus: Time Travel to Ancient Judea.* Pp. 1–19. Louisville, Ky.: Westminster John Knox.

Pilch, John J. 1993. " 'Beat His Ribs While He Is Young' (Sir 30:12): A Window on the Mediterranean World." *Biblical Theology Bulletin* 23:101–13.

ORDERING

Order as a value encompasses the entire range of cosmic and human relationships whereby one is embedded in family, society, culture, and universe. As a perceived mode of relating, it is right relationship, the opposite of chaos, which is disordered or carries no relationship. From the primeval chaos God brought forth order by separating light from darkness, sky from earth, land from water; only then could living creatures flourish (Gen 1:1–13). This notion of order as separating persists in Jewish ritual, e.g., the *Havdalah* (separation) by which the end of Sabbath is celebrated, and sacred time separated from the rest of the week. In this way humans participate in divine cosmic ordering and conquer chaos.

Ordering in human society includes time, place, and specifics of what one does and with whom. The ordering of time is most clearly demonstrated by the weekly cycle of times of prayer, especially the Sabbath for Jews and the first day of the week for Christians. Ordering of place governs notions of holiness (e.g., the temple) and cleanliness (e.g., personal hygiene, waste disposal). Ordering of behavior in a context of strictly-interpreted Jewish law determines, besides moral relationships, minute details of how one is to avoid ritual contamination by appropriate cleansing and storage of cooking and eating utensils, food preparation, and association only with those who will not cause defilement (see **PURITY**). Order is beauty.

Law in human society is simply the extension of the need for order into the realm of social behavior. It creates and forms a way of life that is in harmony with God's ordering of the world, which is the starting point and, in the ancient view, necessitates clear hierarchical arrangement of status. A well-ordered family is a microcosm of a well-ordered society (Eph 5:21–33; 1 Tim 3:4–5); a well-ordered society is a microcosm of God's well-ordered universe (Gen 1; Ps 8; Job 38).

Western post-Enlightenment cultures tend to begin at the opposite starting point, seeing law as the consensus arrangement whereby humans agree to order their behavior so as to live together in peace. Our notions of separation are more economically than chronologically or spatially based: what separates people from each other and determines modes and possibilities of behavior is financial status. Sacred time and space have very little meaning in American culture, though Super Bowl Sunday might serve as a good example of both. (Carolyn Osiek)

Bailey, Clinton. 1982. "Bedouin Religious Practices in the Sinai and Negev." *Anthropos* 77/1–2:65–88.

Cohen, Robert S. 1977. "Cosmic Order and Human Disorder." In *Cosmic Order and Human Disorder.* Ed. W. Yourgrau. Pp. 335–45. New York: Plenum.

Cohn, Robert L. 1980. *The Shape of Sacred Space: Four Biblical Studies.* Chico, Calif.: Scholars.

Douglas, Mary. 1966. *Purity and Danger: An Analysis of the Concepts of Pollution and Taboo.* London: Routledge & Kegan Paul.

Kearney, Michael. 1984. *World View.* Novato, Calif.: Chandler & Sharp.

Lenski, Gerhard. 1966. *Power and Privilege: A Theory of Social Stratification.* New York: McGraw Hill.

Neyrey, Jerome H. 1988. "Unclean, Common, Polluted, and Taboo: A Short Reading Guide." *Forum* 4/4:72–82.

_____. 1990. *Paul in Other Words: A Cultural Reading of His Letters.* Louisville, Ky.: Westminster John Knox. Pp. 21–74.

Neusner, Jacob. 1978. "History and Purity in First-Century Judaism." *History of Religions* 18:1–17.

Sack, Robert D. 1986. *Human Territoriality: Its Theory and History.* New York: Cambridge University Press.

Over-Assertion—see Dramatic Orientation

Pain—see Authoritarianism; Parenting

Parenting

This is a secondary value by which adults socialize their offspring in the core value of family, a kinship reality (see **Family-Centeredness**). It is intimately related to the core values of honor and shame, since kinship honor consists in loyalty to the family. Thus, the parenting process seeks to instill appropriate positive values in the offspring in order to strengthen group or family cohesion.

The cornerstone of the patriarchal and patrilineal social edifice is the father. Children are taught at a very early age to subordinate personal ego to the authority of the father and/or actual male head of the family. "If one aspires to the office of elder . . . he must manage his own household well, keeping his children submissive and respectful in every way" (1 Tim 3:2, 4, author's trans.). The children of an elder ought not to be open to the charge of being profligate or insubordinate (Titus 1:6).

Frequent and severe physical punishment is the means of instilling such obedience and subordination. Many proverbs repeat and affirm this as a key element of parenting: "He who spares the rod hates his son, but he who loves him is diligent to discipline him" (Prov 13:24) and "Do not withhold discipline from a child; if you beat him with a rod, he will not die" (Prov 23:13) are but two explicit examples (see also Prov 10:13; 12:1; 13:1; 15:5; 17:10; 19:18; 19:29; 22:15; 26:3; 29:15, 17; Sir 7:23; 30:1, 12). King David's record as a parent recounted in 2 Samuel—1 Kings is a stirring illustration of a parent who failed to discipline his children and reaped sad consequences.

Such harsh discipline pertains to adolescent boys, since infants and children remain under the mother's influence for the first seven to nine years and are pampered. "I am reminded of your sincere faith, a faith that dwelt first in your grandmother Lois and your mother Eunice . . ." (2 Tim 1:5). Mothers in this culture are also the ones who instill belief in the world of spirits. Notice in the New Testament that the majority of possession and exorcism reports concern men. Even in the maternal sphere, however, boys are pampered while girls are hastened toward womanhood. Boys are breast-fed twice as long as girls are, until long after they can speak. Hannah first weaned her son when he was old enough to remain at Shiloh and minister to the Lord with Eli the priest and his sons (1 Sam 1:21–28; 2:11).

Girls are seen as posing a life-long headache (Sir 42:9–14). Sirach advises fathers not to indulge them (7:24–25) and to keep a close watch on them. The girl is socialized early on to adopt the life-long female role: to be subordinate ("Let a woman learn in silence with all submissiveness," 1 Tim 2:11), to recognize that a woman is of little value ("from a woman sin had its beginning, and because of her we all die," Sir 25:24), and to remain always subservient to men ("Wives, be subject to your husbands, as to the Lord," Eph 5:22). Indeed, the destiny of women in general and particularly of those in the family

circle is to serve the men and obey them. That Jesus was
accompanied on his journeys by women "who provided
for him out of their means" (Luke 8:1–3) is a cultural
commonplace. Recall also Esther's obedience to her Uncle
Mordecai until Haman's threat developed and immobi-
lized Mordecai.

Clearly, the father is viewed as severe, stern, and
authoritarian (see **AUTHORITARIANISM**); the mother is
viewed as loving and compassionate (see **COMPASSION**).
Children respect and fear the father but love the mother
affectionately even after they are married. In the adult
years of their children, mothers continue to play a very
influential role, often promoting competitiveness and sib-
ling rivalry that proves to be an enduring source of conflict and division: recall Rebekah's meddling between
Jacob and Esau (Gen 27) or Bathsheba's machinations to
promote Solomon rather than the first-born to succeed
David as king (1 Kgs 1).

Boys are pampered from birth by all women-kin at
every opportunity. At puberty, the boy is moved from the
warm and loving world of the women into the harsh and
hierarchical world of the men. The shock is so great,
boys run back to the women but have to be redirected to
the men's world. The stern, severe, and authoritarian
ways of elder men, especially the father, leave a strong
impression on the young son. As the proverbs testify,
adolescent boys fourteen to sixteen years old are punished physically rather routinely for the purpose of inur-
ing them to physical pain. The authentic male in this
culture is one who can endure pain. It is highly significant that Jesus is reported to use the word "Abba"
(correctly translated "Father" and never "daddy"; see
PATRONAGE) in the gospels only once: during his agony in
the garden where he prays, "Abba, Father . . . remove
this cup from me; yet not what I will, but what thou
wilt" (Mark 14:36). Mark's report that Jesus did not speak
from the cross until after he had hung on it for six hours,
and then immediately after that he shrieked and died, is

highly plausible from a Mediterranean cultural perspective. The manner in which Jesus died was very manly, and the onlookers would be as impressed as was the pagan centurion (see **AUTHORITARIANISM**).

Given the U.S. cultural value preference for the future (see Introduction), all children, boys and girls, are considered to be the hope and promise of that future. They are socialized into that perspective and expected always to do better than their parents. At the same time, physical punishment of children is not only frowned upon but may subject parents and other adults to litigation and legal punishment for child abuse. In modern times, children of both sexes are considered to have equal and unlimited opportunities for all social goods. (John J. Pilch)

Barr, James. 1988. "Abba Isn't Daddy." *Journal of Theological Studies* 39:27–47.

Levinson, David. 1989. *Family Violence in Cross-Cultural Perspective.* Newbury Park, Calif.: Sage.

Levinson, David, and Martin J. Malone. 1980. *Toward Explaining Human Culture: A Critical Review of the Findings of Worldwide Cross-Cultural Research.* New Haven, Conn.: HRAF Press. Esp. ch. 17: "Cross-Cultural Variations in Child Rearing," and ch. 18: "Child Rearing, Adult Personality, and Expressive Systems."

Pilch, John J. 1989. "Your Abba is Not Your Daddy." *Modern Liturgy* 16 (March, #1): 26.

———. 1991. *Introducing the Cultural Context of the Old Testament.* Mahwah, N.J.: Paulist. "Session Four: Parenting (Discipline)."

———. 1993. " 'Beat His Ribs While He Is Young' (Sir 30:12): A Window on the Mediterranean World." *Biblical Theology Bulletin* 23:101–13.

———. 1995. "Death with Honor: The Mediterranean Style Death of Jesus in Mark." *Biblical Theology Bulletin* 25:65–70.

PATIENCE

The virtue of patience is highly esteemed in the Bible and the cultural world that produced it, for two principal reasons. The first is that patience bears so close a resemblance to resignation that distinctions between them virtually collapse (the classic example is Job

1:21–22; 2:9–10; 7:1; cf. Eccl 1:12–18). The second flows
from the first: i.e., the attitude of resignation derives
from the assumed permanence of religious, cultural, and
cosmic structures, conceived of as unified in a divinely
ordained whole (e.g., Job 9:2–21; Matt 5:10–12).

Resignation in Mediterranean culture should not be
mistaken for either pessimism or despair. On the contrary, resignation, understood as patience, indicates acceptance of status and condition of the individual and/or
family or tribe, and nation as a whole, together with the
course of events which affect them all, as ordered by
God (see ORDERING). Everything comes from the hand of
God, and he is the author of all events (Job 1:21; Deut 28;
Josh 24:19–20; Judg 3:7; Matt 5:45; Luke 24:25–27; Acts
2:22–25; see also Introduction).

Since this is the case, it is clear that in Mediterranean culture, the context in which the Bible originated,
human experience is what it is precisely because God has
so ordered it. Nothing happens in this world apart from
God's will. His commands, by definition, are immutable
(Isa 45:22–23; 46:9–11; Matt 5:18). Therefore, any illness,
suffering, adversity, fall from the favor of the powerful,
estrangement from family or friends, or reversal of
fortune—virtually any calamity—must be met with patience (Ps 56; 130; 140–44). The only alternative attitude
the Bible seems to recognize is rebellion born of pride, a
particularly despised and dangerous attribute (1 Sam
12:13–15; Ezra 4:12–22; Job 5:2; 24:13; Prov 8:32–36,
17:11; Ezek 20:38; Ps 78:8). Thus, patience is an expression of humility, and both are characteristics of biblically
approved persons, from the great (e.g., Deut 17:14–20
[the king]; 1 Sam 15:24–31 [Saul]; 2 Sam 12:13–23
[David]; Mark 10:42–45 [disciples]; Phil 2:6–11 [Jesus],
to the small [1 Kgs 17:7–13 (widow of Zarephath)]; Prov
15:33 [instruction aimed particularly at the youth]; Mark
12:41–44 [the widow and her coins]; Luke 2:22–38 [Simeon
and Anna]). Pride and rebellion are despised because at
their core they represent the rejection of God and an

attempt to usurp his place (Gen 3:1–7; 11:1–6, cf. Jer 13:17; Ezek 12:1–3; Matt 27:40–44; Mark 14:60–64; Luke 4:5–12). The prophets' denunciations of injustice, therefore, are aimed at those who, in their pride, have forgotten God. The prophets call for a renewed and uncompromised fidelity to the authentic covenantal tradition (Isa 5:7–8; Jer 8:8–12; 9:22–23, NAB; Hos 5:6–7; Amos 5:24–25). Patience, then, is acknowledgement of God's ultimate authority and power, and it trusts in or waits for God to judge, vindicate, punish, or reward: "For the LORD, the Most High, the awesome, is the great king over all the earth" (Ps 47:3, NAB; see also Ps 33:13–22; Sir 28:1).

In contrast to the patience manifested in biblical culture, God's own patience is frequently portrayed as a limited tolerance for rebellion (2 Chron 12:1–12; Isa 5:1–19; Jer 2:30; Amos 5:18–27). God, who humbles the proud and punishes the rebellious (1 Sam 2:3–10; Luke 1:51–53), is nevertheless also capable of long suffering patience with his unruly people. Unlike human patience (=resignation), God's patience is identified with compassion, generosity, and generativity (Ps 62; 103:8–13; 106; Isa 43:22–44:5; 55; Jer 33:2–26; Sir 18:6–22).

Patience, as understood in the Bible, is sharply at odds with contemporary Western ideas. Today, the term is usually understood in an evolutionary or developmental way and is applied to the processes of growth and change (rearing children, education, increasing business, etc.). In contrast, the culture in which the Bible originated usually understood the term to apply to fixed conditions unlikely to change significantly, and which therefore must be borne with an attitude of resigned acceptance. This understanding of patience persists as a firmly entrenched feature of modern Mediterranean peasant societies, where God's will, to which one must be resigned, is constantly invoked as the only realistic, and therefore ultimately satisfactory, explanation for phenomena ranging from plane crashes to misplaced keys. (Mark McVann)

Eickelman, Dale. 1981. *The Middle East: An Anthropological Approach.* Englewood Cliffs, N.J.: Prentice Hall.

PATRONAGE—SEE ALSO GRACE/FAVOR

This value characterizes patron-client relationships. It is a form of "justice" rooted in generalized reciprocity, similar to the justice meted out by relatives to each other in kinship systems. To understand it, one must begin with the patron-client relationship.

The patron-client relationship is a social, institutional arrangement by means of which economic, political, or religious institutional relationships are outfitted with an overarching quality of kinship or family feeling. The word "patron" derives from the Greek and Latin word for father, *patēr*. In the Bible, anytime anyone is called a "father" who is not a biological father, the title refers to the role and status of a patron. God is called "father" relative to Israel as a whole (Deut 32:6) and to the Davidic king (2 Sam 7:14). Elisha calls Elijah "father" (2 Kgs 2:12), as does Joash for Elisha (2 Kgs 6:21; 13:14). Similarly, Naaman the Syrian is called "father" by his servants (2 Kgs 5:13). The future king of Isaiah 9:6 is called "everlasting father," that is, abiding patron; similarly Eliakim: "and he shall be a father to the inhabitants of Jerusalem and to the house of Judah" (Isa 22:21).

The God of Israel was the central and focal symbol of Israel's traditional political religion, duly worshipped in Jerusalem's temple. By calling this God "Father," Jesus introduces the kinship title typical of patron-client behavior. God, the "Father," is nothing less than God the Patron. The "kingdom of heaven" proclaimed by Jesus was God's patronage and the clientele bound up in it (Matt 4:17, 23; 10:7; Mark 1:15). To "enter the kingdom of heaven" meant to enjoy the patronage of God, the heavenly Patron, hence, to become a client (Matt 7:21; 8:11; 18:4; 19:23, etc.). And the introductory phrase: "the kingdom of heaven is like" would come out as "the way God's patronage relates and affects his clients is like the following scenario . . ." (Matt 13:24, 31, 33, 44, 45, 47; 18:23; 20:1, etc.). Jesus excoriates scribes and Pharisees as shameful for denying people access to God's patronage (Matt 23:13).

Matthew's frequent title for God the Patron is the "Father who is in heaven" (Matt 5:16 and frequently elsewhere). John, on the other hand, prefers simply "the Father" (John 1:14 and frequently elsewhere). The tradition recalled Jesus' Aramaic usage for the divine patron, "Abba," meaning either "The Father," or "Oh, Father" (never "Daddy" [see PARENTING]: Rom 8:15; Gal 4:6; see Mark 14:36). This reference to God as Patron covers the whole of the New Testament. On the other hand, John accuses opponents of having the devil as their patron (John 8:38–44).

The patron is like a father, and clients are like loving and grateful children, no matter what their age. The client relates to his patron according to the social norms of child relations to actual parents, while the patron is expected to relate to clients as a parent would to his (more rarely, her) actual children. In Mediterranean societies of the past (as in most traditional societies), there was not the faintest trace of human equality, whether before the law or even in some ideal equality of all males. Institutionalized relationships between persons of unequal power statuses and resources were and are highly exploitive in nature (see AUTHORITARIANISM). The "better" families exerted power, applied vertically or hierarchically, as force, in harsh and impersonal fashion. People of higher status sought to maximize·their gains without a thought to the losses of those with whom they interacted. To survive in some meaningful way in such societies, patronage emerged to the mutual satisfaction of both parties: clients had their needs met, especially in fortuitous and irregular situations, while patrons received grants of honor and the accolades of benefaction. Patrons were to treat clients as family members might, with both having special concern for each other's welfare, even though separated sometimes by vast differences in status and power.

Patron-client relations permeated the whole of ancient Mediterranean society. Herod, "the king" of the Judeans in Matthew's infancy account (Matt 2) was a client king of his patron, Caesar Augustus. The Capernaum centurion was a patron who sent word to Jesus through some "friends," a Roman name for client (Luke 7:6). Festus the procurator acted like a patron of his client chief priests and principal men of Judea by doing them a favor (Acts 25:2–3). The title "Friend of Caesar" (John 19:12, NAB) was an official acknowledgement of imperial clientage. But by and large the most common form of patron-client relationship was between a landowner and *some* of his tenants. This special relationship assured the landlord of conspicuous deference and loyalty and provided the tenant with requisite favor.

A "favor" (see **GRACE/FAVOR**) is something received either on terms more advantageous than those that can be obtained from anyone else or which cannot be obtained from anyone else at all. From the client's point of view, favoritism is the main quality of such relationships. Clients seek out patrons, earthly and heavenly, essentially for the purpose of obtaining favors. What the inferior client lacks is *assurance* of aid in various emergencies and a *guarantee* of permanent access to resources. This lack of assurance bespeaks a lack of and need for commitment on the part of one who might do a special favor. No superior is obliged to provide such assurance or guarantee. Clients in this system know that their relation to patrons is highly unequal; patrons have much higher status and greater power and resources. Patrons provide their favors and help in exchange for items of a qualitatively different sort: material for immaterial, goods for honor and praise, force for status support, and the like. The subordinate has no obligation to treat the superior with respect or affection or to accept any offer of abiding commitment.

Within a kinship group, "justice" means enduring loyalty to one's kin. Regardless of the conduct of a kinsman, of a son or daughter, family members are expected to stand behind their kinsmen and support them in the event of any threat of evil from the outside. Similarly, "justice" sought of a patron is the justice of kinship. Anyone who has pledged him or herself to the patron's protection will experience the loyalty of the patron. God is regularly considered a patron (i.e., a heavenly "Father"). It is such patronage, such justice, that faithful Israelites have traditionally sought from their heavenly patrons.

By taking up the task of proclaiming the kingdom (Matt 4:17; Mark 1:15), Jesus presents himself as a broker or middleman of God's patronage. To this end he seeks other brokers to assist him in the task and outfits them with similar authorization (Matt 10:1–16; Mark 3:13–19; Luke 6:12–16). The term "mediator" means a broker who gives access to a patron; it is applied to Jesus in 1 Timothy 2:5: "There is only one broker between God and humankind" (author's trans.). In Hebrews (8:6; 9:15; 12:24) Jesus brokers a new covenant, ostensibly like the role Moses played with the old one (Gal 3:19–20).

Americans are familiar with the idea of patrons and brokers from films such as "The Godfather" or "Prizzi's Honor." The Mediterranean institution known as patronage and brokerage finds nuanced expression in the Italian status of "Godfather." For mainstream U.S. citizens, especially those who are not of Mediterranean ancestry, this institution is curious and intriguing but certainly not to be imitated. This kind of an institution is deemed unnecessary and therefore lacking in individualistic American culture where each person must stand on his or her own two feet and achieve success in a very personal fashion. One is normally expected to pull oneself up by one's own bootstraps in this culture. (Bruce J. Malina)

Barr, James. 1988. "Abba Isn't Daddy." *Journal of Theological Studies* 39:27–47.

Elliott, John H. 1987. "Patronage and Clientelism in Early Christian Society: A Short Reading Guide." *Forum* 3/1:39–48.

Eisenstadt, Shlomo N., and Louis Roniger. 1980. "Patron-Client Relations as a Model of Structuring Social Exchange." *Comparative Studies in Society and History* 22:42–77.

_____. 1984. *Patrons, Clients and Friends: Interpersonal Relations and the Structure of Trust in Society.* Cambridge: Cambridge University Press.

Malina, Bruce J. 1988. "Patron and Client: The Analogy Behind Synoptic Theology." *Forum* 4/1:2–32.

Wallace-Hadrill, Andrew, ed. 1990. *Patronage in Ancient Society.* London: Routledge.

PEASANT

The term "peasant society" refers to a set of villages socially bound up with preindustrial cities (see **AGRARIAN SOCIETY**) in which the overwhelming portion of the population lives in the villages and makes a living from the land. Villages were small and usually related to a preindustrial city which functioned as both an administrative center and a central place of worship. These preindustrial cities lived off the crops of agricultural people in the surround.

Peasant freeholders, that is, peasants who owned and farmed their own land, had economic obligations that severely limited prospects for moving beyond a bare subsistence level. Obligations were both internal and external to the family.

Internal obligations included the following:

Subsistence: Though it can vary from person to person, people living in modern industrial societies require approximately 2,500–2,800 calories per day to meet basic needs. Estimates for Roman Palestine vary from 1,800–2,400 calories per person per day, primarily obtained from grain. Up to one-fourth of the calories came from alcohol. The availability of calories from grain and produce in a peasant family in antiquity would have varied inversely with the number of mouths to feed.

Seed and Feed: Seed for planting and feed for livestock could amount to a substantial portion of the annual produce. In medieval peasant societies where records exist, seed could consume one-third of grain production and feed an additional one-fourth.

Trade: A farm cannot produce everything needed for subsistence. Some produce, therefore, had to be reserved for acquiring equipment, utensils, or food the family did not produce.

External obligations included the following.

Social/Religious Dues: Participation in weddings or other local festivals and the requirements of cultic or religious obligations required yet another portion of the annual produce. This could vary substantially from place to place and year to year.

Taxes: Most agrarian societies expropriated between ten and fifty percent of the annual produce in taxes. Recent estimates for Roman Palestine, including a variety of both civil and religious taxes, put the figure there at 35–40 percent.

Since it is difficult to arrive at precise figures for each of the various obligations, drawing conclusions about what might have been available for family subsistence can be only an estimate at best. Nonetheless, recent attempts to do that for Roman Palestine in the first century suggest that in good years freeholding peasant families may have had as much as 10–20 percent of the annual produce available for meeting subsistence needs. Large families or small landholdings thus placed peasant families close to the margin of survival. In the case of tenant farmers who owed land-rent in addition to the above, the amount available would have been far less.

It is very difficult for contemporary United States citizens who live in an industrialized and highly technological culture to appreciate the distinctive characteristics of peasant societies. Life in the modern world is radically different from peasant life, yet a genuine appreciation for the people who populate the pages of the Bible requires that strong efforts be made to understand peasantry and its characteristics because this is the world in which Jesus lived and ministered. (Richard Rohrbaugh)

Bernstein, Henry, et al, eds. 1994. *The Journal of Peasant Studies: A Twenty Volume Index 1973–1993*. London: Cass.

Hobshawm, Eric J. 1973. "Peasants and Politics." *Journal of Peasant Studies* 1/3:3–22.

Mintz, Sidney E. 1973. "A Note on the Definition of Peasantries." *Journal of Peasant Studies* 1/1:91–106.

Nash, Manning. 1966. *Primitive and Peasant Economies*. San Francisco: Chandler.

Oakman, Douglas E. 1991. "The Countryside in Luke–Acts." In *The Social World of Luke–Acts: Models for Interpretation*. Ed. Jerome H. Neyrey. Pp. 151–79. Peabody, Mass.: Hendrickson.

Potter, J., M. Diaz, and G. Foster, eds. 1967. *Peasant Society: A Reader*. Boston: Little, Brown & Co.

Redfield, Robert. 1963. *The Little Community and Peasant Society and Culture*. Chicago: University of Chicago Press.

Scott, James C. 1985. *Weapons of the Weak: Everyday Forms of Peasant Resistance*. New Haven: Yale University Press.

Shanin, Teodor. 1971. *Peasants and Peasant Society*. Baltimore: Penguin.

Wolf, Eric. 1966. *Peasants*. Foundations of Modern Anthropology Series. Englewood Cliffs, N.J.: Prentice Hall.

PITY

This quality leads a person to perform some significant kindness for another person who is in need, notably when that other has no right to the kindness and cannot repay it. Pity is therefore a secondary value by means of which a person achieves honor. People moved by pity are prompted to act honorably toward one in need. (This notion would be related to the biblical notions of mercy [see **GRACE/FAVOR**] and lovingkindness [see **STEADFAST LOVE**].) The quality inheres in a person's eyes and/or heart (see **EYES-HEART**; Deut 7:16; 19:13, 21; Ps 17:10) and is revealed by what a person *does* (see **HANDS-FEET**) on behalf of others in need (e.g., Ps 111:4–9; Mark 1:41; 8:2). One who acts out of pity is said to be compassionate or gracious. Such pity is a quality of God (Exod 34:9; Rom 9:15; Jonah 4:2; Ps 103:8, 13; 111:4; Jas 5:11); its withdrawal is a sign of God's judgment (e.g., Jer 13:14; Ezek 5:11; 7:4,

9). It normally marks the behavior of fathers toward their children (Ps 103:13; but see Ezek 5:10). Prophets expect it of God's people in dealing with their less fortunate fellows and resident aliens (e.g., Zech 7:8–10), and Jesus uses it as the touchstone of his picture of the final judgment (in Matt 25:31–46). Pity is undoubtedly part and parcel of the care and concern for neighbor that Jesus sought (Matt 5:43–47; Luke 6:27–28).

Americans are frequently stirred to pity and are motivated to act out of this feeling, but with a significant difference. Their pity-motivated behavior is most often directed to the faceless or anonymous needy and is rendered in impersonal fashion (writing a check, sending a donation, leaving a bag of food in the church vestibule, and the like; see **Altruism**). There are of course exceptions to this pattern, but the sparsity of examples confirms the general pattern described. (Bruce J. Malina)

Bultmann, Rudolf. 1964. "eleos ktl." *Theological Dictionary of the New Testament* 2:477–87.

Dupont, Jacques. 1973. *Les Béatitudes.* 3:604–33. Paris: Gabalda.

POWER

This is the ability to exercise control over the behavior of others. It is obviously necessary that power be recognized and accepted by those whose existence is being controlled. When subordinates accept and respect the power of superiors, the superior is considered to be honorable. Thus, power is a means value which facilitates the realization of the Mediterranean core values of honor and shame. Power can be analyzed in the two formal institutions of the Mediterranean biblical world: kinship and politics.

In the family circle (real kinship) those who exercise control over the individual child are: father, mother, aunts, uncles, siblings, cousins, and other members of the extended family. Joseph and Mary were not negligent but rather very ordinary Mediterranean parents in travelling a day's journey from Jerusalem without worrying about Jesus because they could reasonably suppose that "kinsfolk and acquaintances" were keeping track of the lad (Luke 2:44). Even in adulthood, family members continue to exercise power over other family members: Jesus' [extended?] family responds to reports that he is crazy by trying to seize him (Mark 3:21). Surprisingly, Jesus refuses to answer the call of his mother and brothers to come out and speak with them (Mark 3:31–35 and parallels). The answer to Cain's [rhetorical?] question to God: "Am I my brother's keeper?" (Gen 4:9) is Yes! One brother is to "redeem" another brother who might need it (Lev 25:48) or avenge his death when and if that becomes necessary (Num 35:16–21).

Beyond the family circle (extended family and fictive kin), adult lives are controlled by the group that camps and wanders together. Abraham's retinue included his brother's son Lot, "and the persons that they had acquired in Haran" (Gen 12:5). Abraham and Lot had to keep order in the group (Gen 13:7ff.). Moses' father-in-law, Jethro, advised that Moses establish rulers over groups in the Exodus to help Moses settle disputes among them (Exod 18:18–27). In settled times, the Sadducee chief priests and scribes became concerned about the damage Jesus' teaching caused and sought to have him arrested and killed (Matt 26:3–5 and parallels). Such behavior is necessary in order to defend or protect the group and/or maintain peace in it.

The second formal institution in which one can see power at work in society is politics, for politics by definition is the institution by means of which members of a group achieve and use power to implement public goals. In the NT, except for his exorcisms, Jesus generally has no power at all. Thus, Jesus' exorcisms can be correctly understood as political actions performed for the purpose of restoring correct order to society.

Each society's identified illnesses constitute a sign or emblem that marks what that group values, disvalues, and preoccupies itself with. In Jesus' Mediterranean world, human beings possessed by a spirit are in a disvalued state. Moreover, the relationship of spirits to this world and their involvement in it certainly preoccupies Jesus and his contemporaries.

The process of healing involves diagnosing the problem, prognosing the outcome, and applying the suitable therapy. In other words, healers seek to explain, predict, and control reality. In the Beelzebub episode (Luke 11:14–26), the problem diagnosed or the reality explained (by all parties) is a case of demon-possession. The prognosis or predicted outcome is that the cast-out demon might return with seven more powerful ones. The therapy Jesus applies or the reality he seeks to control is "he who is not with me is against me, who does not gather with me scatters" (Luke 11:23). Since Jesus has effective power against demons, he has the power to maintain order in society as it should be. Anyone who would stand in the way of that stands in the way of the order that properly belongs in society.

Another instance in the political institution wherein some people have power is the mediation of disputes. This is a difficult but highly honorable task best accomplished by a kinsperson removed from the situation by about five links. The mediator most often is sought to settle blood feuds. Recall how Joab sent the woman of Tekoa to David to play the role of mediator and bring the blood feud between David's sons to an end (2 Sam 14).

Sometimes the challenge is less than that as when a man asked Jesus to mediate between him and his brother by instructing the brother to share the inheritance (Luke 12:13). Though Jesus declined to accept this role on this occasion, (perhaps because he recognized the request as unfair, see Deut 21:17), he appreciated the general political value of mediation and included it among the beatitudes: "Blessed are the peacemakers [i.e., mediators], they shall be called sons of God" (Matt 5:9). Beatitudes, after all, are culturally valuable lines of conduct quite obvious to anyone familiar with the workings of the culture. "Peacemaker" is another name for mediator, a relatively distanced and disinterested third party, highly regarded by the aggrieved parties, and skilled in the art of bringing hostile parties to a mutually honorable truce. In the agonistic Mediterranean culture reflected in the Bible, this is a very powerful and important role.

In mainstream United States culture, power resides with the people who delegate it to leaders. In a certain sense, people have the ability to determine just who is able to control their existence and to what degree. In the cultural world of the Bible, the power resided in leaders who lasted "forever." (John J. Pilch)

Fogelson, Raymond D., and Richard N. Adams, eds. 1977. *The Anthropology of Power*. New York: Academic Press.

Levinson, David, and Martin J. Malone. 1980. *Toward Explaining Human Culture: A Critical Review of the Findings of Worldwide Cross-Cultural Research*. New Haven, Conn.: HRAF Press. Esp. ch. 21: "Aggression."

Lewellen, Ted C. 1983. *Political Anthropology: An Introduction*. South Hadley, Mass.: Bergin & Garvey.

Mann, Michael. 1986. *The Sources of Social Power*. Vol. 1, *A History of Power from the Beginning to A.D. 1760*. Cambridge: Cambridge University Press.

Nelson, C. 1973. "Women and Power in Nomadic Societies in the Middle East." In *The Desert and the Sown: Nomads in the Wider Society*. Ed. C. Nelson. Berkeley: Institute of International Studies, University of California.

Pilch, John J. 1991. "Values and Nature." In *Introducing the Cultural Context of the New Testament*. Pp. 189–218. Mahwah, N.J.: Paulist.

———. 1995. "Insights and models from medical anthropology for understanding the healing activity of the Historical Jesus." *Hervormde teologiese studies* 51:314–37.

Rogers, S. 1975. "Female Forms of Power and the Myth of Male Dominance: A Mode of Female/Male Interaction in Peasant Society." *American Ethnologist* 2/4:727–56.

PROGRESS ORIENTATION

Societies and their sub-groups evaluate developmental change differently on the basis of two sets of variables: whether societal members are understood as embedded in a group or as individuals; and whether or not the social values of the group can be realized. The different combinations of these variables produce four scenarios for evaluating change as "progress," or as "deviance" and "deterioration." (1) Those who are embedded in a group and can realize their values tend to be "conservative"; society should change only organically and by its own mechanisms (evolution). Progress is thus a slow and natural change for the better. (2) The orientation of those who are embedded in a group but find it difficult to realize their values is considered "radical," since it calls for society to be completely restructured (revolution). For them, values no longer match experience, and thus progress is understood as drastic change in order to bring about a match. The orientation of early Christians illustrates a "radical" stance: this is clearly how they were perceived by those outside their group. (3) Individualistic societies which can achieve their values are "liberal": society continuously seeks progress defined as fine-tuning in order to maximize efficiency (convolution). (4) Those who are individualistic and are frustrated in realizing their values can be characterized as "anarchist"; progress is the dismantling of society and replacing the present order with a universal humanity (devolution).

While ancient Israel and Judah were societies oriented to groups rather than individuals (see Introduction), some OT books are the products of segments of society which were able to realize their values (e.g., Proverbs), and other books are from those whose values were out of step with the dominant culture (e.g., Job). The books originating among the urban establishment (e.g., legislative codes, the Priestly writings, Proverbs) clearly presuppose that the group's members can realize their values. Job, the prophetic writings (with some exceptions), etc., are the products of groups which were frustrated in realizing their values. This fundamental difference accounts for different answers to the question:

"What should we do about our situation?" and therefore conflicts within Israelite and Judean societies. Depending upon one's place in society, either evolutionary or revolutionary change was evaluated as progress.

Foundational myths (those that undergird the basic beliefs and behaviors of a society) such as Genesis 1:1–2:4a (Priestly) and Genesis 2:4b–3:24 (Yahwistic), even though from different periods and social groups, are examples of an orientation to members embedded in a group who are able to realize their values. They establish not only "origins," but social values (e.g., symmetry), and they confirm distinctions. The same is true of legal "codes" (e.g., the Covenant Code, Exod 20:22–23:33). Deviants are "sinners" or "criminals." Wisdom literature such as Proverbs and Ben Sira share this view of progress. They too perceive an orderly world that affirms the status quo. Change is suspect and is generally evaluated negatively as some form of deviance: it leads to destruction (Prov 1:29–32), family shame (Prov 28:7; Sir 5:14–6:1), or poverty (Prov 13:18). Deviants are called "fools" or "wicked" and those who comply are called "wise" or "righteous" (see Prov 10–15). Anything other than slow, organic change, then, is a negative value, standing for deviance.

Most of the classical prophets (e.g., Elijah, Amos, Jeremiah) can be identified with groups who are frustrated in realizing their values. The books which recount prophetic narratives and speeches indicate that their goal was the "repentance" of the people and leaders: behavioral, structural, or policy changes in response to a value critique. The prophetic "calls to repentance" and the "prophecies of disaster" point up a fissure between values and experience, cultural ends and institutional means, and therefore they can be termed "radical." They are repeatedly depicted in conflict with the political and temple authorities due to their critiques of Israelite and Judean social structures, policies, and failures in value compliance (e.g., 1 Kgs 21:1–29; Isa 20:1–6; Jer 26:1–24). Concretely, they often predicted disaster for failure to respond to their critiques: the collapse of the monarchy, invasion by foreigners, death of leaders, destruction of the temple, drought and famine, and loss of the land. The following of leaders and performance of rites is often depicted by the prophets as ineffectual for purification or turning away disaster (e.g., Amos 4:4–5; Isa 1:11–13). Justice, righteousness, purity, and loyalty are what Israel or Judah fails to uphold. What only Yahweh can provide is "a new covenant" (Jer 31:31), "a new heart and a new spirit" (Ezek 18:31), and "a new name" (Isa 62:2). But the new thing which Yahweh will accomplish is not in the immediate present, but only "in the latter days" (Isa 2:2; Jer 30:24). Consistent with their perspective, the "best times" are imminent (on the horizon), but not yet here. For an example of institutional prophets who affirm the status quo in conflict with a classical prophet, see 1 Kings 22:5–28. The Deuteronomistic History (Deuteronomy–2 Kgs) is the systematic account of Israel's and Judah's national stories in light of their failures to heed the prophetic message of repentance, with a few exceptions (see 1 Kgs 17:13).

Like most of the prophetic writings, the NT is the product of communities oriented toward group embeddedness but whose values were out of step with the dominant cultures (both Roman and Jewish). Its overarching ideological perspective can also be termed "radical." The early Christians looked for a reorientation and restructuring of society in the near future. Thus, drastic change had the positive connotation of progress—as rightly perceived by the Jerusalem establishment (Acts 6:14; 4:19–21).

Parallel to the prophetic stance in the OT, the message summaries of John the Baptist (Mark 1:1–4; Luke 3:7–14) and Jesus (Mark 1:15; Luke 4:18–21) are calls to repentance and a new order, signalled by a new rite: baptism. Legitimate authority was no longer in the hands of those who held office, or traditional authority. Furthermore, Jesus challenged the primary authority of the biological family (Mark 3:31–35) and conservative Torah interpretation (Matt 5:21–22).

Paul contends that Christians, as a group, are in an ongoing process of change (literally a "metamorphosis") into God's likeness—a process effected by God (2 Cor 3:18) and characterized as a "new creation" (2 Cor 5:17; Gal 6:15). In Galatians 3:28 he challenges the distinctions based upon ethnic group, status, and gender. Thus, "progress" is moving beyond these barriers.

The Gospel of John is oriented to individuals who are unable to realize their values. Consequently, its ideological mode is "anarchist": the destruction of society in favor of a universal humanity. It is interested not in the slow process of social change, but in the transformation of values. Unlike the Synoptics, John emphasizes the personal encounters of Jesus with *individuals* who are more fully developed characters (e.g., the Samaritan woman), the transcending of Jewish rites and sacred space (John 4:21–23), "believing into" (and unmediated attachment to) Jesus as sole mode of divine relationship (11:25–26, see also **LOVE**), and the immediately recoverable remote past in the present (6:32–34). The "new commandment" is love: mutuality to others in the loose aggregation of believers (13:34–35).

Whatever the perspective on social and value change, a theme which appears in both the OT and NT is: God is consistent and unvarying (Num 23:19; 1 Sam 15:29; Jas 1:17). The writer of Hebrews accords this same consistency to Jesus (Heb 13:8). When God does change/repent/ turn, it is not a change in character, goal, or purpose, but a change in action in response to human change or pleading (e.g., Exod 32:14; 1 Sam 15:35; 2 Sam 24:16).

United States society is oriented to individuals who can realize their values, and therefore can be characterized as "liberal": society should be refined for maximum efficiency. Because our society is fundamentally oriented to the future, change and progress are expected to be constant and as fast as possible: refining, enhancing, perfecting. Technology is seldom called into question prior to reaching a crisis point (e.g., toxic waste dumps, global warming). And the resolution to these crises is envisioned not as a return to a prior simplicity, but as more creative, sophisticated progress and better techniques. (K. C. Hanson)

Downing, F. Gerald. 1995. "Common Strands in Pagan, Jewish and Christian Eschatologies in the First Century." *Theologische Zeitschrift* 51:196–211.

——. 1995. "Cosmic Eschatology in the First Century: 'Pagan,' Jewish and Christian." *L'Antiquité classique* 64:99–109.

Hanson, K. C. 1996. "Group, Individual, and Personality." In "Greco-Roman Studies and the Social Scientific Study of the Bible: A Classified Periodical Bibliography (1970–1994)." *Forum* 9/1–2: 63–119.

McLuhan, Marshall. 1989. *The Global Village: Transformations in World Life and Media in the 21st Century.* New York: Oxford University Press.

Moore, Wilbert E. 1968. "Social Change." In *International Encyclopedia of the Social Sciences.* Ed. D. L. Sills. 14:365–75. New York: Macmillan.

Toffler, Alvin. 1970. *Future Shock.* New York: Random.

——. 1980. *The Third Wave.* New York: Morrow.

PROMINENCE

This evaluative label is used in acclaiming a person or thing to be of social worth and, hence, worthy of priority. The opposite of prominence is deviance. Prominence is best thought of as an English gloss for a broad range of semantic fields related to honor and shame (see **HONOR/SHAME**) rather than as a translation of a single term or concept. Examples of this intersection of fields are "glory" (*doxa* in John 17:5, 24; 1 Cor 2:7), "favor" (*charis* in Luke 2:52), and "prestige" (*exousia* in 3 *Macc* 7:21; Acts 25:23).

As a form of ascription, prominence is a mode of classification which confers limit-breaking or limit-defining status to a person or thing. Because of this, acclamations of prominence often occur within the context of a status transformation ritual. A promotion with the result of increased honor and prestige, as in Esther 5:11, is one such instance. Thus, prominence is a value that serves as a means for establishing and/or confirming honor.

Prominence implies an ordering of priority on the basis of time, space, or rank, and it may occur as a formal title. This sequencing of priority-evaluation is often indicated in the Bible by the categories "first" and "last." Any such categorization obviously presumes an honor/ shame evaluation. For example, those who are "first" in a kingdom "see the king's face" (Esth 1:14); "face" is a body-symbol for honor. Similarly, the Hebrew word for "first" is *re'šit*, which is a derivative of the word for "head" (*ro'š*) hence, the association with honor. Another example of the equation of "first" with honor can be found in Genesis 49:3: "Reuben, you are my first-born, my might, and the first fruits of my strength, pre-eminent in pride and pre-eminent in power."

In an agonistic society (see **POWER**), such as that of Mediterranean antiquity, labels of prominence also carry a contestive slant. The Greek word *proerchomai*, meaning "to come into prominence" also means "to have advantage over."

Indicators of prominence on the basis of firstness are present throughout the Greco-Roman world. For example, the official title for Caesar, "princeps," means "first citizen." Josephus uses *hoi prōtoi* to refer to the leaders of any political organization (e.g., tribe, nation, priesthood). In nearly all cases the priority-evaluation of firstness expresses the structure of social relations.

In the Synoptic Gospels, occurrences of this category as the indicator of social structure are manifold. Simon Peter is ranked first among the disciples, (Matt 10:2) but in John's Gospel it is the beloved disciple who outruns Peter and reaches the empty tomb first, replicating the Johannine ideological stance of prominence relative to other Christian groups who base their legitimacy on Peter's prominence (John 20:4, 8). The prominent position of women within the structure of early Christian groups is expressed when the risen Jesus appears to Mary Magdalene first (Mark 16:9). The center and periphery of the Jesus faction is expressed when Jesus confers information upon the twelve disciples first (Luke 12:1).

In the Pauline letters, firstness not only expresses but legitimates social relations. Adam was created first, therefore men have priority over women (1 Tim 2:13). God appointed apostles first, therefore apostles have priority over other church roles (1 Cor 12:28). The household of Stephanus was the first in Achaia to be converted, therefore Stephanus has priority over other households (1 Cor 16:15–16). Paul's group was the first to proclaim the gospel in Corinth, therefore they have priority access to the loyalty of the Corinthians (2 Cor 10:14–15). In every case priority implies legitimation and the power to wield social commitment.

The institution of primogeniture is an important indicator of prominence in the Hebrew Bible. The firstborn male child (*bekor*) is acclaimed prominent through the status transformation ritual of the blessing, by which the child is accorded double the normal inheritance and priority over other siblings (Gen 27). The relationship of Israel to Yahweh is also expressed in this framework: Israel is the Lord's firstborn, delivered from slavery. By killing the Pharaoh's firstborn son Yahweh demonstrates his Lordship and priority over Egypt (Exod 4:22–23). This act of patronage toward Israel is reciprocated by Israel in the redemption of all firstborn and firstfruits (in essence, all socially valued "goods") from Yahweh (Exod 13:11–16).

The Hebrew Bible contains other instances of firstness as indicative of prominence. In begging a favor from the king, it is the first of the household who comes forward (2 Sam 19:20). Whoever smites the enemy first gets to be chief (1 Chron 11:6). The most unfaithful to the covenant (the most deviant) is to be exiled first (Amos 6:7). The witness to a crime gets to cast the first stone

(Deut 13:6–9; 17:7). A leader is referred to as "one who goes up first for us" (Judg 1:1).

Prominence labelling expresses not only priority but also time preference. In Mediterranean antiquity, where the past figures as the primary or secondary time orientation, firstness as an indicator of prominence serves to reinforce this preference pattern on the principle "older is better, oldest is best." That which is first possesses power, wisdom, or authority (Job 40:19; Prov 8:22–26; Col 1:15; Heb 7:2; Rev 1:17). Because God is without precedent, he is worthy of worship (Ps 90:2). Finally, time preference determines the primary aim of past-oriented society: restoration of the past or first conditions (Jer 33:7; see TIME ORIENTATION).

A highly significant facet of prominence labelling in both the Hebrew Bible and first-century Christian literature is prominence reversal: the reversal of the expected order of priority. This pattern is present in the gospel proclamation "the first shall be last . . ." (Matt 19:30; 20:16; Mark 10:31, 44). In Acts 13:46 the gospel is proclaimed first to the Jews, but their rejection of it causes the Gentiles to receive the benefits of God's patronage first instead.

The priority reversal ritual can be conceptualized as an act of patronage (see PATRONAGE) on the part of Yahweh which disrupts established priorities and structures: a status-levelling mechanism which is contingent upon a perception of limited good (see LIMITED GOOD; ENVY). This pattern is evidenced in Zechariah 12:7, where Judah's victory levels the honor status of Jerusalem and the king. The reversal of primogeniture status can be seen constantly throughout the Genesis narratives: Abel over Cain, Jacob over Esau, Joseph/Judah over Reuben, Ephraim over Manasseh, Moses over Aaron, David over his brothers, Solomon over Adonijah, etc. The disruptive effect this intervention has on established priority structures is seen in Genesis 48:17–19.

While priority and prominence are characteristics of any classification system, their location within that system differs widely according to social structure and time preference. Contemporary American society is future-oriented (in contrast to Mediterranean past-orientation) and, hence, is based upon the principle "newer is better, newest is best" (see Introduction). There was no concept of progress in antiquity (see **PROGRESS ORIENTATION**); any novelty had to be legitimated by precedent (Jesus legitimated his reputational authority through recourse to a venerated prophetic tradition). Even theology proper is subject to time preference: while the biblical Yahweh is worthy of worship because of his firstness, a significant trend of American and European theology seeks to establish God's prominence in a future-oriented society by acclaiming evolution, progress, and change to be divine attributes.

Prominence indicators often do not communicate to contemporary Bible readers because the hierarchical priority-order presumed in the texts is dissonant with U.S. egalitarian social structure. (Chris Seeman)

Gilmore, David D. 1982. "Anthropology of the Mediterranean Area." *Annual Review of Anthropology* 11:175–205.

———. 1987. *Honor and Shame and the Unity of the Mediterranean.* American Anthropological Association Special Publication 22. Washington: American Anthropological Association.

Malina, Bruce J., and Jerome H. Neyrey. 1988. *Calling Jesus Names: The Social Value of Labels in Matthew.* Sonoma, Calif.: Polebridge. Pp. 93–131.

PURITY—SEE ALSO NUDITY; WHOLENESS

This value directs each member of a society to respect and observe the system of space and time lines that human groups develop to have everything in its place and a place for everything. In Mediterranean biblical society, purity marks a person who knows how to be clean rather than unclean, pure rather than polluted—in other words, how to maintain honor and avoid shame. Purity thus is a means value because it facilitates the realization of the core values of honor and shame.

Purity is threatened in four ways: (1) from outside; (2) from inside; (3) at the margins or boundaries; and (4) from inconsistencies or internal contradictions. (1) Shecaniah observed that God's holy (pure, clean) people had polluted themselves by taking as wives foreign women among the peoples of the land. Ezra accepted his suggestion to dismiss all foreign wives and the children born of them, and he enforced it in order to remove this impurity that came "from the outside" (Ezra 9–10). The holy community was polluted when foreign women were brought inside from the outside. By removing the foreign women from within, and prohibiting the introduction of other foreign women, God's people were holy once again, the inside was pure.

(2) Inside the system there are lines that create distinct places and roles for everyone. Crossing these lines renders a person impure and unclean. Sex–linked roles are part of this purity concern. Men should behave like men and women should behave like women. This is why Leviticus 20:13 decrees that "if a man lies with a male as with a woman, both of them shall be put to death for their abominable deed" (NAB). This is also why Paul (1 Cor 11) insists that men and women should wear the hair-style appropriate to each gender: short for men, long for women. Members of society who disregard internal lines are impure and unclean.

(3) Purity is threatened at the margins when boundaries become porous and permeable. Leviticus 11 (clean and unclean foods), 12 (childbirth), 13–14 (repulsive scaly condition) and 15 (male and female bodily effluvia) all concern body openings at the very margins of the human body. The discussion in these laws is precisely about purity: how it is threatened and how it might be regained. In the NT, Jesus of course changes the rules, for he does not agree that purity threats are located at the

margins but teaches rather that they are within (see next paragraph).

(4) Inconsistencies or internal contradictions putting a system at apparent war with itself are perhaps the most common threats to purity. Jesus attacked one such inconsistency when the Pharisees who would agree with the commandment to "honor father and mother" also allowed a male to declare his goods *qorban*, that is, dedicated to God, and therefore unavailable to his parents, should they need it (Mark 7). Yet the same Jesus said: "If anyone comes to me and does not hate his own father and mother and wife and children and brothers and sisters, yes, and even his own life, he cannot be my disciple" (Luke 14:26; cf. Matt 10:37). In the former case, he is clearly concerned with internal contradictions. In the latter case he is concerned with the potential stranglehold this culture imposes on males (notice the word "wife"). While upholding kinship obligations, Jesus does not want them to render a person totally helpless.

Concepts of purity in the United States mainstream community are somewhat different. We even use different words such as "deviant" (describing someone outside socially agreed lines), "normal" (describing someone inside the lines, or "legal" (describing anything or any person within explicitly articulated boundaries sanctioned by the political institutions) and "illegal" (situated outside those legal lines). Thus, we have concerns about "illegal aliens" or "illegitimate healers" whom we call "quacks," "charlatans," "purveyors of snake oil," and the like. (John J. Pilch)

Douglas, Mary. 1968. "Pollution." In *International Encyclopedia of the Social Sciences*. Ed. D. L. Sills. 12:336–42. New York: Macmillan.

_____. 1966. *Purity and Danger: An Analysis of Concepts of Pollution and Taboo.* New York: Praeger.

Frymer-Kensky, Tikva. 1983. "Pollution, Purification, and Purgation in Biblical Israel." In *The World Shall Go Forth: Essays in Honor of David Noel Freedman in Celebration of His Sixtieth Birthday.* Ed. Carol L. Meyers and M. O'Connor. Pp. 399–414. Winona Lake, Ind.: Eisenbrauns.

Neyrey, Jerome H. 1986. "The Idea of Purity in Mark's Gospel." *Semeia* 35:91–128.

_____. 1988. "Unclean, Common, Polluted, and Taboo." *Forum* 4/4: 72–82.

_____. 1990. *Paul, In Other Words: A Cultural Reading of His Letters.* Louisville, Ky.: Westminster John Knox.

Pilch, John J. 1981. "Biblical Leprosy and Body Symbolism." *Biblical Theology Bulletin* 11:119–33.

_____. 1988. "Understanding Biblical Healing: Selecting the Appropriate Model." *Biblical Theology Bulletin* 18:60–66.

PURPOSIVENESS/END ORIENTATION

Twentieth-century Americans and Europeans are preoccupied with effective means and expeditious gratification of wants. Technology is in constant ferment in the modern world, so that through effective means human wants may be gratified as quickly as possible. Modern economies are "productive," quickly able to transform raw materials into finished products, distribute those products, and sell them. The satisfaction of individual wants takes precedence over the group's well-being. Aggressive individual striving is encouraged by Madison Avenue's "have it all now" advertising designed to stimulate more and greater immediate wants (see Introduction).

By contrast, the ancient world of the Bible thought in terms of effective ends and causes leading to the eventual satisfaction of the wants of the group. Only a very few in antiquity could ever contemplate immediate personal gratification. The many had to be patient. There was no focus upon effective means in the ancient world, because it was believed typically that no such means existed. The zero-sum nature of ancient economy—the persistent belief that if some part increased, another part had to decrease—led to a rather static productive and technological picture. This fact is well illustrated by a story about Vespasian (69–79 CE). The Roman Emperor refused to utilize a new invention, because it would have led to unemployment (Suetonius, *Vespasian* 18). Production of goods in such societies was always limited in comparison with modern standards. Furthermore, the ancient individual was "embedded" in society; the ancient societies were comprised of "dyadic personalities" for the most part, i.e., people whose cultural scripts needed constant interpretation by reference to others, especially superiors (see **DYADISM**). Normal individuals did not "get ahead" in such societies; their hopes, dreams, and needs were perennially subordinated to those of their leaders, families and communities.

These broad considerations help us to understand specific biblical values and concerns as expressions of a purposive cultural orientation. In the Synoptic Gospels there is the central image of the harvest (e.g., Mark 4:8, 29; Luke 10:2). Jesus focuses upon a familiar "end" to talk about the Kingdom of God. There is little here about effective means—no discussions, as it were, of better methods of tillage, more effective fertilizers, improved pesticides. The Kingdom's coming is mysterious and almost inexplicable in terms of the "means," yet the harvest is sure. With such patient confidence Jesus invites the disciples to become oriented to that end (cf. John 4:35). This "conforming to the end" or "effective cause" is realized through reoriented behavior. Paul thinks of the Law (see **TORAH ORIENTATION**) not as a means to righteousness, but as an effective cause toward conformity to Christ (Rom 10:4).

It is important thus to notice the New Testament stress upon the present effects of behavioral "ends." Normal anxieties in the face of limited production can be confidently relinquished in the face of the Kingdom of God (Luke 12:31). James 5:7 similarly articulates the typical attitude of the end-oriented early Christians. Words like "patience," "endurance," "steadfastness," "confidence," "faith," and "hope" express the purposive orientation of early Christianity. Romans 5:3–5 is particularly instructive in this regard. Notice how Paul sees hope emerge from character: the properly formed (we moderns would say socialized) character—the one oriented to the proper end—will have the qualities appropriate to that end. In very similar terms Aristotle speaks of virtue, moderation, and the goal of all ethical behavior in happiness (e.g., *Nicomachean Ethics* I.i [1094^a]; I.vii.5 [1097^b]).

Two other New Testament words significantly express the purposive orientation under discussion: "Sin" and "maturity." The Greek word for sin, *hamartia*, meant in Homeric Greek "to miss the mark," as when a javelin was thrown and missed its target (*Iliad* 5.287). Aristotle thought of ethical failure as comparable to the failure of an archer to hit the mark (*Nicomachean Ethics* I.ii.2 [1094^a]; II.vi.14[1106^b]). Viewed in this way, human behavior is deficient primarily because the intended ends of behavior have been missed altogether, not because of technical infractions (inadequate means). For this reason, New Testament people were more likely culturally to fear being shamed by God because of wrong orientations than to be preoccupied with guilt for specific transgressions (consider Phil 3:8–9).

Conversely, mature behavior—the end, purpose, or goal of *teleioi anthrōpoi* (Greek for "mature people")—is that behavior which is aimed in the right direction. The "perfection" (*teleios*) of the Sermon on the Mount (Matt 5:48) really signifies this end-oriented quality of maturity. This quality does not necessarily imply that the end has been reached, but emphasizes simply that the end is always in view and determinative of present activity.

The emphasis in mainstream United States culture upon goal-setting, future-planning, and similar strategies is linked intimately with the belief and fact that individuals, rather than groups, can shape the future rather than just suffer it. It is ever the individual, not the group, who is master of personal fate.

Moreover, the speed with which one's goals can be accomplished leads many to adopt and live by a "now" orientation. "Do it now" was, in fact, the motto of the Mayor of Baltimore who spearheaded urban renewal in his city with the conversion of the Inner Harbor from rotted docks to Mediterranean-style walk-ways and shopping areas along the harbor. (Douglas E. Oakman)

Dover, K. J. 1994. *Greek Popular Morality in the Time of Plato and Aristotle.* Berkeley: University of California Press, 1974. Reprint, Indianapolis: Hackett.

Finley, Moses I. 1979. *The World of Odysseus.* 2d ed. Harmondsworth, Middlesex: Penguin.

————. 1981. "Technical Innovation and Economic Progress in the Ancient World." In *Economy and Society in Ancient Greece.* Ed. with an intro. by Brent D. Shaw and Richard P. Saller. Pp. 176–95. Harmondsworth, Middlesex: Penguin.

Grundmann, Walter. 1964. "Sin in the NT, s.v. ἁμαρτάνω, κτλ." In *Theological Dictionary of the New Testament.* Ed. G. Kittel and G. Friedrich. Trans. G. W. Bromiley. 10 vols. Grand Rapids: Eerdmans, 1964–1976. 1:302–316.

Kautsky, John H. 1982. *The Politics of Aristocratic Empires.* Chapel Hill: University of North Carolina Press.

MacIntyre, Alasdair. 1981. *After Virtue: A Study in Moral Theory.* South Bend, Ind.: University of Notre Dame.

Staehlin, Gustav, and Walter Grundmann. 1964. "Sin and Guilt in Classical Greek and Hellenism, s.v. ἁμαρτάνω, κτλ." In *Theological Dictionary of the New Testament.* Ed. G. Kittel and G. Friedrich. Trans. G. W. Bromiley. 10 vols. Grand Rapids: Eerdmans, 1964–1976. 1:296–302.

RELATEDNESS

The assumption of the social sciences is that premedieval Mediterranean society was "dyadic," that is, that the solidarity of social groups was of greater value than the prosperity or survival of the individual (as is still true in Koranic law, for example), and that individuals' sense of themselves was much more strongly influenced by common group perceptions than ours would be (see **DYADISM; GROUP ORIENTATION**). Thus, the sense of oneself as capable of making independent judgments and decisions, while certainly not non-existent, was not esteemed as a social value. Without some sense of personal responsibility, however, the great Israelite prophets could not have functioned; Jeremiah could not have entertained the thought of ceasing to prophesy (Jer 20:9).

Members of an extended family saw themselves and were seen by others as embedded in the head of the family. Women, unless widowed and beyond remarriageable age, were productive assets to fathers and husbands, on whom they were socially dependent, and from whom they derived their identity. Children were the means to ensure continuation of the family and legitimate transfer of property. Thus, it was not unusual for whole families to suffer the fate of their male head. Blood was thicker than marriage; primary loyalty remained with one's family of origin (see FAMILY-CENTEREDNESS).

These are structural social perceptions. This is not to say that tender and loving relationships were not present within marriages and families, but generally the social institutions did not first presume such relationships as a basis for their existence. In spite of the general pattern in which decisions were made for everyone by the head of the household (Acts 11:14; 16:33), there is ample evidence in early Christianity and its surrounding culture that religious conversion also happened individually, even on the part of wives and slaves (1 Cor 7:12–16; 1 Tim 6:2; 1 Pet 3:1).

Though the household codes suggest that one's membership in the church is mediated through one's biological family, there is already beginning in the New Testament the tendency for the church to replace the family as the primary relationship of embeddedness: preservation of Jesus' sayings regarding renouncement of family for the sake of the gospel (e.g., Mark 3:21, 31–35; 10:28–30); Paul's image of the church as the body of Christ in which all have a direct role (1 Cor 12); the family-oriented language of the Pastoral Epistles for relationships in the church as a whole (1 Tim 5:1–2; Titus 2:2–6). Even so, primary relationship was generally to one's social group rather than to an individual person, or *with* one's social group to a person in the case of the disciple-master relationship.

Dominant American culture, with its intensive individualism, forms its expectations of relatedness quite differently, on the basis of personal attraction, supposedly (though not actually) independent of others' expectations. Many ethnic subcultures, as well as the adolescent subculture, operate more consciously out of the awareness of social grouping (see **Group Orientation** and the Introduction). (Carolyn Osiek)

Abu-Hilal, Ahmad. 1982. "Arab and North-American Social Attitudes: Some Cross-Cultural Comparisons." *Mankind* 22:193–207.

Buchanan, George W. 1963. "The Role of Purity in the Structure of the Essene Sect." *Restoration Quarterly* 4:397–406.

Duling, Dennis. 1995. "BTB Readers Guide: Social-Scientific Small Group Research and Second Testament Study." *Biblical Theology Bulletin* 25:179–93.

Firth, Raymond W. 1973. *Symbols: Public and Private.* Ithaca, N.Y.: Cornell University Press.

Malina, Bruce J. 1979. "The Individual and the Community: Personality in the Social World of Early Christianity." *Biblical Theology Bulletin* 9:126–38.

_____. 1989. "Dealing with Biblical (Mediterranean) Characters: A Guide for U.S. Consumers." *Biblical Theology Bulletin* 19:127–41.

_____. 1992. "Is There a Circum-Mediterranean Person? Looking for Stereotypes." *Biblical Theology Bulletin* 11:66–87.

_____. 1995. "Early Christian Groups: Using Small Group Formation Theory to Explain Christian Organizations." In *Modelling Early Christianity: Social-Scientific Studies of the New Testament in its Context.* Ed. Philip F. Esler. Pp. 96–113. London: Routledge.

Sharabi, Hisham, with Mukhtar Ani. 1977. "Impact of Class and Culture on Social Behavior: The Feudal Bourgeois Family in Arab Society." In *Psychological Dimensions of Near Eastern Studies.* Ed. L. Carl Brown and Norman Itzkowitz. Pp. 240–56. Princeton, N.J.: Darwin.

Scheflen, Albert, and Alice Scheflen. 1972. *Body Language and the Social Order: Communication as Behavioral Control.* Englewood Cliffs, N.J.: Prentice Hall.

Taylor, Nicholas H. 1995. "The Social Nature of Conversion in the Early Christian World." In *Modelling Early Christianity: Social-Scientific Studies of the New Testament in Its Context.* Ed. Philip F. Esler. Pp. 128–36. London: Routledge.

Reliability—see Faith/Faithfulness

Resignation—see Patience

SECRECY—SEE DECEPTION

SELF-SACRIFICE

The strong group orientation of ancient and contemporary traditional societies lends itself to the expectation that individual interests and desires hold second place to the common good and common concerns. In the earlier eras depicted in the Bible, survival often depended on a strongly cohesive group in which strong patriarchal leadership held sway. On the other hand, the frequent appeals to harmony and relinquishing of one's own way in the Pauline churches (e.g., Rom 13:3; 14:15; 1 Cor 11:18–19; Phil 2:1–4; 4:2; Col 3:13–14) would suggest that self-sacrifice did not come naturally in an urbanized Hellenistic context. Thus, self-sacrifice is a value that serves as a means of preserving honor which is rooted in the group and shared in by individual members of that group (see **HONOR/SHAME**).

In later years the ideal of self-sacrifice was urged more strongly on women and children than on free males, while slaves represented the epitome of it; this tendency is already visible in the New Testament (Eph 5:22; 6:5; Col 3:18, 22; 1 Pet 2:18). But the ideal of submission (see **OBEDIENCE**), where appropriate (Eph 5:21; 1 Pet 2:13–14), and especially the ideal of self-surrender, are addressed to all (Mark 8:34–35; Matt 16:24–25; Luke 9:23–24; John 12:23–26).

The discipleship passage in Mark 8:34–35 and parallels presents a problem for considerable transcultural interpretation. To "deny oneself" or to "lose one's *psyche*" (self, soul, personality) must have meant something very different before the psychological revolution of the early twentieth century. In a dyadic culture the concept of self as an individual entity is closely attached to the experience of self as part of a social grouping (see **DYADISM; GROUP ORIENTATION**). The pursuit of individual paths regarding such things as personality development and career choice is not socially reinforced and probably meets with strong social sanction. Thus, the concept of self in such a culture cannot convey the sense of unique individuality and basis for inalienable rights that it does in a modern culture.

Still, the laying down of personal preferences for the sake of the common good, even to the point of death, a very high ideal in any culture, is workable only when accompanied by some belief in ultimate compensation and reciprocity.

In contemporary American culture, the call to sacrifice or deny oneself without a healthy psychological context makes little sense and can be dangerous, for it has been a contributing source to unhealthy self-deprecation and unnecessary endurance of abusive situations. (Carolyn Osiek)

Dubisch, Jill, ed. 1986. *Gender and Power in Rural Greece.* Princeton, N.J.: Princeton University Press.

Harré, Rom. 1989. "The 'Self' as a Theoretical Conception." In *Relativism: Interpretation and Confrontation.* Ed. Michael Krausz. Pp. 387–417. South Bend, Ind.: University of Notre Dame.

Harris, Grace Gredys. 1989. "Concepts of Individual, Self, and Person in Description and Analysis." *American Anthropologist* 91:599–612.

Malina, Bruce J. 1990. "Mother and Son." *Biblical Theology Bulletin* 20:54–64.

_____. 1994. " 'Let Him Deny Himself' (Mark 8:34): A Social-Psychological Model of Self-Denial." *Biblical Theology Bulletin* 24:106–19.

_____. 1995. "Power, Pain and Personhood: Asceticism in the Ancient Mediterranean World." In *Asceticism.* Ed. Vincent L. Wimbush and Richard Valantasis. Pp. 162–77. Oxford: Oxford University Press.

Milavec, Aaron. 1995. "The Social Setting of 'Turning the Other Cheek' and 'Loving One's Enemies' in Light of the *Didache.*" *Biblical Theology Bulletin* 25:131–43.

Pilch, John J. 1995. "Death with Honor: The Mediterranean Style Death of Jesus in Mark." *Biblical Theology Bulletin* 25:65–70.

Schwartz, Shalom H. 1990. "Individualism-Collectivism: Critique and Proposed Refinements." *Journal of Cross-Cultural Psychology* 21:139–57.

Stendahl, Krister. 1976. "The Apostle Paul and the Introspective Conscience of the West." In *Paul among Jews and Gentiles and Other
Essays.* Pp. 78–96. Philadelphia: Fortress.
Whyte, Martin King. 1978. *The Status of Women in Preindustrial Societies.* Princeton, N.J.: Princeton University Press.

SELF-SUFFICIENCY

This is the state of being content or satisfied with
what one has and not craving for gain from one's fellows
(see ALTRUISM; COOPERATIVENESS; ENVY; FATE; LIMITED
GOOD; PURPOSIVENESS/END ORIENTATION). The cultures of
Mediterranean antiquity placed a high value upon self-
sufficiency = self-contentment (Greek: *autarkeia*). Everywhere, however, one sees a tension between self-reliance
and the need for community. For instance, Hesiod con-
cludes a discussion of "the good neighbor" by remarking:
"It is a good thing to draw on what you have; but it
grieves your heart to need something and not to have
it . . ." (*Works and Days*, 366–67; cf. Prov 11:24–26). The
attainment of self-sufficiency involves not only internal
productivity and control of want, but effective manipulation of external social relations as well.

The ancients envisioned the goods of life as being in
limited supply. It is not only wealth produced from agriculture, but also cultural "goods" like honor and interpersonal "goods" like love and esteem that fall within this
purview. This predominantly peasant world operates
upon zero-sum principles (see PURPOSIVENESS/END ORIEN-
TATION; AGRARIAN SOCIETY; PEASANT). When something
increases, something else must decrease. When someone
is perceived to have gotten ahead, everyone else must
necessarily have lost out (Matt 20:1–15).

Therefore, there are informal and institutional
mechanisms within peasant societies to keep things in
balance: gossip and envy function to shame into sharing
families who have unusual luck in the harvest. Community festivals institutionalize redistribution (Luke 15:9).
Conformity to the lowest common denominator of society is the safe route to avoid sanctions and envy. The

value of self-sufficiency also is designed to keep people oriented to just what they need out of life and not to seek self-aggrandizement.

The biblical tradition knows this value well: Exod 16:16–19; 20:17; Neh 5:14–19; Luke 3:10–14; Phil 4:11; and 1 Tim 6:6. Jesus, like Hesiod, opposes individualistic self-sufficiency or self-reliance. He melds into his message of the kingdom of God both a notion of God as - Patron (see **PATRONAGE**) or Provider (Matt 6:25–33 = Luke 12:22–31; cf. Prov 10:3) and the universal claim of the neighbor to hospitality and charitable treatment (Luke 10:29–37; 11:5–13; Matt 5:44//Luke 6:27; see **HOSPITALITY**). The Christian movement continues this dual emphasis of material contentment within community (2 Cor. 9:8).

American society strongly encourages self-sufficiency as it tallies well with its emphasis on individualism, achievement, and the like. Though the common belief is that these values contribute to the welfare of the community and nation, in actuality some who strive for achievement and self-sufficiency do so at the expense of the common good, as banking deficiencies and crises appear to testify. (Douglas E. Oakman)

Austin, M. M., and P. Vidal-Naquet. 1977. *Economic and Social History of Ancient Greece: An Introduction.* Trans. M. M. Austin. Berkeley: University of California Press.

Booth, William James. 1993. *Households: On the Moral Architecture of the Economy.* Ithaca, N.Y.: Cornell University Press.

Critchfield, Richard. 1983. *Villages.* Garden City: Anchor.

Finley, Moses I. 1985. *The Ancient Economy.* 2d ed. London: Hogarth.

Foster, George. 1967. "Peasant Society and the Image of Limited Good." In *Peasant Society: A Reader.* Ed. Jack M. Potter, et al. The Little, Brown Series in Anthropology. Pp. 300–323. Boston: Little, Brown.

Kittel, Gerhard. 1964. "αὐτάρκεια, αὐτάρκης." In *Theological Dictionary of the New Testament.* Ed. G. Kittel and G. Friedrich. Trans. G. W. Bromiley. 10 vols. Grand Rapids: Eerdmans, 1964–1976. 1:466–467.

Montmarquet, James A. 1989. *The Idea of Agrarianism: From Hunter-Gatherer to Agrarian Radical in Western Culture.* Moscow, Idaho: University of Idaho Press.

Scott, James C. 1976. *The Moral Economy of the Peasant: Rebellion and Subsistence in Southeast Asia.* New Haven, Conn.: Yale University Press.

White, K. D. 1977. *Country Life in Classical Times.* Ithaca, N.Y.: Cornell University Press.

Wolf, Eric R. 1966. *Peasants.* Foundations of Modern Anthropology Series. Englewood Cliffs, N.J.: Prentice Hall.

SERVICE

In the Bible, service normally refers to something to be done by a slave, i.e., servile work. Servile work was servile because slave and non-slave belonged to two different species, so to speak, similar to the way humans differed from God. Service refers to tasks performed by lesser persons for those who control their existence. Relative to God, service looks to temple worship and its rituals (e.g., Exod 31:10; 35:19; 1 Esd 6:18; Luke 1:23), while relative to men it pertains to forms of bondage (e.g., Gen 30:26; Exod 1:14). "It is a duty not only to repay a service done but also to take the initiative oneself in doing a service" (Aristotle, *Nicomachean Ethics* V.v [1133^a]). Note how for Paul, the slave service (see **FREEDOM**) owed God in temple worship is now to be displayed in the Christian's service to neighbor, which is service to Christ (Rom 12:1–2; 14:17–18; Gal 5:13; see also 1 Cor 9:19; 2 Cor 4:5).

In the United States, there has been a long tradition of service to the needy. Customs such as barn raising are one illustration. Neighbors helped a person to build a barn within one day so that productive activity would not be held up for long. Service to the needy who are "economically poor" is somewhat similar but also very different. One serves these needy people in an effort to help them become productive citizens again. Such service is clearly voluntary and based on self-interest. Finally, there is an ambivalence toward the value of "service" in the United States. Citizens generally pay lip service to its importance, acknowledge that many do not volunteer for any kind of service, but resist efforts to "require" service from students or others for specific purposes. The Pauline concept of slave service which derives from Christian freedom baffles Americans when it has to be applied in concrete circumstances. (Bruce J. Malina)

Collins, John N. 1990. *Diakonia: Re-Interpreting the Ancient Sources*. Oxford: Oxford University Press.
Patterson, Orlando. 1982. *Slavery and Social Death: A Comparative Study*. Cambridge: Harvard University Press. Pp. 17–101.

SHAME—SEE HONOR/SHAME

SIN—SEE FREEDOM; PURPOSIVENESS/END ORIENTATION

SOUL—SEE EYES-HEART; SELF-SACRIFICE

STEADFAST LOVE—SEE ALSO GRACE/FAVOR; AUTHORITARIANISM

This is a value that governs human interactions in the Mediterranean world. Because kinship is one of the major social institutions in this culture, and family-centeredness a major value, steadfast love draws its meaning primarily from interactions in this social context. English translations of the Hebrew word *ḥesed* correctly reflect this reality. The KJV and ASV translate this word "lovingkindness"; the RSV and NRSV gloss it as "steadfast love," "loyal love," and "loyalty," which is often in parallelism with "mercy." The Greek translation of the Hebrew Scriptures renders this word as "mercy," and it is this "mercy" rather than "steadfast love" which occurs in the New Testament.

In the conflict-ridden (see **POWER**) and competitive (see **HONOR/SHAME**) Mediterranean world, the one certain and reliable source of support is one's family and relationships that replicate the family situation. Abraham persuades his sister/wife Sarah to go along with his strategy of passing her off as his sister by saying: "This is the loyalty [steadfast love; lovingkindness] that you must do me: at every place to which we come, say of me, 'He is my brother' " (Gen 20:13). When Abraham's servant finds Rebekah, the appropriate marriage partner for Isaac [in this instance a second cousin, see TRUST], he says to Rebekah's brother Laban: "Now then if you will deal *loyally* and truly with my master, tell me; and if not, tell me . . ." (Gen 24:49). Jacob relies on the loyalty or steadfast love of Joseph, his son, not to bury him in Egypt but rather to bury him with his ancestors in Hebron (Gen 47:29–30). Naomi prays that God will be as loyal to her daughters-in-law Orpah and Ruth as they were to her and their deceased husbands (Ruth 1:8).

This same steadfast love or loyalty was also demanded in situations that replicated the kinship context. Host and grateful guests were expected to be bound by this kind of steadfast love or loyalty, as Lot was with his guests (Gen 19:18–19) or Rahab was with the spies she hid (Josh 2:12, 14, see HOSPITALITY). Friends such as David and Jonathan (1 Sam 20:8, 14) were also bound to such loyalty, which makes betrayal of friendship so shocking, as in the case of Hushai and David (2 Sam 16:15–19) and Judas and Jesus (see John 13:26–27; cf. Ps 41:10). In all of these instances, loyalty is reciprocal or mutual. It is expected that one will repay the loyalty experienced.

But this highly desirable ideal was not always practiced in Israel. The prophet Hosea reports God's complaint that "there is no faithfulness [see FAITH/FAITHFULNESS) or loyalty, and no knowledge of God in the land. Swearing, lying, and murder, and stealing and adultery break out" (4:1, author's trans.). What God desires, says this prophet, is "steadfast love and not sacrifice" (6:6), a theme Jesus echoes with nuance in his preaching as well: "I desire mercy, and not sacrifice" (Matt 9:13; 12:7).

Mercy is a value or quality that flows naturally from loyalty or steadfast love. "Have mercy on me, O God, according to your steadfast love" (Ps 51:1, NRSV). Thus, while the explicit term "steadfast love" in the sense of "loyalty" does not seem to appear in the New Testament, its expression in "mercy" occurs instead. The idea is that kinship bonds stir confidence that one can expect an emotionally-prompted response from God who is the source and model of mercy (2 Cor 1:3; Eph 2:4; Rom 15:9; Phil 2:27) as well as from Jesus who provides rescue from dire straits (Matt 15:22; 17:15; 20:30–31).

Weak kinship ties characterize the culture that prevails in the United States; individualism is the dominant value. Loyalty or steadfast love in the prevailing culture is rooted in self-interest rather than in kinship or fictive-kinship bonds. For this reason, loyalty or steadfast love in the United States is linked with expedience. The values last as long as they are useful; when no longer useful, loyalty or steadfast love is discarded or transferred to another individual or group so long as that replacement will prove expedient. This is illustrated by the very recent legal "breakthrough" whereby a child was acknowledged to have the right to "divorce" an unworthy parent. Such a behavior is entirely unimaginable in the ancient Mediterranean world. If it occurred, as in the story of the so-called prodigal son, that father was entitled to kill the son on the spot. If the father did not fulfill this cultural requirement, then another son and very definitely the villagers would do it for him. (John J. Pilch)

Hatfield, Elaine, and Richard Rapson. 1993. "Love and Attachment Processes." In *Handbook of Emotions*. Ed. Michael Lewis and Jeannette M. Haviland. Pp. 605–16. New York: Guilford.

Sakenfeld, Katharine Doob. 1977. *The Meaning of Hesed in the Hebrew Bible: A New Inquiry.* Harvard Semitic Museum 17. Missoula, Mont.: Scholars.

SUBMISSION—SEE OBEDIENCE

THRIFT (GREEK *OIKONOMIA*, MANAGEMENT, STEWARDSHIP)

Originally this term referred to a state of prosperity, but now it is used in the sense of economical management to avoid waste. It is the prudent and clever management of resources, particularly with a view to accumulating savings in order to secure the future. The thrifty person does not indulge in luxuries and may even deprive him/ herself to the point of niggardliness, although thriftiness itself is not miserliness.

Several factors are pertinent to the practice of thrift in the Mediterranean world. First, the concept of limited good, that is, that there were limited resources in the world (see ALTRUISM; COOPERATIVENESS; ENVY; FATE; LIMITED GOOD; PURPOSIVENESS/END ORIENTATION); second, the prevailing conditions of unequal distribution of wealth (see PATRONAGE); third, the occurrence of natural disasters, such as famine, drought or locust infestation; fourth, the havoc left by human warfare together with the phenomenon of social banditry; fifth, the critical matter of the water supply: migrants often had to buy water (Deut 2:28), and the offer of a cup of water was considered both a significant deed of lovingkindness, a sign of hospitality (Job 22:7) and an honor (Matt 10:42). In the ancient world, water was regarded as the primal cosmic element and the source of all life. These factors not only encouraged but mandated the practice of thrift in matters of food, water, clothes, and equipment.

However, thrift was also a means of increasing solidarity within the community (cf. the thrifty housewife in Prov 31). Strict economy was practiced in the family and in the marketplace, in selling, buying, and hiring workers. Thrift or *oikonomia* was expected of the leaders of the Christian communities with regard to both spiritual and worldly goods (e.g., 1 Cor 9:17; 1 Cor 4:1; Eph 3:2). An important aspect of a market place economy was bargaining. But thrift would be practiced differently in the city, country, and desert areas, the latter demanding strict thrift in the usage of water for human beings and animals. Usually the thrift of the country and wilderness can be contrasted with the thriftless luxury of the life of many rich city dwellers.

Yet much of the New Testament teaching appears to repudiate the practice of thrift, possibly in light of the imminent *parousia*. Jesus advocated storing treasures not on

earth but in heaven (Matt 6:19–21) and taught his disciples that they should cease to be anxious about providing materially for the future (Matt 6:25–34), but
rather depend upon God for their sustenance. This *modus
vivendi* characterized the first rural Christians and the
itinerant preachers and prophets. Jesus himself appears
to have implemented his own teaching with regard to
this perspective (Matt 8:18–22; Luke 9:57–62). In their
first mission, the disciples rely wholly on hospitality (see
HOSPITALITY) for their sustenance (Matt 10:5–15; Mark
6:7–13; Luke 9:1–6), and some of Jesus' parables breathe
an atmosphere of thriftlessness, e.g., the treasure in the
field, the pearl of great price (Matt 13:44–46). They teach
"profligacy" rather than thrift in matters of the Kingdom
of God although, of course, this type of rhetoric must not
be taken literally. However, the incidents of the widow's
mite (Luke 21:1–4) and Jesus' anointing by women (Matt
26:6–13; Mark 14:3–9; John 12:1–8) show a complete lack
of thriftiness. During the time of Jesus' ministry and perhaps in the early stages of the Christian community
these guidelines may have been followed because of the
eschatological crisis (cf. Paul's teaching on marriage in
1 Cor 7). The selling of property and communal sharing
of good in Acts 1–5 suggests an abandonment of personal
thrift with regard to the future. But Jesus' counsel to the
disciples at the Last Supper, according to Luke, is different: the disciples must now take thought for their future
(Luke 22:35–38). Similar teaching is conveyed in the Parable of the Talents or Pounds (Matt 25:14–30; Luke
19:11–27): the Lukan account is clearly in the context of
the delay of the *parousia*. The appointment of the seven
(Acts 6:1–7) and the Pauline exhortation to liberal giving
(e.g., 2 Cor 8:1–9:15) show a provident care for others.
Paul and his companions supported themselves by their
own handiwork (Acts 18:1–3; 1 Cor 9:6).

In the first blush of the Christian movement Mediterranean thriftiness was "thrown to the wind." When
Christianity spread, especially to the urban areas, the

practice of thrift came into play once again. In American culture where the prevailing belief is "there's always more where this came from" (in contrast to the Mediterranean understanding of limited good as "there is no more where this came from"), thrift is not highly prized. Americans are notorious in the contemporary world for poor saving habits relative to all the goods of life, and not just money. (Josephine Massyngbaerde Ford)

Oakman, Douglas E. 1991. "BTB Readers Guide: The Ancient Economy in the Bible." *Biblical Theology Bulletin* 21:34–39.

TIME ORIENTATION

When the people described in the pages of the Bible were faced with some vital problem, their choice of solution was usually rooted in the present. Like other peasant societies, the societies of the Hebrews, Israelites, Judeans, Galileans, and Pereans all held the present as their first-order temporal preference; the past was their secondary preference; and the future was a very distant and nearly unthinkable third choice. The exception for the ancient Mediterranean region would be the successful city empires, such as Assyria, Babylon, Persia, and Rome, whose elites sought to live up to their ancestors; hence, they had an ostensible past orientation as their primary preference, an orientation to the present as their secondary choice, and a future perspective as an extremely remote third. Yet even such elites showed complete indifference to the future; they simply were not concerned with long-range planning in any field (see Introduction).

Thus, to read the Bible is to enter a world immersed in the present. Invariably, the people we read about looked to the present, to their present experiences, and the people presently around them. God is addressed as though being with them, in the present. And if a solution was not available in the present, they looked to the past, for example, the God of their notable ancestors, Abraham, Isaac, and Jacob. Mention of such ancestors served to root the present pleas to God in past relations. Rarely, if ever, did they bother with the future.

The whole purpose of the recorded story of Israel was to direct present experience. The creation stories compiled in Genesis 1–11 explained, then, present behavior such as the role of women, the reason for agricultural work, and especially the origin(s) of shame. The story of Abraham (Gen 12ff.) explained who we are in terms of our father Abraham and his descendants. The story of the patriarchs explained the reason for our tribal affiliations. The story of the Exodus gave basis for our obligation to God and "the sons of your own people" (Lev 19:18), while the Laws given to Moses directed our present, daily living. In fact, for the people who are pictured in the Bible and who preserved the Bible, there was only one, large, present orientation.

Should the present turn problematic, one would look to the past: "remember the former things of old; for I am God, and there is no other; I am God, and there is none like me" (Isa 46:9). One could remind God of the past: "Awake, awake, put on strength, O arm of the LORD; awake, as in days of old, the generations of long ago. Was it not thou that didst cut Rahab in pieces, that didst pierce the dragon?" (Isa 51:9). And God would respond: "Then he remembered the days of old, of Moses his servant" (Isa 63:11). Yet for the doings of God, the present was preferable: "Remember not the former things, nor consider the things of old" (Isa 43:18).

Similarly, the world of Jesus was a present-oriented world, with the past as second preference (witness quotes from the Bible depicting the past). Proverbs such as the following underscored the present: "Tomorrow will be anxious for itself. Let the day's own trouble be sufficient for the day" (Matt 6:34); "Do not be concerned from morning until evening, and from evening until morning about what you will wear" (*Gospel of Thomas* 36; Oxyrhynchus Papyrus 655.1). And whether one prayed: "Give us this day our daily bread" or "Give us today tomorrow's bread" (Q Matt 6:11; Luke 11:3), emphasis was still on the present. Such preference is typical of non-elites in agrarian societies in general (see AGRARIAN SOCI-ETY; PEASANT). Present orientation as first-order prefer-ence meant not only that there were no schedules or time tables, it meant also that "it is not for you to know times or seasons which the Father has fixed by his own authority" (Acts 1:7).

Secondary past preference might be seen in the Magnificat where Mary is described as saying: "For be-hold, henceforth all generations will call me blessed" (Luke 1:48). The Lukan reader knew the obvious mean-ing of the passage: all people from all past generations up to Mary's present were to acclaim her. The appar-ently "past" reference in Hebrews 13:8: "Jesus Christ is the same yesterday and today and forever," actually forms part of a phrase that expresses an endless today, hence, an abiding present. The thanksgivings at the opening of the Pauline letters move from the past to an extended present. Likewise, statements about those who "have their reward" in contrast to those who receive a "reward from your Father who is in heaven" (in Matt 6:2, 5–6, 16) are both about reward now, underscoring the fact that those who already have their own sort of reward are not to receive a reward from God at present. The present time orientation explains why Jesus' state-ments on the rewards of discipleship include "a hun-dredfold now in this time" or "manifold more in this time" (Mark 10:28–30; Matt 19:27–29; Luke 18:28–30). There simply is no concern for the future; no mention of some next generation, or future generations, or future time periods, in the NT. We read of this age and the age to come, but nothing of ages to come nor of a new gen-eration in the age to come! It seems quite clear, for ex-ample, that Matthew's "close of the age" (Matt 28:20) was to have been witnessed by "some standing here," belonging to "this generation" (Matt 16:28; 24:34), again with no other generation in sight.

The fact is there really is no expressed concern for the future in the gospel story. And it would appear that the same holds for the entire NT, since any time description consisting of this age and a rather proximate age to come has no room for a future of the sort we speak of. For example, a book such as Revelation was to console a present generation. It looked to their present. It did speak of events and persons who were forthcoming but not future. Something is forthcoming when its later presence is already guaranteed by its present presence: a child is forthcoming as a present fetus; a field of grain is forthcoming in a presently plowed and planted field; a symphony is forthcoming in a present opening movement. A present that includes the forthcoming is a broad present, embracing "this generation," for example. The future, on the other hand, is the merely possible, the conceivable, something not ostensibly rooted in the present. For the people in the Bible, such a possible, merely conceivable future is known only to God, just like the past for which there are no living witnesses. Such future and past is known to God alone.

The conceivable, possible past and the conceivable, possible future are domains exclusive to God, for whom all things are possible (Gen 18:14; Jer 32:27; Matt 19:26; Luke 1:37; Rom 4:21). It is true that at God's command, these domains might impinge on present human experience. Yet to say that all things are possible for God means all those things presently not possible for human beings will forever remain so. The past and the future as the possible, then, cannot belong and never will belong to human beings. They are God's. To glimpse the world of the distant past or of the future, the world of the possible, is to assume divine prerogatives. For Jews such insolence was idolatry, while for Greeks it was hubris. The possible past and the possible future are simply closed to human beings.

Thus, on the one hand, the need for prophets in Israel to tell about distant origins, whether of the human family or of the people of Israel. Only God could know that distant period for which there were no living witnesses, hence, only God could reveal it through his prophets. As the preserve of God alone, information about the past must be given by God to men as in the "Former Prophets" headed by the great prophet Moses, then Joshua, Judges, Samuel, and Kings. As for the Later Prophets, given the fact that they and their audience were concerned exclusively with the present and what comes forth from the present, they too were present oriented. If God tells of the possible future, it is for the present reason of avoiding idolatry (see Isa 44:7–8; 45:21; 48:5).

This possible future is that which falls outside the purview of what comes forth from the present, known to God alone (see Mark 13:32; Matt 24:36; Acts 1:7). On the other hand, statements such as "Behold, he is coming with the clouds, and every eye will see him, every one who pierced him; and all tribes of the earth will wail on account of him" (Rev 1:7) indicate something rooted in present human experience. "Everyone who pierced him" was still available. The same holds for Paul's reference to "we who are alive, who are left until the coming of the Lord" (1 Thess 4:15). The process set under way with the death and resurrection of Jesus is viewed as present and experienced.

So for members of Jesus movement groups, God's kingdom was forthcoming, Jesus' emergence as Messiah with power was forthcoming, the transformation of social realities in favor of God's people was forthcoming. Yet for the audiences of Mark, Matthew, and Luke, things obviously changed. The coming of Jesus is moved now into the realm of possibility, into the imaginary future known only to God. The coming of the Son of Man with power in Mark and Matthew, for example, moves present experience into some possible future, a piece of imaginary time known only to God: "But of that day or that hour no one knows, not even the angels in heaven, nor the Son, but only the Father" (Mark 13:32; Matt 24:36). And the same with hopes for social transformation in Luke's group: "It is not for you to know times or seasons which the Father has fixed by his own authority" (Acts 1:7). In the NT writings, we can see how the forthcoming rooted in present experience became future, rooted in possibilities known only to God.

In contrast, mainstream United States culture is predominantly focused on the future. Newer is better, the future belongs to the youth. Our society has invented and refined future planning, even to the extent of distinguishing between a linear plan (if all goes well) and a discontinuous plan (wherein unforeseen but imaginatively anticipated contingencies could cause different outcomes). Such confidence in the ability to prognosticate and shape the future stands in stark contrast with the Mediterranean world. It is very difficult but very necessary for American readers of ancient Mediterranean texts to keep future considerations out of these ancient texts. (Bruce J. Malina)

Eviatar, Zerubavel. 1981. *Hidden Rhythms: Schedules and Calendars in Social Life.* Chicago: University of Chicago Press.
Lauer, Robert H. 1981. *Temporal Man: The Meaning and Uses of Social Time.* New York: Praeger.
Malina, Bruce J. 1989. "Christ and Time: Swiss or Mediterranean." *Catholic Biblical Quarterly* 51:1–31.
Munn, Nancy. 1992. "The Cultural Anthropology of Time: A Critical Essay." *Annual Review of Anthropology* 21:93–123.

TORAH ORIENTATION (LAW-MINDEDNESS)

If "beliefs" are "the way things are," if "values" are what a social group shares that are rooted in its beliefs, and if "norms" are the more or less explicit rules or guidelines that express those "values," then "law" is the more or less formalized, systematic statement ("codification") of those norms, often but not always in written form, the object of which is to maintain social institutions. Law is normally regulated by a person or persons in authority (kings, judges, the military) and enforced by powers (police).

In the U.S., law is traditionally based on eighteenth-century revolutionary beliefs about "self-evident truths" or the universal "Law of Nature" thought to be known by human reason, namely, that individuals are "created equal" and have "inalienable rights"; that these rights include life, liberty, and the pursuit of happiness, and that the mutual self-interest of "the people" leads to their forming a "social contract" (Rousseau), that is, the people agree either to preserve such values by common consent (Locke) or to establish safeguards against destroying each other (Hobbes). The majority rules, but minority rights are protected regardless of race, color, religious creed, sex, or national-ethnic origin (the Bill of Rights). Such beliefs include the view that the state shall not establish or interfere with an individual's private religious beliefs or practices (the First Amendment: "separation of church and state").

"Law-mindedness" in the Bible must be understood on the basis of a different set of beliefs, values, and norms. The Hebrew term translated "law" in English is usually *torah*. Torah can mean all written and oral revelation, but in the more restricted sense it normally refers to the "Law of Moses" (cf. Neh 8:1), that is, the Pentateuch, or first five books of the Jewish Scriptures. The Pentateuch contains not only "laws," but tribal myths and legends, genealogies, and a whole range of instructions about morality and ritual purity for a particular group of people, the Israelites or Jews. From this perspective, "law" is divinely revealed "instruction" for all of life within a particular "national-religious-ethnic" social group that believes itself chosen to be the "light to the nations" (cf. Isa 49:6); it enshrines beliefs and values about the group that are related to sexual, social, and religious hierarchies in families, households, ancient tribal units, monarchies and empires. While the equivalent Greek word *nomos* in the New Testament occasionally takes on certain Greco-Roman overtones that come closer to the English word "law," and while some early Christians challenged what they perceived to be meanings of the Torah (for example, the Gospel of Matthew) or extended "law" to a more general sense (for example, Paul), *nomos* in the New Testament often continues to be influenced by the Jewish idea of torah, and early Christian writers frequently quote it and interpret it. In the Bible, "law-mindedness" includes these different beliefs and values.

To illustrate the contrast between biblical torah and modern democratic, individualistic ideals about law, consider the biblical beliefs, values, norms, and laws about the sexes. In the kinship system, male ("patrilineal") genealogies are important for determining whom one can or cannot marry, inheritance laws, the legitimacy of kings (e.g., the tribe of Judah, the lineage of David), and the maintenance of priestly purity. In families, sons rank ahead of, and are generally more desirable than, daughters, and are designated by their fathers' names (e.g., Jesus, son of Joseph). The occasions for female impurity are much more numerous than those for male impurity (Lev 15; cf. Mark 5:25–34; Luke 2:22) and taboos about sexual incest are seen from the male perspective (Lev 18; cf. 1 Cor 5:1–8). In families the man/husband/father is "lord" or "master" over the woman/wife/mother (e.g., "Household Codes": Col 3:18; Eph 5:21–33; 1 Pet 2:11–3:12). A man can divorce a woman because he finds something "indecent" in her (Deut 24:1; cf. Matt 19:3). Though Jesus is portrayed as challenging this law by forbidding divorce altogether (Mark 10:1–9), which may be a kind of protection for women, there is no legal recourse for a Jewish woman until Greco-Roman legal ideas make their appearance (Mark 10:11; 1 Cor 7:10–16). In short, there is care and concern for wives and widows, but laws about marriage, divorce, adoption, bearing children, inheritance, female purity and impurity, the legitimacy of kings, the purity of priests, and the like are all expressions of cultural beliefs, values, and norms about male dominance.

More concretely, the earliest biblical law codes appear to have been modelled on the "suzerainty treaties" of the ancient Hittites (in modern Turkey) in which "Great Kings" agreed to protect their vassal or "client kings" in return for their loyalty. In Israel, such a legal agreement, or "covenant," was believed to have been formed between Yahweh/God, the "Great King," and his client-people, "Israel," whom he had delivered from Egyptian slavery. The law codes contained unconditional negative prohibitions ("apodictic" laws) such as those found in the familiar Ten Commandments ("Thou shalt not . . ."; cf. Deut 5:5–21; Exod 20:1–17; cf. Exod 22:18–23:19). But there were also laws that spelled out specific conditions with the formula "When/if (the case) . . . then (the consequence)" ("casuistic" or case laws). The following example, which also illustrates the dominant patriarchalism, comes from the well known "Covenant Code" (Exod 20:22–23:33):

> When a man sells his daughter as a slave, she shall not go out as the male slaves do. If she does not please her master, who has designated her for himself, then he shall let her be redeemed; he shall have no right to sell her to a foreign people, since he has dealt faithlessly with her. If he designates her for his son, (then) he shall deal with her as with a daughter. If he takes another wife to himself, (then) he shall not diminish her food, her clothing, or her marital rights. And if he does not do these three things for her, (then) she shall go out for nothing, without payment of money (Exod 21:7–11).

The famous "an eye for an eye and a tooth for a tooth" (Latin: *lex talionis*, "law of the claw") falls into this "casuistic" category. There are also many regulations with a humanitarian flavor, that is, that protect the widow, the orphan, the stranger, and the poor.

As noted, "law-mindedness" includes the sphere of purity/impurity (see **PURITY**). In the "Holiness Code" (Lev 17–26) the major theme is, "You shall be holy to me; for I [Yahweh] am holy, and have separated you from the peoples, that you should be mine" (Lev 20:26). Correspondingly, there are a number of priestly laws in Exodus, Leviticus, and Numbers that deal with sacrifice, menstruation, birth, forbidden sexual relations, and contact with outsiders.

In the period of the Davidic monarchy (ca. 1000–587 BCE), it appears that everyday justice was administered by city elders sitting at the city gate. Yet, specific decisions employing these laws are difficult to find, leading some modern interpreters to think that they were not based on actual cases, but were ideal legislative guidelines promulgated by kings. By New Testament times the eastern monarchical tradition that the king is the law, or at least the "incarnation" of Divine Law, had superseded the classical Greek philosophical ideal (e.g., Aristotle) that the "rule of law" is superior to the rule of men.

In the period prior to the rise of Christianity, the Torah as "instruction" for all of life had achieved the status something like "Scripture." Professional legal experts who interpreted it were called "scribes" (Ezra 7:6, 11; Sir 38:24–39:11). There had emerged a system of courts, the most prestigious and well known of which was the "Supreme Court" in Jerusalem (the Sanhedrin).

There were a number of factions and movements whose scribes sought to interpret the Torah. The wealthy, aristocratic, priestly Sadducees, a faction which controlled the Sanhedrin, were, to use a modern term, "strict constructionists," that is, they held to a very literal interpretation of only the written "Law of Moses" and rejected what they perceived to be innovations, such as the resurrection of the dead, based on other, non-Torah, books they considered to be of lesser importance.

In contrast, the non-priestly Pharisees accepted other books ("the prophets" and "the writings") and may have believed that their own oral legal "tradition" (the New Testament's "tradition of the elders"?) had also come directly from Moses. The Pharisees sought to extend temple purity laws to everyday life, believing that they should be observed in the kitchen, the bedroom, the street, and the field. Pious Jews, for example, should avoid impure persons, places, and foods (Kosher practices). The Pharisees developed rules for interpreting the sacred texts and sought to protect the people from transgressing the heart of the Torah (by "building a fence around the Torah"). Whether they were more quietistic or were zealously active in attempting to impose their oral tradition on the masses is debated.

Though not mentioned in the Bible, a third faction, called the Essenes, whose writings were discovered in 1947 (the Dead Sea Scrolls), was also "law-minded." Taking literally the prophetic text, "In the wilderness prepare the way of the Lord" (Isa 40:3; cf. Mark 1:3; Matt 3:3; Luke 1:76; 3:4–6; John 1:23), the Essenes retreated to the wilderness along the Dead Sea where they awaited the end of the world in a type of monastic scribal community that interpreted the books of the Torah and other sacred books within and outside the Hebrew Bible to apply specifically to themselves as the chosen people. Especially noteworthy is their method for applying these texts to their own times (*pesher* or "interpretation"). As a priest-led community, they especially emphasized purity and sabbath laws.

There were also a variety of popular socio-political revolutionary groups and movements in Palestine during the first century. Josephus, the Jewish historian, calls one of them the "zealots," which refers specifically to their extreme "zeal" for the Torah to the extent that they would fight, kill, and die for it (Num 31:13–20; 25:6–9; 1 Macc 2:26). Those who adhered to this sort of "law-mindedness" became leaders in the war of liberation against the Romans (66–70 CE).

What of "law-mindedness" among everyday Palestinian folk? As noted above, the Pharisees sought to extend laws about temple purity to everyday life. While it is likely that the Jewish peasantry of Palestine observed the most important laws (e.g., circumcision, the Sabbath, festivals, and avoidance of non-kosher foods such as pork), the sources about their daily adherence to ritual purity laws are so limited that the question is debated.

There are a variety of attitudes toward "law-mindedness" in the New Testament. Jesus is portrayed on the one hand as observing the Sabbath law (Mark 1:21 and parallels) and the festivals (Mark 11:1ff. and parallels). Matthew 5:18–19 has Jesus say, "For truly I tell you, until heaven and earth pass away, not one letter, not one stroke of a letter, will pass from the law (*nomos*) until all is accomplished. Therefore, whoever breaks one of the least of these commandments, and teaches others to do the same, will be called least in the kingdom of heaven; but whoever does them (the Law) and teaches them will be called great in the kingdom of heaven" (NRSV). Yet, Jesus is also portrayed as blurring Torah distinctions between clean and unclean (Mark 7:1–23 and parallels; see **PURITY**), as challenging the law on divorce (Mark 10:2–12 and parallels), and the Matthean passage just cited continues by showing that Jesus reinterprets laws/ legal traditions about murder, adultery, divorce, swearing oaths, forgiveness, love, and hate ("You have heard that it was said . . . But I say to you"). Similarly, the Gospel of Luke has Jesus say, "The Law and the Prophets were until John; since then the good news of the Kingdom of God is preached" (Luke 16:16), and the book of Acts portrays the Hellenistic Christian Stephen as being martyred for his opposition to the temple and the Torah (Acts 6:13ff.).

Perhaps the most distinctive view of "law-mindedness" in the New Testament is that of the apostle Paul, who claims to have been a Pharisee (Phil 3:5). On the one hand he says that "the law is holy, and the commandment is holy and just and good" (Rom 7:12); on the other hand he claims that ". . . Christ is the end of the law, that every one who has faith may be justified" (Rom 10:4). For Paul, the legal agreement, or "covenant," that was made with Abraham was based on Abraham's faith or trust that God would fulfill his promise (Gen 15:6),

namely, that through Abraham's "seed" the "nations"—
the term in Greek that can also mean "Gentiles"—would
be blessed (Gen 12:3; 18:18; Gal 3:6; Rom 4:3). Circumcision, the sign of the covenant (Gen 17:9–14), came only
after Abraham's faith (Rom 4:10–11). Indeed, the "Law of
Moses," a new covenant, did not come until 430 years
after Abraham's faith (Gal 3:17), and it was only temporary, like a "disciplinarian/child-sitter" or "custodian"
(Gal 3:24) for the young, to point out "sin" (Rom 5:20).
When Christ came, the law of Moses symboled by circumcision, though not in itself sinful, was no longer necessary for believing Christians. For Paul, Christ as the
true "seed" of Abraham (Gal 3:16) accomplished by his
sacrificial death and resurrection what the law could not
do. All those who believe in him are likewise "sons" of
Abraham (Gal 3:29), the model of faith. Paul generalized:
"For we hold that a man is justified by faith apart from
works of the law" (Rom 3:28). At the same time, Paul
limited freedom wherever it seemed to him to go to un-
ethical extremes or to threaten Christian unity; in such
cases he emphasized the model of weakness and humility
symboled by the crucifixion of Jesus, as well as the responsibility to love others within the new Christian group
(esp. 1 Corinthians). (Dennis Duling)

Black, Donald. 1976. *The Behavior of Law.* New York: Academic Press.
Derret, J. Duncan M. 1977–1989. *Studies in the New Testament.* 5 vols.
    Leiden: Brill.
Malina, Bruce J. 1981. "The Apostle Paul and Law: Prolegomena for an
    Hermeneutic." *Creighton Law Review* 14:1305–39.
Selznick, Philip, et al. 1968. "Law." In *International Encyclopedia of the
    Social Sciences.* Ed. D. L. Sills. 9:49–78. New York: Macmillan.

TRADITION—SEE GROUP ORIENTATION; FAMILY-CENTEREDNESS

TRUST (PERSONAL AND GROUP)

The Mediterranean cultural conviction that human
beings do not control nature is underscored by their

daily experience in which many other aspects of human life are similarly beyond their control. People who live in such circumstances understandably search for security, for someone or something in which they can trust, in which they can place their allegiance, upon which they can base their hope. Trust or hope is thus a value that serves as a means to attaining an honorable existence, so long as the source is trustworthy and reliable (see **PATRONAGE**).

Relative to persons, trust (also known as hope or allegiance) is rooted in the security that derives from a solidly reliable, interpersonal relationship. The nouns "hope," "trust," "confidence," "allegiance," as well as the verbs "to have hope" and "to hope," refer to the social experience of security and trustworthiness that characterize relationships. As a social bond, it works along with the value of (personal and group) attachment (translated "love") and the value of (personal and group) loyalty (translated "faith").

In the family-centered culture of the Mediterranean world (see **FAMILY-CENTEREDNESS**), one would naturally expect to trust, hope in, or rely upon one's kin-folk. An ideal female marriage partner in patriarchal and patrilocal society typical in this world is a close relative, often a first cousin (a father's brother's daughter, or a similar relative (see Gen 24:1–4, 15–16; 28:1–5). The ancient Hebrews also recognized the role of a redeemer in each family, a next of kin, who would avenge the tarnished honor of a family member when that should become necessary (Num 35:9–12). But experience testified that sometimes one's family was unreliable (Jer 9:4; Job 8:14; 18:14).

In addition, many other seemingly solid sources of trust and hope proved to be illusory: riches (Prov 11:28; Ps 62:10; Luke 18:18–25), fortified cities (Jer 5:17; Deut 28:52), horses and chariots (Isa 31:1), armor (Luke 11:21–22), even friends (Jer 9:4–6; Mic 7:5; Ps 41:9)!

Only God is reliable and trustworthy. "Blessed are those who trust in the LORD, whose trust is the LORD" (Jer 17:7, NRSV) but "cursed are those who trust in mere mortals" (17:5, NRSV). Trust in God is preferable to specious self-confidence (Prov 3:5; 16:20; Ps 25:2; 26:1; 28:7) as Jesus noted in directing a parable against the Pharisees "who trusted in themselves that they were righteous" (Luke 18:9–14).

Abraham hoped "against hope" (Rom 4:18). Paul testifies during his trial before the governor: "I have a hope in God . . . that there will be a resurrection of both the righteous and the unrighteous" (Acts 24:15, NRSV; see also Acts 26:6–7). So secure does Paul feel in his allegiance to God that he boasts "in our hope of sharing the glory of God" (Rom 5:2).

Sometimes abiding trust, steadfast allegiance, and unshaken hope in God seem to outside observers to be mistaken or misplaced. Those standing around the cross mocked Jesus by saying: "He trusts in God; let God deliver him now, if he wants to . . ." (Matt 27:43, NRSV). The choice to maintain secure hope is rooted in the sense of the reliability of the one in whom such allegiance is placed. Paul writes: "He who rescued us from so deadly a peril (near death) will continue to rescue us; on him we have set our hope that he will rescue us again" (2 Cor 1:10, NRSV). Such a sense of security allows a person to act with great boldness (2 Cor 3:12; Heb 3:6), without fear of being shamed (Phil 1:20).

The staunch individualism that characterizes United States culture, along with the pride of personal achievement, prompts us rather to suspect others as unreliable and perhaps even hostile to personal aspirations. In addition, excessive confidence in technology and human ability causes Americans to turn to God only when science fails, that is, in moments of desperation. Such an attitude is a stark contrast to the cultural values reflected in the Bible. (John J. Pilch)

Heise, David R., and John O'Brien. 1993. "Emotion Expression in Groups." In *Handbook of Emotions.* Ed. Michael Lewis and Jeannette M. Haviland. Pp. 489–98. New York: Guilford.

WHOLENESS

This concept, which pervades ancient Jewish culture, finds linguistic expression in many phrases, such as *holos* (whole), *hygies* (sound), even the terms for "one" nd "all." It also finds expression in terms depicting its opposite, "dividedness" or "blemished/maimed." Wholeness is a fundamental value expressed in the creation story in Genesis 1: God made no hybrids, no mixture of creatures, no blemished or imperfect beasts, but rather true, perfect birds, fish and animals. For example, a "perfect" bird is defined as one that satisfies all the conditions of being a true bird: it stays in a bird's place (the air), moves like a bird (flies) and eats a bird's diet (seeds). Holy animals, which may be offered in sacrifice to God or eaten by holy people, come only from the class of creatures which fill completely the definition in Genesis 1 of an ideal animal and which remain bodily whole. An animal with three or five legs is not whole and so is unholy; an androgynous person is not wholly male or female and so is unholy. "Too much" or "too little" means unwholeness. What is unwhole cannot be offered to God and so is considered unholy; conversely what is whole and unblemished can be offered in the temple and so is holy.

Wholeness finds expression in many ways. The premier commandment according to Jesus is love of God with the whole "heart . . . soul . . . mind . . . strength" (Mark 12:30). God demands total loyalty, a totality of the inner faculties (heart/soul) and outer limbs (strength), a wholeness of thought and action. The same sense of wholeness is expressed in Paul's prayer that God sanctify us "wholly," which means that God will keep our "spirit and soul and body" sound and blameless (1 Thess 5:23). People cannot serve both God and mammon, and so must be wholly devoted to one or the other (Matt 6:24). Jesus demands that God be served by the whole person, both in bodily action and in interior desires (Matt 5:21–48).

Wholeness finds expression in all-or-nothing patterns (see also **AUTHORITARIANISM; EMOTION/DEMONSTRATION OF FEELINGS**). If one bodily member is dark, the whole body is dark (Matt 6:22–23). If one has bathed, then only the feet need to be washed, for one is clean all over (John 13:10). Conversely, a little leaven leavens the whole batch (1 Cor 5:6). People, then, are either saints or sinners (see John 9:31). "Either make the tree good, and its fruits good; or make the tree bad, and its fruits bad" (Matt 12:33); but a tree cannot be both good and bad. Hence, "whoever keeps the whole law but fails in one point has become guilty of all of it" (Jas 2:10).

Wholeness finds vivid expression in terms of the human body. One aspect of a "holy" body is that it must be bodily whole; blemished, maimed or defective bodies lack wholeness and so are unqualified for the presence of God (Lev 21:17–20). The thrust of Jesus' healings is to make persons "whole" once more (Luke 7:10). Jesus makes bodily limbs "whole," whether paralyzed legs (John 5:6–15; 7:23) or withered arms (Matt 12:13). His miracles, then, make whole by restoring what was lost ("the mute speaking, the maimed whole, the lame walking, the blind seeing," Matt 15:31, NRSV).

Wholeness is concerned as well with the integrity of human thought and action. James states that true religion must include correct actions, so that what enlivens heart and mind shows up in hands and feet as well (1:26–27; see **EYES-HEART; HANDS-FEET**). James would describe any distinction between "faith" and "works" as nonsense, for true righteousness means a wholeness of belief and behavior (2:17–26). In this vein, Paul calls for a wholeness of conversion when he exhorts the church to "live a life worthy of your calling" (1 Thess 2:12). Conversely, there is a horror at hypocrisy, the very sin of dividedness, whereby what one does with hands and feet, external behavior, is divorced from the heart's interiority (Matt 6:1–18; 23:13, 23–30).

Wholeness as a paramount value informs many areas of life. In regard to marriage, the two become one flesh, a wholeness ordained by God at creation (Mark 10:6–8). Hence, divorce is prohibited because it divides that wholeness (10:9). Concerning the church, Paul stresses that it is "one," that is, it has a certain wholeness which includes rich and poor, wise and foolish, noble and peasant; divisions based on boasting or arrogant claims make some feel as though they do not belong, thus wounding the wholeness of Christ's body and threatening its holiness (1 Cor 12:14–26). Paul's rationale for remaining unmarried rests on his belief in the value of wholeness: the unmarried are totally devoted to the affairs of the Lord, whereas the married are "divided" in loyalty (1 Cor 7:32–35).

On occasion, divorce and unwholeness are tolerated as a lesser evil: it is better to pluck out the scandalizing eye and to cut off the offending hand or foot, than to enter "whole" into Gehenna/Hell (Mark 9:43–48). It is better for a believer to divorce an unbeliever who objects to the spouse's faith; better divorce than apostasy (1 Cor 7:15).

Wholeness applies also to Christian teaching. 1 Timothy speaks of "whole" doctrine in contrast with heresy. Heretics promote a single idea and make an unwarranted emphasis, whereas true believers hold to all that has been handed down (1:10b–11). Jesus claimed that he did not come to abolish the law and the prophets by so much as one iota or dot (Matt 5:17–18). Wholeness of traditional doctrine remained important for him. True believers, moreover, insist that for doctrine to be "whole," what one teaches must be in accord with what one does.

The converse of wholeness is dividedness. Some dividedness results from deception (see **DECEPTION; EQUIVOCATION**), when hypocrites mask a bad heart with correct external behavior. Other dividedness results from incomplete conversion. James chides some saying, "cleanse your hands, you sinners, and purify your hearts, you . . . of double mind" (4:8); hands and heart should both be clean, even as the heart must be totally loyal to God. James also notes that some who pray are double-minded (1:8) and so do not receive what they pray for. A heart full of faith is a whole heart; those who pray with single-mindedness are heard (see Mark 11:23). Lack of wholeness might be spoken of as hardheartedness, that is, a divided condition when the heart does not believe what the eyes see (see Mark 3:5; 8:17; John 12:40). Allied with hardheartedness is the quality of being stiff-necked (Acts 7:51), the refusal to accept the yoke of God despite instruction. What passes through the eyes and ears, then, does not form a whole with either the heart, the mind, or the hands. Such a person remains divided (see **Hands-Feet; Eyes-Heart**).

Western culture in general has gloried in specialization. By reducing things, problems, and just about everything to its component parts, westerners generally believe solutions are easier to find. That this very helpful outlook has been often taken to extremes is evident in the growing popularity of "holistic" approaches in the United States including, for example, "holistic" approaches to skiing! The unremitting criticism of "holistic" (sometimes spelled "wholistic") approaches to life in its many dimensions in the United States confirms that this outlook is neither dominant nor prevalent in this culture. (Jerome H. Neyrey)

Douglas, Mary T. 1966. *Purity and Danger: An Analysis of the Concepts of Pollution and Taboo.* London: Routledge & Kegan Paul.

_____. 1968. "Pollution." In *International Encyclopedia of the Social Sciences.* Ed. D. L. Sills. 12:336–42. New York: Macmillan.

Elliott, John J. 1993. "The Epistle of James in Rhetorical and Social Scientific Perspective: Holiness-Wholeness and Patterns of Replication." *Biblical Theology Bulletin* 23:71–81.

Neyrey, Jerome H. 1986a. "The Idea of Purity in Mark's Gospel." *Semeia* 35:91–128.

_____. 1986b. "Body Language in 1 Corinthians: The Use of Anthropological Models for Understanding Paul and His Opponents." *Semeia* 35:129–70.

_____. 1988. "Unclean, Common, Polluted, and Taboo." *Forum* 4/4:72–82.

_____. 1991. "The Symbolic Universe of Luke–Acts: 'They Turn the World Upside Down.' " In *The Social World of Luke–Acts: Models for Interpretation.* Ed. Jerome H. Neyrey. Pp. 271–304. Peabody, Mass.: Hendrickson.

WORSHIPFULNESS

The Greek word for worshipfulness, *eusebeia*, denoted wide-ranging relationships in the Hellenistic world. It designated the respect due to divine beings, including Fate and Chance. Since human beings believed that such beings, and not they, were able to control nature and life-events (see Introduction), they held such beings in high regard.

Worshipfulness was also to be extended toward valued objects, such as parents, country, good deeds, even one's personal demon. The word designates not an abstract attitude but rather an ongoing display of acts of piety (1 Tim 5:4). This value permeated the lives of those who believed that one God is the source of all goodness and blessings.

Worshipfulness of this one God displayed itself not only in a daily program of prayer but in all conduct. God's constant care evokes continuous worshipfulness as the public mark of the faithful. The pious person is contrasted with the sinner as the lamb with the wolf (Sir 13:17). Followers of the God of Israel were designated as worshipers/pious (Acts 13:43, 50; 17:4, 17; 18:7; see Josh 4:24, LXX), equivalent to the Hebrew idiom of those who "fear the Lord."

To engage in ritual without worshipfulness in the heart is hypocrisy (Matt 15:8–9, citing Isa 29:13; see EQUIVOCATION). The worshiper of the Lord does not say anything deserving of death (Sir 23:12) but engages in wise conversation (Sir 27:11) and keeps God's commandments (Sir 37:12). The centurion Cornelius, graced with a vision for his prayer and good works, exemplifies this style of life (Acts 10:2).

The term acquired special significance in the early catholic Christian communities, which extolled this value as a summary of the life of Jesus (1 Tim 3:16). Piety is useful in every way because it has the promise of life both now and in the future (1 Tim 4:8). Aspiring leaders of the church are called to be models of worshipfulness. It makes them a target for persecution (2 Tim 3:12) because they reject the values of this world. This mode of living gives public witness that their loyalty is to the divine. It nourishes in believers hope for the glorious return of "our great God and Savior Jesus Christ" (Titus 2:13). God will rescue from the final judgment those who worship him (2 Pet 2:9). Worshipfulness rests upon belief in a stable order worthy of honor, reverence, and loyalty. It nourishes within its possessors a cultivation of the values worshiped; they stand out in a society that lacks self-control (Titus 2:12).

A life of worshipfulness proposes demands that are no longer the cornerstone of modern American culture, such as respect for parents, who no longer wield power and influence, and fidelity to the God who condemns all worship of creatures. Parents must earn whatever reverence they hope to receive. Self-reliance, higher education, and whatever spells success occupy the place of honor that reverence held in Judeo-Christian societies at the time Jesus was first proclaimed. (†James M. Reese)

Malina, Bruce J. 1993. "The Perception of Limited Good: Maintain One's Social Status." In *The New Testament World: Insights from Cultural Anthropology.* Pp. 90–116. Louisville, Ky.: Westminster John Knox.

ZEAL/JEALOUSY

The term refers to the internal emotional disposition and the corresponding external behavior which an honorable person is expected to exhibit toward that to which s/he is perceived to possess exclusive access. Zeal thus is a value that serves as a means for preserving and maintaining honor.

Within a context of honor and shame (see **HONOR/ SHAME**) and a perception of limited good (see **ALTRUISM; COOPERATIVENESS; ENVY; FATE; LIMITED GOOD; PURPOSIVE- NESS/END ORIENTATION**), zeal/jealousy refers to the concern for maintaining possession and control over that to which one claims to have honorable and exclusive access. Envy (see **ENVY**), in contrast to zeal/jealousy, constitutes the de- sire to possess, or the resentment of, the honorable and ex- clusive possession of another. From the perspective of envy, zeal/ jealousy is the expected, honorable response of a per- son perceived to have been dishonored, afflicted, violated, or otherwise injured by envious intentions and/or actions.

The English word "jealousy" derives from the word "zeal" (Greek: *zēlos*), of which it is a transliteration. The equivalent in Hebrew is the verb root *qana'* and its de- rivatives. No English version of the Bible is 100 percent consistent in its translation of *zēlos/qana'*. The reason for this is that the terms have a multivalence of meaning which can incorporate either zeal/jealousy or envy, de- pending on the context and the perspective of the biblical author. The only context which never warrants the trans- lation of "envy" occurs when the subject or agent of the action is God (who, by definition, has honorable claim to all limited goods, hence, is incapable of envy). Among translations of the biblical texts, the KJV tends to read envy more frequently than the RSV and other versions (cf. Isa 11:13, 26:11; Job 5:2).

Zeal/jealousy is best understood as a process involv- ing three steps. The first step is the perception of an action to have been motivated by a desire to possess something belonging honorably and exclusively to the perceiver by means of a crossing or violation of a purity line. Purity lines demarcate and separate that which is exclusive (and, hence, worthy of zeal/jealousy) from that which is common or unclean. Purity lines are often correlated with holiness (Josh 24:19; Isa 65:15). The condition of zeal/jealousy presumes a state of perceived injury or af- front to one's honor (Deut 32:16; 1 Kgs 14:22; Ezek 8:3, 5).

The second step in the zeal/jealousy process is the ignition of *zēlos/qana'* as a transforming agent of the emotional state in the person who perceives self to be the victim (Num 5:14; Prov 6:34). *Zēlos/qana'* is an autonomous emotive agent which *activates* a person to behave in a possessive and protective manner against the perceived injustice. This step is labelled "ignition" because it is invariably conceptualized through metaphors of fire, heat, indignation, wrath, provocation and the like (Num 25:11; Deut 4:24, 6:15; 29:20; Job 36:32–33).

The third step in the zeal/jealousy process is the retaliatory response of the injured party against the offender. Punishment, vengeance, and satisfaction are all typically honorable responses (Ps 69:9; Isa 26:11; Ezek 5:13; 16:42). When God retaliates against such injustice, he is often called the Lord of Hosts in conjunction with the aggressive and warlike spirit of retaliation (Isa 9:7; Zech 1:14; 8:2). All three of these steps presume an honorable claim to zeal/jealousy. A dishonorable response would be considered either shameful or envious.

What, then, generates honorable zeal/jealousy? All of the biblical references to zeal/jealousy are based on purity lines having to do with property and ownership of limited goods (see **PURITY; ENVY; LIMITED GOOD; PURPOSIVENESS/END ORIENTATION**). The model for describing these limited goods is the covenantal marriage image laid out in Numbers 5. A NT passage providing a similar conceptual scenario is 2 Corinthians 11:2: "I feel a divine jealousy for you, for I betrothed you to Christ to present you as a pure bride to her one husband."

Since that which is pure is also holy, much of what generates such a jealous response is associated with God, who is the ultimate source of holiness and purity. Thus, in the OT, limited goods capable of generating zeal/jealousy include: God (Num 25:11, 13; 1 Kgs 19:10, 14; 2 Kgs 10:16) who is himself an agent of jealousy (Exod 20:5; 34:14; Deut 5:9; 6:15); God's name (Ezek 36:6); God's household (Ps 69:9); God's holy Torah (Gal 1:14); God's holy land (Ezek 36:5; Joel 2:18; Nah 1:2); God's holy city and mountain (Zech 1:14); and God's holy remnant (2 Kgs 19:31; Isa 26:11). In the NT both Christians and Jews are called *zēloi* (Acts 5:17; 13:45; Rom 11:11; 2 Cor 7:7; 9:2; cf. 2 Pet 1:10; 3:14). Jealousy sometimes occurs in the "vice lists," although it might be more appropriate to translate the Greek word as "envy" here (2 Cor 12:20; Gal 5:20; Jas 3:16).

In twentieth-century American usage, jealousy has a negative connotation, while zeal maintains some degree of autonomy as a positive term (except when encountered in excess, as "fanaticism"). In the first-century Mediterranean world, zeal/jealousy is expected, encouraged, honorable, and always righteous. (Chris Seeman)

Pilch, John J. 1996. "A Window into the Biblical World: Slow to Anger and Long of Nose." *The Bible Today* 34/5:305–10.
Schweder, Richard A. 1993. "The Cultural Psychology of Emotions." In *Handbook of Emotions.* Ed. Michael Lewis and Jeannette M. Haviland. Pp. 417–31. New York: Guilford.

Index of Ancient Sources

Old Testament

Genesis

1	66, 144, 204
1–11	190
1:1–13	143
1:1–2:4a	163
2:4b–3:24	163
2:4ff.	99
2:7	99
2:8	99
2:15	99
2:19	99
2:21	99
2:24	127
2:25	136
3:1–7	150
3:5–7	71
3:8	99
3:21	136
3:24	13
4:9	159
6:5	69
6:8	89
9:20–27	76
11:1–6	150
12:3	201
12:5	159
12ff.	190
13:7ff.	159
15:6	200
17:9–14	201
18:3	89
18:4	100, 116
18:14	192
18:18	201
19:1–10	116
19:2	100, 116
19:3–14	82
19:4–5	116
19:18–19	185
20:12	30
20:13	184
21:8	82
21:19	71
22:2	128
22:12	99
24:1–4	202
24:15–16	202
24:27	94
24:32	100, 116
24:45	69
24:49	185
26:14	61
26:26–31	82
27	147, 168
27:4	127
28:1–5	202
29:20	128
29:22	83
29:32	128
30:1	61
30:26	183
31:5	89
32:5	89
33:8	89
33:10	89
33:15	89
34	76
34:2	119
34:11	89
37:11	61
39:4	89
40:20	83
43:14	32
43:24	100
44:1–34	80
45:22	22
47:29	89
47:29–30	185
48:14	99
48:15–49:27	76
48:17–19	169
49:3	167
49:10	101
50:4	89

Exodus

1:14	183
2:11–12	35
2:23	85
3:5	24, 99, 100
3:21	89
4:21	69
4:22–23	168
4:25	101
5:1	85
6:5–9	85
7:3	69
7:4	99
7:13	69
7:14	69
7:16	85
7:22	69
7:23	69
8:1	85
8:15	69
8:19	69
8:20	85
8:21	85
8:32	69
9:1	85
9:7	69
9:12	69
9:13	85
9:14	13
9:34	69
9:35	69
10:1	69
10:3	85
10:12	76
10:20	69
10:27	69
11:3	89
11:10	69
12:11	99
12:26	76
12:36	89
13:8	76
13:11–16	168
14:4	14, 69
14:8	69
16:16–19	182
18:18–27	159
19:2–8	76
19:10	25
19:14	25
20:1–17	34, 86, 197
20:2–6	76
20:5	60, 211
20:6	129
20:7	27
20:12	76, 93, 108
20:14	20
20:16	27
20:17	20, 182
20:22–23:33	163, 197
20:26	136, 138
21:7–11	20, 197
21:15	93, 108
21:17	93, 108
22:17–19	20
22:18–23:19	197
24:7–8	3
25:31–35	80
28	24
28:5–6	22
28:42	24, 136
29:10	99
29:15	99
29:19	99
30:19	100
30:21	100
31:10	183
32:14	165
33:12–13	89
33:16–17	89
33:19	31
34:6	94
34:9	89, 157
34:14	60, 211
35:19	183
40:31	100

Leviticus

3:2	99
3:8	99
3:13	99
5:1–13	34
5:13–15	34
10:8–11	34
11	171
11:1–43	27
11:40	25

11:44–45   27, 32, 104
12   171
13–14   104, 171
13:6   25
13:34   25
13:45–46   105
14:8–9   25
14:9   25
15   171, 196
15:5–8   25
16:26   25
17–26   197
17:15   25
18   3, 196
18:6–18   140
18:24–25   77
19:3   93
19:18   8, 17, 128, 190
19:19   24
19:34   128
20   3
20:11   140
20:13   171
20:17   137
20:17–21   140
20:26   198
21:17–20   205
23:2–44   82
24:10–16   20
24:14–16   29
25:10   86
25:18   77
25:48   159
26:41   69, 119

Numbers
1:2–3   76
1:17–19   76
5   211
5:14   60, 211
5:30   60
8:10   99
8:12   99
11:11   89
11:15   89
12:3   131
15:39   71
19:7–10   25
23:19   165
24:3   71
25:11   211
25:13   211
26:55–56   80
27:8   76
27:23   99
31:24   25
33:54   80
34:13   80
35:9–12   202
35:16–21   159
36:2–3   80

Deuteronomy
2:28   187
2:30   69
3:21   71
4:3   71
4:9   71, 76
4:24   60, 211
4:34   14
4:39   69
5:5–21   197
5:6–10   76
5:6–21   34, 86
5:9   211
5:10   129
5:11   27
5:15   14
5:16   76, 93, 108
5:20   27
5:28–32   29
5:28–33   3, 77
5:32–33   38
6:1–3   20
6:4–9   19, 38
6:5   13, 70, 128
6:7   76
6:12–15   20
6:15   60, 211
6:20–25   76
7   34
7:1–6   76
7:8   85
7:9   72, 129
7:9–12   93
7:16   157
7:17   69
7:19   14, 71
8:1–6   77
8:2   119
8:16   119
8:17   69
9:4   69
9:29   14
10:16   69
10:21   71
11:1   128, 129
11:2   14
11:18   69
13:5   85
13:6   30, 77
13:6–9   169
13:18   31
15:7   69
15:9   62, 69
15:12–18   34
17:7   169
17:14–20   149
18:21   69
19:11   77
19:13   157
19:14   77
19:21   157
20:15–18   77
21:17   160

21:18–21   34, 76, 108
22:5   22
22:10   24
22:11   24
22:13–23:1   76
23:2–9   34
24:1   89, 196
25:5–10   33
25:6–9   199
26:8   14
27:15–26   17
27:16   108
28   149
28:48   137
28:50   89
28:52   202
28:54   62
28:56   62
28:65   71
28:67   71
29:5   99
29:19   69
29:20   211
30:3   31
30:6   70
30:15–20   77
31:13–20   199
32–33   20
32:6   151
32:7   76
32:9   79
32:16   210
32:46   69, 76
33:2–29   17
34:9   99

Joshua
2:2–3   116
2:12   185
2:14   185
4:24 (LXX)   208
5:15   99, 100
9:5   99
10:24   101
14–21   80
22:5   127, 129
24   3
24:7   71
24:14–18   76
24:19   60, 210
24:19–20   149

Judges
1:1   169
3:7   149
7:2   126
8:21   60
8:26   60
14:10   83
14:12–13   22
14:16   128
19:21   100

Ruth
1:8   185
3:4   101
3:7   101
3:8   101

1 Samuel
1   14
1:21–28   146
2:3–10   150
2:11   146
2:33   71
8   19
8:11–18   14
11:2   71
12:13–15   149
15:22–23   4
15:24–31   149
15:29   165
15:35   165
18:15–17   77
18:22   128
19:24   138
20:8   185
20:14   127, 185
20:30   137
25:41   100

2 Samuel
1:26   94
2:30   23
3:20   82
6:20   138
7:14   151
10:4   137
11:8   100
12:1–12   76
12:13–23   149
13:4   127
13:15   128
14   160
15:20   94
16:15–19   185
19:6   129
19:20   168
22:28   119
22:37   100
22:39   100
24:14   31
24:16   165

1 Kings
1   147
2:5   99
3:6   94
5:3   100
8:23   93, 94, 129
8:42   14
8:47   69
8:50   31
9:3   71
11:2   127

13:26   66
14:7–16   19
14:8   71
14:22   210
17:7–13   149
17:13   164
19:10   211
19:14   211
21:1–29   163
21:29   119
22:5–28   164

2 Kings
2:12   151
5:13   151
6:21   151
10:16   211
10:30   71
13:14   151
13:23   31
17:36   14
19:22   71
19:31   212
22:8–20   119
25:7   71
25:27   46
25:29   46

1 Chronicles
11:6   168
19:4   137

2 Chronicles
6:14   93, 94
6:32   14
6:37   69
7:16   71
12:1–12   150
16:9   71
19:2   129
25:2   71
30:9   31
33:23   119
36:12   119
36:13   69

Ezra
4:12–22   149
7:6   198
7:11   198
8:21   119
9–10   171
10:9–14   19
10:44   19

Nehemiah
1:5   93
1:6   71
1:11   31
5:14–19   182
8:1   195
9:17   94
9:32   93
10   38

13:1–2   33
13:23–31   19, 33

Esther
1:3–9   82
1:14   167
2:17   23
2:18   82
5:1–7:10   82
5:11   167
8:15   23

Job
1:21   149
1:21–22   149
2:9–10   149
5:2   62, 149, 210
7:1   149
8:14   202
9:2–21   149
12:5   100
12:11–12   28
12:17   137
12:19   137
15:12   71
18:8   100
18:14   202
22:7   187
22:22   69
22:26–27   10
24:13   149
31:7   70
36:32–33   211
38   144
38–42:6   21
40:19   169
41:24   69

Psalms
2:4   134
5:1   28
5:11   128
8   144
8:6   100
10:13   69
10:17   131
11:6   80
12:2   70
14:1   69
16:5   80
17:5   100
17:10   157
18   28
18:27   119
18:36   100
18:38   100
19:8   70
22:8   29
23:5   80
24:3–6   28
24:4   70
25:2   203
25:10   93, 94

25:15   100
26:1   203
26:3   94
26:8   128
28:7   203
32   28
33:5   127
33:13–22   150
35:4   109
36:1   71
36:5   94
37   21, 131
37:1   62
37:11   131
37:13   134
40:10–11   94
40:16   127
41:9   202
41:10   185
44   109
44:1–8   108
44:9–16   108
44:13–16   108
44:16   109
44:17–22   108
46:11   3
47:3   100, 150
50:16–21   28
51   28
51:1   185
52:3–4   127
52:6   134
53:1   69
54   108
55   108
55:19   119
56   149
56:13   100
57:3   94
57:10   94
59:8   134
62   150
62:10   202
66:9   100
69   109
69:9   211
69:10   119
70:2   109
71:13   109
73:2   100
73:3   62
78:8   149
83:16–17   109
86   28
88:2   28
89   28
89:28   93
90:2   169
91:14   127
96   28
102   28
103:7   76
103:8   157

103:8–13   150
103:13   31, 157, 158
105:4–11   76
105:23–25   76
105:42–45   76
105:44–45   19
106   150
106:45   93
106:46   31
109:17–19   29
109:28–29   109
111:4   157
111:4–9   157
115   3
116:8   100
116:13   80
119   3, 20, 127, 142
119:9–10   19
119:11   69
119:17   77
119:25   77
119:35–37   19
119:50   77
119:88   77
119:92   77
126   77
128   77
129   77
130   149
131   38
131:1   71
136:12   14
137   77
140–144   149
147:19–20   76

Proverbs
1:20–23   127
1:29–32   163
2:1–2   28
2:20–22   77
3:1–2   77
3:5   203
3:13–18   39
3:31   62
3:34   119
4:1–4   33
4:6   127
4:10–12   33
4:21   69
4:25–27   38
5:1   28
5:7   28
5:19   127
6:1–3   116
6:16–19   34
6:34   211
6:35   39
7:1–4   77
7:21–27   38
8:7   28

8:17	127
8:21	127
8:22–26	169
8:32–36	149
9:1–6	38
9:11	38
10–15	163
10:3	182
10:13	146
10:18	28
11:9	28
11:22	21
11:24–26	181
11:28	202
12:1	146
13:1	146
13:18	163
13:24	146
15:2	29
15:5	146
15:21	38
15:30	70
15:33	119, 149
16:20	203
16:33	80
17:10	146
17:11	149
17:24	38
18:6–7	29
18:12	119
18:15	28
18:18	80
19:18	146
19:26	108
19:29	146
20:20	108
21:2	71
21:4	71
21:17	38
22:1	39
22:11	70
22:14	28
22:15	146
23:6	62
23:12	39
23:13	146
23:17	62
23:26	71
24:1	62
24:19	62
26:3	146
27:4	62
28:4	39
28:7	163
28:9	19
28:14	69
28:22	62
28:24	108
29:5	100
29:13	71
29:15	146
29:17	146
30:17	76

30:20	28
30:32–33	28
31	187
31:10–31	21

Ecclesiastes

1:12–18	149
2:10	71
7:26–29	20
11:9	70
12:13–14	39

Isaiah

1:10	28
1:11–13	164
2:2	164
2:6–3:26	108
2:9	119
2:11	119
2:17	119
3:16	101
3:20	60
5:1–19	150
5:7–8	150
5:8	77
6:2	101
6:10	70
9:2–5	77
9:6	151
9:7	211
11:4	131
11:13	61, 210
16:5	94
19:9	22
20:1–6	163
20:2	100
20:3–5	109
20:4	137
22:21	151
26:11	210, 211, 212
29:13	208
29:18	71
29:19	131
30:3–5	109
31:1	202
32:3	70
32:11	137
37:17	28
37:26	79
40–55	109
40:3	199
40:13–14	21
41:1	3
43:1–7	108
43:8	70
43:18	190
43:22–44:5	150
44:7–8	193
45:21	193
45:22–23	149
46:9	190
46:9–11	149

47:3	137
47:5	3
47:7	69
47:8	69
48:5	193
49:6	195
49:7	72
49:13	31
49:15	31
49:21	69
51:9	190
51:17	80
51:22	80
53:7	15
54:4	110
54:8–10	31
54:10	93
55	150
55:8–9	21
55:11	66
57:1	69
57:15	119
58:5	119
59:1–19	108
59:17	22
61:1	87
61:7	110
61:8	129
62:2	164
63:11	190
63:17	69
65:11–12	80
65:15	210
66:2	119

Jeremiah

2:30	150
5:17	202
6:18–21	19
6:23	31
7:1–7	20
8:8–12	150
9:2	28
9:4	202
9:4–6	202
9:7	28
9:22–23	150
9:26	70
10:9	22
11:1–13	19
12:1–4	21
12:11	69
13:14	157
13:16	100
13:17	150
13:22	69
13:25	79
13:26–27	109
16:7	80
17:5	203
17:7	203
18:22	100
20:9	176

21:7	31
22:17	70
23:40	109
25:15–28	81
26:1–24	163
27:5	14
30:24	164
31:31	164
32:17	14
32:18	14
32:21	14
32:27	192
33:2–26	150
33:7	169
33:26	31
34:8	86
34:17	86
35	77
42:12	31
49:12	81
50:42	31
51:7	80
51:51	109

Lamentations

1:8	137
1:13	100
5:17	71

Ezekiel

4:12–15	28
5:10	158
5:11	157
5:13	211
6:9	71
7:4	157
7:9	158
8:3	210
8:5	210
10–11	4
12:1–3	150
16:8	127
16:10	22
16:11–12	23
16:13	22
16:36	137
16:36–54	109
16:37	109
16:42	211
18:31	164
20:33	14
20:34	14
20:38	149
21:6	71
22:10	119, 137
23:17	127
23:26–30	137
23:31–33	81
23:42	23
24:17–23	100
34:18–19	101
36:5	212
36:6	211

36:26   70
44:25   127
48   80

Daniel
1:9   31
9:4   93

Hosea
2:3   138
2:10   109, 138
3:1   127
4:1   185
5:6–7   20, 150
6:6   92, 185
8:1–4   19
9:15   19, 129
14:2–10   20

Joel
2:18   212

Amos
1:11   30
4:2–3   46
4:4–5   164
5:15   129
5:18–27   150
5:24–25   150
6:7   168

Obadiah
1:3   69

Jonah
1:7   80
4:2   157

Micah
1:11   137
3:2   129
7:5   202
7:6   127
7:20   94

Nahum
1:2   212
3:5   109, 138

Habakkuk
2:15   80

Zephaniah
3:12   119

Zechariah
1:14   211, 212
2:17   3
7:8–10   158
7:9–10   30
8:2   211
8:19   127
9:9   119
12:2   80
12:7   169

13:4   23

Malachi
2:2   69
4:3   100

OT Apocrypha

1 Esdras
6:18   183

1 Maccabees
1:14   141
1:15   141
2   19
2:26   199
4:23   22
11:13   23

2 Maccabees
4:12   22, 140
4:9–15   141
6:7   141
6:18–7:41   19
6:28–31   15
7   77
7:1–42   15
8:18–31   33

Sirach
1:21–24   19
1:24–29   39
3:1–16   21
5:11–13   28
5:14–6:1   163
6:5   28
7:1–17   3
7:23   146
7:24–25   146
7:26   20
7:27–28   76
8:9   20
8:15   38
9:2   20
10:20–22   20
11:20–21   39
13:17   208
14:3   62
14:6   62
14:8   62
14:9   62
14:10   62
17:17   79
18:6–22   150
18:18   62
23:12   208
25:12–26:18   20
25:24   146
27:11   208
28:1   150
30:1   146
30:12   146
31:13   62

35   33
37:10   62
37:12   208
37:12–15   39
38:24–39:11   198
40:1–11   21
41:14–42:8   33
42:9–14   146

Tobit
4:7   62
4:16   62

Wisdom of Solomon
4:12   62
5:1   10
6:12–21   39
9:13   21

OT Pseudepigrapha

Jubilees
3:21   137
3:27   137
3:30   137
3:31   141

3 Maccabees
7:21   166

4 Maccabees
6:2   138

Dead Sea Scrolls

1QS 7:13–14
138

New Testament

Matthew
1:1–18   53
2   153
2:3   58
2:16   58
2:18   58
3:2   87
3:3   199
3:7   133
3:7–10   43
3:7–12   20
3:9   77, 133
4:4   16
4:7   16
4:10   16
4:17   20, 87, 151, 154
4:23   151
5–7   134
5:3–11   17
5:5   131

5:8   70
5:9   160
5:10–12   19, 78, 149
5:11   112
5:15   133
5:16   152
5:17–18   206
5:17–48   29
5:18   52, 149
5:18–19   34, 200
5:21–22   165
5:21–48   205
5:22   17
5:23   17
5:24   17
5:27–30   39
5:29   71
5:29–30   51
5:33–37   27
5:43–47   158
5:44   129, 182
5:45   149
5:47   17
5:48   175
6:1–18   66, 206
6:2   42, 52, 191
6:5   42, 127
6:5–6   191
6:9–13   20
6:11 (Q)   191
6:16   42, 191
6:16–18   119
6:17–18   42
6:19–21   188
6:22   71
6:22–23   62, 205
6:24   129, 205
6:25–33   182
6:25–34   188
6:30   73
6:34   15, 190
7:3   133
7:7   8
7:13–27   129
7:21   64, 151
8:2–3   105
8:10   73
8:11   135, 151
8:12   58
8:18–22   188
8:26   73
9:2   74
9:10   116
9:13   92, 185
9:14–17   119
9:22   73
9:24   135
9:27   93
9:28   74
9:29   73
9:36   32
10:1–16   154

10:2   167
10:5–6   17
10:5–15   188
10:6   87
10:7   151
10:14–23   115
10:24   15
10:24–25   112
10:26   44
10:35   127
10:37   78, 112
10:37–38   73
10:42   187
11:10   16
11:18–19   52
11:19   42
11:21   23
11:28–29   73
11:29   57, 119,
131
12:1–12   42
12:7   92, 185
12:13   205
12:22–45   105
12:30   17
12:33   205
12:43–45   43
13:1–9   135
13:15   70
13:24   152
13:31   152
13:33   152
13:42   58
13:44   152
13:44–46   188
13:45   152
13:45–46   135
13:47   152
13:50   58
13:55   54
13:57   15
14:14   32
14:26   58
14:31   73
15:4   93
15:4–6   108
15:8–9   208
15:22   53, 93, 186
15:28   73
15:31   205
15:32   32
16:8   73
16:13   16
16:17   53
16:24–25   179
16:27   73
16:28   191
17:15   93, 186
18:1   112
18:4   120, 151
18:5   118
18:6   73
18:15   17

18:15–17   34, 77
18:21   17
18:23   152
18:23–25   9
18:27   32
18:33   92
18:35   17
19:3   196
19:5   127
19:8   69
19:19   128
19:23   151
19:24   51
19:26   192
19:27–29   191
19:30   15
19:30   169
20:1   152
20:1–15   181
20:1–16   37
20:15   62
20:16   16, 169
20:27   113
20:28   87
20:30   93
20:30–31   186
20:31   93
20:34   32
21:3   49
21:5   119
21:13   16
21:21   74
21:23   105
21:28–31   51
21:28–32   64
21:32   73
21:33–46   113
21:42   16, 133
22:2–10   83
22:11–14   22
22:29   16
22:37   70, 128
22:39   128
22:44   101
23:2   33
23:3   41
23:5   23, 140
23:6   128
23:8–10   113
23:11–12   113
23:12   119, 120
23:13   152, 206
23:13–34   17
23:15   133
23:23   73, 92
23:23–30   206
23:24   133
23:25   41
23:27   41
23:28   42
24:4   44
24:4–5   43
24:11   43

24:23   74
24:23–24   43
24:26   74
24:34   191
24:35   20
24:36   193, 194
24:43–51   33, 57
24:51   58
25   xxi
25:14–30   188
25:30   58
25:31–46   17, 57,
158
25:36   23
25:38   117
25:43   117
26:3–5   105, 159
26:6–13   188
26:24   16
26:28   87
26:31   16
26:52–54   131
26:53   14
26:54   16
26:56   16
26:64   14
26:67–68   113
26:75   58
27:18   62
27:27–30   47
27:27–31   114,
134
27:28   138
27:31   138
27:40–44   150
27:42   73
27:43   114, 203
27:46   48, 58
27:50   58
27:54   15
28:19   17
28:20   191

Mark
1:1–4   164
1:3   199
1:6   23
1:7   119
1:11   54
1:15   87, 151, 154,
164
1:19   53
1:21   200
1:30–31   116
1:40–42   105
1:41   157
2:1–12   112
2:5   74
2:8   43, 69
2:13–14   42
2:15   42
2:15–17   112
2:18–20   119

2:18–22   112
2:23–28   112
3:13–19   154
3:1–6   112
3:5   69, 207
3:20–35   112
3:21   159, 177
3:23–24   19
3:31–35   78, 159,
165, 177
4:8   174
4:11   21
4:29   174
4:40   73
4:41   142
5:17   116
5:19   93
5:23   99
5:25–34   196
5:34   73
6:3   54
6:4   15
6:5   104
6:7–13   188
6:8   117
6:10   116
6:21   83
6:34   32
6:50   58
7   xxix, 172
7:1–6   34
7:1–8   112
7:1–23   200
7:3–5   95
7:6   42
7:6–13   20
7:9–13   108
7:10   93, 97
7:15   140
7:18–19   27
7:18–23   28
7:19   78
7:20–22   xxix
7:22   62
7:34   57
8:2   32, 157
8:17   73, 207
8:23   99
8:27   16
8:27–29   55
8:31   55
8:32   11
8:34   95
8:34–35   179
8:38   73, 112
9:3   25
9:7   54
9:22   32
9:34   112
9:37   117, 118
9:40   17
9:42   73
9:43–48   206

10:1–9   196
10:1–12   112
10:2–12   200
10:5   69
10:6–8   206
10:7   127
10:9   206
10:11   196
10:16   99
10:27   21
10:28–30   78, 177, 191
10:31   169
10:35–41   33
10:37   172
10:38–39   81
10:42–45   78, 149
10:44   113, 169
10:45   87
10:47–48   93
10:52   73
11:1ff.   200
11:15–16   42
11:23   207
11:24   74
11:27–33   112
12:1–12   113
12:13–17   112
12:18–27   112
12:30   13, 70, 204
12:30–31   128
12:36   100
12:41–44   149
13:1–2   42
13:5   44
13:9–13   19, 78
13:21–23   19
13:32   193, 194
14:3–9   188
14:12–25   83
14:23–25   81
14:33–35   47
14:36   55, 81, 147, 152
14:50   47
14:51–52   47
14:60–64   150
14:60–65   29
14:62   14
14:65   113
14:72   58
15:10   62
15:16–20   47, 113, 134
15:21   53
15:24   22
15:29–31   114
15:29–32   29, 114
15:32   73
15:34   48
15:39   15, 54
16:8   3

16:9   168

Luke
1   90
1:5   53
1:9   80
1:12   58
1:23   183
1:27   53
1:32–33   xxvii
1:37   192
1:39–41   60
1:48   191
1:50   93
1:51–53   150
1:52   119
1:54   93
1:54–55   xxvii
1:58   133
1:72   93
1:72–73   xxvii
1:76   199
1:78   93
2   90
2:11   xxvii
2:19   69
2:22   196
2:22–38   149
2:25–26   xxvii
2:34   xxvi
2:38   xxvii
2:44   159
2:46–47   51
2:48–50   xxvii
2:51   69, 142
2:51–53   150
2:52   166
3:4–6   199
3:7–14   164
3:10–14   182
3:11   9
3:17   xxvi
3:23–38   53
4:5–12   150
4:18–19   xxvi, 87
4:18–21   164
4:21   xxvii, 51
4:24   15, 122
4:27   53
4:28–30   58
4:36   xxviii
5:12–13   105
5:15   133
5:20   74
5:22   69
5:29   82, 116
5:33–39   119
6:6–11   50
6:12–16   154
6:20–26   57
6:22   112
6:27   129, 182
6:27–28   158

6:35   9
6:36   32
7:6   153
7:9   73
7:10   205
7:11–15   xxvi
7:13   32
7:21   90
7:25   22
7:36–50   116, 117
7:37–50   xxvi
7:40–42   117
7:42   90
7:43   90
7:44   100
8:1–3   147
8:3   54
8:11–15   xxvi
8:19–21   xxvii
8:24–25   xxviii
8:25   73
8:44   60
8:48   73
9:1–6   188
9:18   16
9:23–24   179
9:26   73
9:46   112
9:48   112, 118
9:50   17
9:57–62   xxvii, 188
10   93
10:2   174
10:8   116
10:27   70, 128
10:29   xxvi
10:29–37   36, 129, 182
10:30   22, 140
10:33   17, 32
10:37   93
10:40–42   116
11:3   191
11:14–26   160
11:21–22   202
11:23   xxvi, 17, 160
11:34   62
11:41   9
11:43   128
11:5–13   182
12:1   42, 168
12:13   160
12:13–21   9
12:15   8
12:22–31   182
12:28   xxviii, 73
12:31   174
12:42–48   33
12:50–53   xxvii
12:53   127
13:10–17   42

13:15   42
13:16   xxvi
13:28   58
13:30   41
13:32–33   xxviii
14:7–11   41, 113, 119
14:8   116
14:11   120
14:13–14   9
14:26   73, 112, 172
14:26–27   xxvii
14:28–30   112
14:28–33   66
15:8   23
15:9   181
15:20   32
15:22   22
16:13   129
16:14   135
16:16   200
16:19   22
17:6   142
17:10   45
17:13   93
17:20–21   xxviii
18:9–14   203
18:14   41, 119, 120
18:18–25   202
18:28–30   191
18:38–39   93
18:42   73
19:6–7   42
19:9   xxviii
19:11–27   188
19:41   58
19:45   50
20:9–19   113
20:19   99
20:20   42
20:46   128
20:47   50
21:1–4   188
21:8   44
21:12   99
22:26   41, 113
22:35–38   188
22:44   47
22:62   58
22:63–65   47, 113
22:69   14
23:11   47
23:27   58
23:35   114
23:43   xxviii
24:25–27   149
24:37   58

John
1:11   118
1:14   90, 152

1:16–17   90
1:23   199
1:35–51   39
1:46   18
2:3   64
2:4   64
2:4–5   33
2:7–8   64
2:10   117
2:13–15   57
2:24–25   43
3:16   128
3:26   125
3:30   125
4:9   53
4:21–23   165
4:21–24   39
4:27   20
4:35   174
4:44   15
4:47   64
4:48   64
4:50   64
5:6–15   205
5:9–16   42
5:42   128
6:32–34   165
6:70   43
7:3–4   64
7:6–8   64
7:10   64
7:12   42
7:16   55
7:23   205
7:24   40
7:26   11
8:15   40
8:29   121
8:31–58   43
8:38–44   152
8:42   128
8:44   43
9   54
9:14–16   42
9:28   54
9:31   205
10:24   11
11:1–4   11
11:25–26   165
11:33   58
11:38   58
11:47–48   125
12:1–8   188
12:23–26   179
12:40   70, 207
13:5–14   100
13:10   205
13:13–16   96
13:20   118
13:26–27   185
13:27–30   43
13:34–35   128, 165

14:10   55
14:15   128, 129
14:21   128
14:23   128
14:24   128
15:10   129
15:12–13   128
15:17   128
15:18–20   96
16:25   11
16:29   11
17:5   166
17:24   166
17:24–26   128
18:20   11
18:28   47
19:1–3   114
19:2–3   47, 134
19:3   47
19:5   47
19:12   153
19:18   47
19:19   47
19:23–24   48
20:4   168
20:8   168
21:15–17   128

Acts
1–5   188
1:1   50
1:7   191, 193, 194
1:26   80
2:21   28
2:29   11
2:45   78
2:22–25   149
2:42–46   78
3:20   88
3:21   88
4:13   11
4:19–21   164
4:29   11
4:31   11
5:17   212
6:1–7   188
6:6   99
6:13ff.   200
6:14   164
7:24–25   35
7:33   99, 100
7:34   57
7:51   70, 207
7:55–56   114
7:57   28
8:8   135
8:17   99
9:12   99
9:17   99
9:27–28   11
10:2   208
10:9–16   27
10:14   140

10:34–35   17
10:35   121
11:1–18   27
11:14   177
11:23   90
11:26   xxvii
12:2   54
12:21   22
13:14–15   116
13:25   99
13:39   87
13:43   208
13:45   212
13:46   11, 169
13:50   208
13:52   135
14:3   11
14:26   90
15:3   135
15:40   90
16:33   177
17:4   208
17:7   117
17:17   208
17:32   134
18:1–3   188
18:7   208
18:24   53
18:26   11
19:8   11
19:16   137
19:23–40   19
19:28   58
19:32   58
20:24   90
21:17   99, 117
22:3   53
22:5   55
22:27   53
24:15   203
25:2–3   153
25:23   166
25:24–27   16
26:6–7   203
26:26   11
26:28   xxvii
27:24   90
28:7   117
28:27   70
28:31   11

Romans
1:7   90
1:11   90
1:17   16
1:24   111
1:26   111
1:28   111
1:29   62
2:5   69
2:24   16
2:29   70
3:4   16

3:10   16
3:28   201
4   95
4:3   16, 201
4:10–11   201
4:17   16
4:18   203
4:21   192
4:23   16
5:2   203
5:3–5   174
5:5   128
5:8   128
5:14–21   74, 97
5:15   90
5:16   90
5:19   142
5:20   201
6:3–11   28
6:12–14   20
6:12–23   28
6:16–22   97
6:22   88
7:12   200
8:7   142
8:8   121
8:15   152
8:23   57
8:26   57
8:32   90
8:34   114
8:36   16
8:39   128
9:13   16
9:15   157
9:17   16
9:18   69
9:33   16, 111
10:4   174, 200
10:5   16
10:6   69
10.11   16
10:12–13   28
10:15   16
11:2   16
11:8   16
11:11   212
11:26   16
11:29   90
11:30–31   93
12:1–2   183
12:3   90
12:6   90
12:8   93
12:10   128
12:13   117
12:19   16
13:1   142
13:1–7   97
13:3   179
13:5   142
13:8–10   128
13:13   62

14:11 16
14:15 128, 179
14:17–18 183
15:1–2 121
15:3 16, 121
15:9 16, 93, 186
15:15 90
15:21 16
15:24 36
15:26–27 122
16:2 36
16:3–16 116
16:20 101
16:23 117
16:26 16

1 Corinthians
1:4 90
1:7 90
1:9 66, 73
1:23–25 41
1:26–28 21
1:26–31 111
1:31 96
2:1–5 110
2:6 65
2:7 166
2:12 90
3:10 90
3:21 96
4:1 187
4:1–5 110
4:5 44
4:6 96
4:6–10 111
5:1–2 96, 140
5:1–8 196
5:2 96
5:6 205
5:6–8 96
5:12–13 16
6:9 44
6:9–10 55
6:19 88, 96
6:20 88, 96
7 188
7:7 90
7:10–16 196
7:12–16 177
7:15 206
7:17–24 33
7:20 55
7:23 97
7:32–34 121
7:32–35 206
8:1 96
8:1–2 96
8:7–11 96
8:7–13 55
8:11 96
9:1 97
9:4 117
9:6 188

9:17 187
9:19 183
9:19–23 65
10:13 73
10:24 96
10:33 122
11 171
11:1 95
11:1–16 34
11:2 95
11:2–16 20, 88
11:3–16 111
11:6 111
11:14–15 22
11:17–30 4
11:17–33 82
11:17–34 117
11:18–19 179
11:19 82
11:21 82
11:23 95
11:25–29 81
12 177
12:4 90
12:9 90
12:12 54
12:14–26 206
12:16 28
12:18 54
12:23 137
12:28 90, 97, 168
12:30 90
12:31 90
13 128, 129
14:1 129
14:3–4 96
14:18 65
14:26–33 96
14:32–33 142
14:33–36 95
15:3 95
15:10 90
15:25 101
15:27 101
15:27–28 142
15:51–57 65
16:15–16 168
16:16 142

2 Corinthians
1:2 90
1:3 186
1:10 203
1:11 90
1:12 90
1:17 65
1:18 73
2:7 90
2:9 142
2:10 90
3:1–3 65
3:12 11, 203
3:18 165

4:5 183
5:1–4 138
5:2 57
5:4 57
5:7 121
5:9 121
5:10 111
5:12 65
5:17 165
6:1 90
6:2 121
7:4 11
7:7 212
7:8 65
8:1 90
8:1–9:15 188
8:12 121
9:2 212
9:8 182
10:1 131
10:10 65
10:11 65
10:14–15 168
11:1–5 19
11:2 211
11:5–6 110
11:12 96
11:14–15 43
11:21ff. 65
11:22 65, 110
11:22–31 19
11:23–28 110
12:10 19, 110, 121
12:13 90
12:20 212
12:21 119

Galatians
1 110
1:1 97
1:1–9 29
1:10 65, 110, 122
1:14 211
1:15–16 97
1:19 54
2 110
2:1–10 78
2:9 90
2:11–14 65
2:13 42
2:21 90
3 95
3:1 62
3:6 201
3:10–14 78
3:16 201
3:17 201
3:18 90
3:19–20 154
3:24 201
3:28 88, 165

3:29 201
4:4–6 54
4:6 152
4:13–14 41
4:15 71
5:7–12 19
5:11 65
5:13 183
5:19–23 xxix, 55
5:20 212
5:21 62
5:26 62
6:13 137
6:15 165

Ephesians
1:20 114
1:22 101
2:4 186
3:2 90, 187
3:7 90
3:8 90
3:12 11
4:2 120, 131
4:7 90
4:15 128
4:18 69
4:24 26
4:32 90
5:21 142, 179
5:21–33 97, 144, 196
5:22 55, 76, 142, 146, 179
5:22–24 20
5:24 142
6:1 142
6:2 93
6:5 70, 142, 179
6:5–8 55
6:14–17 22
6:19 11

Philippians
1:15 62
1:20 11, 203
1:29 90
2:1–4 179
2:5ff. 49
2:5–11 114
2:6–11 28, 149
2:6–12 95
2:8 119, 142
2:9 90
2:27 186
3:3–4 65
3:5 53, 200
3:5–6 110
3:7–8 110
3:7–10 95
3:8–9 175
3:10–11 110
3:17 95

3:19   137
3:20   54
3:21   142
4:2   179
4:11   182
4:15   117

Colossians
1:4   128
1:6   90
1:15   169
2:8   38
2:13   90
2:15   11
3:1   114
3:11   78, 88
3:12   120, 131
3:12–14   32
3:13   90
3:13–14   179
3:18   76, 142,
    179, 196
3:18–19   97
3:20   55, 142
3:22   70, 121,
    142, 179
3:22–4:1   33
4:5   16

1 Thessalonians
1:9   117
2:2   11
2:4   43, 110, 122
2:12   205
3:3   80
3:13   111
4:3–7   141
4:9–10   128
4:12   16
4:15   193
5:12–13   116
5:23   111, 204
5:24   66, 73

2 Thessalonians
1:3   128
2:12   121
2:15   95
3:6   95

1 Timothy
1:5   70
1:10b–11   206
1:13   93
2:1–15   33
2:4   121
2:5   154
2:5–6   87
2:11   146
2:13   168
3:2   145
3:4   145
3:4–5   144
3:7   16

3:16   209
4:8   209
4:14   90, 99
5   39
5:1–2   177
5:3–4   36
5:4   208
5:10   36
5:22   99
6:2   177
6:4   62
6:6   182
6:9–10   39

2 Timothy
1:5   146
1:6   90, 99
1:13–14   95
2:4   121
2:13   73
2:22   70
3:12   209
3:14   95
3:15–17   39
4:3–5   28
4:13   22

Titus
1:6   145
1:12   18, 53
2:2–6   177
2:5   142
2:9   142
2:11   90
2:12   209
2:13   209
2:14   87
3:1   142
3:3   62

Philemon
8   11

Hebrews
1:3   114
2:8   101, 142
2:9   90
3:1–3   74, 97
3:2–6   55
3:6   11, 203
4:16   11, 93, 94
5:8   74, 97, 142
5:9   142
7:2   169
8:1   114
8:6   154
9:15   154
10:7   121
10:9   121
10:12   114
10:19   11
10:35   11
10:38   121
11   95

11:11   73
11:37–38   23
12:2   114
12:15   90
12:24   154
13:8   165, 191

James
1:8   207
1:12   128
1:16   44
1:17   165
1:21   131
1:26–27   205
2:2   23
2:5   128
2:10   205
2:13   92
2:17–26   205
3:1–6   63
3:13   131
3:16   212
3:17   94
4:1–10   62
4:5–7   143
4:8   207
4:10   119
5:7   174
5:11   157

1 Peter
1:3   94
1:8   128
1:18   87
2:1   62
2:11–3:12   196
2:13–14   179
2:18   142, 179
2:20   93
3:1   142, 177
3:1–7   97
3:3   23
3:5   142
4:2–5   39
4:9   117
4:10   90
5:5–6   119

2 Peter
1:10   212
2:9   209
3:14   212

1 John
2:15–17   38, 39
2:16   62
2:28   11
3:19–21   11
3:22   121
4:17   11
4:18   11
5:14   11

Jude
10–19   39

Revelation
1:7   193
1:17   169
2:23   43
3:14–21   57
3:16   17
3:18   137
4:4   23
5:9–13   28
7:14   25
11:3   23
12:1   101
16:15   139
17:4   80
18:2   46
18:7   69
18:8   46
18:10   46
18:12   22
18:12–13   47
18:15   46
18:21–22   47
18:23   47
19:9   83
19:17   83

NT Apocrypha

Gospel of Thomas
36   190

**Mishna, Talmud,
    and Rabbinic
    Literature**

**'Abot de Rabbi
    Nathan**
40   139

m. Yoma
7:5   24, 140

b. Ber.
62a   139

b. Shab.
120b   138

Esther Rabbah
3.14   137

**Hellenistic
    Jewish
    Authors**

Josephus
Against Apion
269   18

Antiquities
3.151–158   24
3.161   24
12.240–241   141
15.268–270   141

Life
11   23
122–123   124
352   18

War
2.129   23
2.148–149   139
2.224   138
2.224   138

Philo
Contemplative Life
66   23

Drunkenness
110   125

Embassy
347   126

Flaccus
29   125

***Greco-Roman
Literature***

**Anonymous
Iamblici**
124

Aristotle
Nicomachean Ethics
I.i [1094^a]   175
I.ii.2 [1094^a]
175
I.vii.5 [1097^b]
175
II.vi.14 [1106^b]
175
V.v [1133^a]   183

Aulus Gellius
X.15.19–20   139

Hesiod
Works and Days
366–67   181

Homer
Iliad
5.287   175

**Oxyrhynchus
Papyrus**
655.1   190

Plato
Philebos
1   132

Plutarch
*Old Men in Public
Affairs*
787D   125

*On Listening to
Lectures*
44B   124

In Praise of Women
258E   137

Roman Questions
274A–B   139

Strabo
Geography
16.2.23   18
16.4.24   18

Suetonius
Vespasian
18   173

Thucydides
Peloponnesian War
I.vi.4–6   136